The Poetics of Conflict Experience

Seventy years after the end of the Second World War, we still do not fully appreciate the intensity of the lived experience of people and communities involved in resistance movements and subjected to German occupation. Yet the enduring conjunction between individuals, things and place cannot be understated: from plaques on the wall to the beloved yellowing relics of private museums, materiality is paramount to any understanding of conflict experience and its poetics. This book reasserts the role of the senses, the imagination and emotion in the Italian war experience and its remembrance practices by tracing a cultural geography of the everyday material worlds of the conflict, and by digging deep into the multifaceted interweaving of place, person and conflict dynamics. Loneliness, displacement and paranoia were all emotional states shared by resistance activists and their civilian supporters. But what about the Fascists? And the Germans? In a civil war and occupation where shifting allegiances and betrayal were frequent, traditional binary codes of friend-foe cannot exist uncritically. This book incorporates these different actors' perceptions, their competing and discordant materialities, and their shared – yet different – sense of loss and placelessness through witness accounts, storytelling and memoirs.

Sarah De Nardi is a Research Associate in Cultural Geography at the University of Durham. Her focus on embodiment and identity frames war and conflict as lived experience in the everyday. She has published in cultural geography, anthropology, history and archaeology journals and volumes, and is Assistant Editor of the *Journal of Community Archaeology and Heritage*. Recently she co-edited *Memory, Place and Identity: Commemoration and Remembrance of War and Conflict* (Routledge, 2016). This book grows out of seven years of research in Italy, the UK and Germany, and is informed by a close personal connection to the topic of resistance due to the fact that her grandfather was a Partisan. Her subjectivity as an Italian, European citizen and scholar is a recurrent theme in the book, lending a nuanced and engaging perspective to the overarching theme and the arguments put forth.

Material Culture and Modern Conflict

Series editors:

Nicholas J. Saunders
University of Bristol

Paul Cornish
Imperial War Museum, London

Modern warfare is a unique cultural phenomenon. While many conflicts in history have produced dramatic shifts in human behaviour, the industrialized nature of modern war possesses a material and psychological intensity that embodies the extremes of our behaviours, from the total economic mobilization of a nation state to the unbearable pain of individual loss. Fundamentally, war is the transformation of matter through the agency of destruction, and the character of modern technological warfare is such that it simultaneously creates and destroys more than any previous kind of conflict.

The material culture of modern wars can be small (a bullet, machine-gun or gas mask), intermediate (a tank, aeroplane or war memorial), and large (a battleship, a museum, or an entire contested landscape). All share one defining feature – they are artefacts, the product of human activity rather than natural processes. In this sense, for example, the First World War's Western Front is as much a cultural artefact as a Second World War V2 rocket, a cold war early-warning radar station, wartime factories and bombed buildings, as are photographs, diaries, films, war souvenirs and a host of conflict-related art forms. Similarly artefactual, though not always understood as such, are people – the war-maimed (sometimes fitted with prostheses), war refugees and their camps, collectors of memorabilia, and the post-conflict 'presence of absence' in towns and cities of large numbers of missing men, women and children. Each in their own way – through objects, memories, attitudes and actions – perpetuate different engagements with conflict and its painful and enduring aftermath.

The material culture of conflict offers a field of study which is both rich and fiercely relevant to the world which we inhabit. Wars and other forms of conflict have formed that world. Today we still live in the shadow of two world wars which set new standards for extremes of violence, and violent conflicts remain in progress across the globe as this series of books is inaugurated. These events have created a truly massive volume of material culture. The ways in which people engage with it is conditioned by society's equivocal attitude to violent conflict itself. As John Keegan wrote, 'We are cultural animals and it is the richness of our culture which allows us to accept our undoubted potentiality for violence but to believe nevertheless that its expression is a cultural aberration' (Keegan, *A History of Warfare*, 1994). Keegan himself knew that the reality was not so clear cut as this reassuring vision. The relationships which people have with the material culture created in a context of violence add weight to this assessment, for they are simultaneously capable of supporting or undermining the perception of warfare as an aberration or exception.

Now as never before, we perceive unfamiliar but underlying truths in the way in which these artefacts reveal infinitely varied interactions with people: a 'social life' created by human engagement with objects. Although overwhelmingly inanimate, they are not merely passive signifiers, reifications or receptors of 'meaning', but can exercise positive agency in forming and embodying human thoughts and emotions. In short, objects make people as much as people make objects. The behaviours provoked by conflict illustrate how an individual's social being is determined by their relationship to the objects that represent them – how objects are a way of knowing oneself through things both present and absent. This is as true for First World War battlefield pilgrims (often widows), survivors of the Holocaust, and Second World War civilian internees and prisoners of war, as it is for uniformed service personnel who took part in both world wars, the Vietnam War, the Sarajevo militia of the Bosnian Conflict, and the war-maimed from Afghanistan and Iraq, to name just a few.

A further incentive to focus on this subject lies in developments in the academic world. For decades, anthropologists and historians have devoted increasing amounts of effort to the study of conflict. Until recently, their studies have followed discrete paths, but change has been afoot since the closing years of the last century. A slow-burning revolution in academic engagement with warfare (not to say a 'rebranding') relocated historians of conflict from the unfashionable suburb of 'military history' to uptown locales like 'war studies' and 'First World War studies'. Everyone now accepts that what we call 'peace' cannot be understood without knowing what happens in wars, any more than wars can be comprehended in isolation. Furthermore, ground-breaking work began to appear in which historians addressed wars from the perspective of their material and cultural milieus or manifestations.

Parallel advances have been occurring in the disciplines of archaeology and anthropology. The re-appraisal of materiality has been at the forefront of these developments. The ways in which we view and think about the things we make, their complex volatility, and their elusive meanings have been brought under academic scrutiny. The transformative quality of the material culture of modern conflict, and its ability to move across disciplinary boundaries, demands a robust interdisciplinary response. Focused on material culture, such an approach offers to revitalize investigations into the physical and symbolic worlds that conflict creates, and that defines us as subjects through memory, imagination, and technology.

Since the turn of the millennium the editors of this series have taken a lead in focusing the gaze of both disciplines on the material culture of conflict. Moreover, they have opened the discussion out to practitioners of the widest possible range of disciplines and vocations, including historians, anthropologists, archaeologists, museum curators and artists. For this growing international group of collaborators, the material culture of conflict represents the nodal point at which their disciplines can meet and cross over. This series of books seeks to build on this foundation and to offer a platform for those wishing to publish new research on the subject.

The series adopts a genuinely interdisciplinary approach to re-appraise the material legacy of twentieth- and twenty-first-century conflict around the world. By conceiving and studying the material culture of conflict, it helps to construct biographies of objects, and explore their 'social lives' through the changing values and attitudes attached to them over time. The series aims to show how objects can survive as expressions of 'war beyond conflict', revitalizing meanings and creating new engagements between and understandings of people and 'war things'. It offers new perspectives on the intricate web of connections that bind and separate people and places in times of conflict and beyond.

In so doing, the series offers a radical departure in the study of modern conflict – proving a truly interdisciplinary forum that draws upon, but does not privilege archaeology, anthropology, military and cultural history, art history, cultural geography, and museum and heritage studies. The complexity of modern conflict demands a coherent, integrated, and sensitized hybrid approach which calls on different disciplines where they overlap in a shared common terrain – that of the materiality of conflict and its aftermath. This approach has extraordinary potential to bring together the diverse interests and expertise of a host of disciplines to create a new intellectual engagement with the understanding of conflict.

The Poetics of Conflict Experience

Materiality and Embodiment in Second World War Italy

Sarah De Nardi

LONDON AND NEW YORK

First published 2017
by Routledge
2 Park Square, Milton Park, Abingdon, Oxon OX14 4RN

and by Routledge
711 Third Avenue, New York, NY 10017

First issued in paperback 2018

Routledge is an imprint of the Taylor & Francis Group, an informa business

© 2017 Sarah De Nardi

The right of Sarah De Nardi to be identified as author of this work has been asserted by her in accordance with sections 77 and 78 of the Copyright, Designs and Patents Act 1988.

All rights reserved. No part of this book may be reprinted or reproduced or utilised in any form or by any electronic, mechanical, or other means, now known or hereafter invented, including photocopying and recording, or in any information storage or retrieval system, without permission in writing from the publishers.

Trademark notice: Product or corporate names may be trademarks or registered trademarks, and are used only for identification and explanation without intent to infringe.

British Library Cataloguing in Publication Data
A catalogue record for this book is available from the British Library

Library of Congress Cataloging in Publication Data
Names: De Nardi, Sarah, author.
Title: The poetics of conflict experience : materiality and embodiment in Second World War Italy / Sarah De Nardi.
Description: Abingdon, Oxon ; New York : Routledge, 2017. | Series: Material culture and modern conflict
Identifiers: LCCN 2016028551| ISBN 9781472486295 (hardback : alk. paper) | ISBN 9781315308876 (ebook)
Subjects: LCSH: World War, 1939–1945—Italy—Literature and the war. | War stories, Italian—History and criticism. | Collective memory—Italy. | War and society—Italy.
Classification: LCC PQ4053.W37 D4 2017 | DDC 850.9/35845091—dc23
LC record available at https://lccn.loc.gov/2016028551

ISBN 13: 978-1-138-33013-9 (pbk)
ISBN 13: 978-1-4724-8629-5 (hbk)

Typeset in Perpetua
by Apex CoVantage, LLC

To Nonno Memi: your courage will not be forgotten.

Contents

List of figures   xii
Disclaimer   xiv
Acknowledgements   xv

Introduction: a poetics of civil war and resistance   1

Baldini dies in the end: journey through a world at war 1
Armchair strategists vs. affective archives 10
The materialities of absence 14
The interview process 16

1   8 September 1943, 'end of days': Italy's capitulation and its dystopian aftermath   18

    1.1   *My family history as a story of the resistance 21*
    1.2   *The genesis of civil war and German occupation 24*
    1.3   *Materiality and memory 33*
    1.4   *The poetics of storytelling: interviewing, imagining, mapping 36*

2   Unsettling identities   40

    1944 41
    2.1   *Identities and the uneasy materiality of conflict 43*
    2.2   *Materialities and the uncanny 44*
    2.3   *The partisan experience 47*
    2.4   *Understanding the Fascists 48*
    2.5   *Who were the Germans, and what did they want? 51*
         2.5.1   Germans . . . or Austrians? 51
         2.5.2   German self-reflections 57
    2.6   *Why weren't the Allies more helpful? 59*
    2.7   *Spies: the ultimate uncanny element 62*

x   Contents

3   The lost bodies of the Italian resistance and civil war   66

   3.1   Bodies in the snow 66
   3.2   The body of the fighter 70
      3.2.1   Sex 71
      3.2.2   Bodily hygiene 73
   3.3   The female body 75
   3.4   The Jewish body in the resistance 80
   3.5   Other bodies 83
   3.6   Saved or dead: the body's tale 85
   3.7   Reconnaissance in no man's memory: the grim legend of Buss de la Lum 87

4   The haunting materiality of storytelling   93

   4.1   Storying affects: wartime rumour as inter-corporeal practice 93
   4.2   The ontogenetic nature of storytelling: the snowball effect 98
   4.3   Action! The historical workings of affect 101
   4.4   Story one: constructing an American OSS agent as the Other 107
   4.5   Story two: the Golden Column of Menarè 109
   4.6   Story three: expected and unexpected emotions 111
   4.7   Conclusion 113

5   Competing materialities: presence and absence in the material world of the war   116

   5.1   The material turn in the social sciences: things 'matter' 116
   5.2   The materiality of the interview 122
   5.3   Wartime tangibilities: on emotional absence-presence 123
   5.4   Frontline materialities: evocative objects and booby traps 126
      5.4.1   The eagle and the death cult: Fascists and their materiality 126
      5.4.2   Frontline objects 129
   5.5   Absence as an affect: the shadow-play of memory 130
      5.5.1   A paper cenotaph: Bruno's memento 131
      5.5.2   The night is a thing: the poetics of sleep and sleep deprivation 134
      5.5.3   'I shouldn't have asked them for it'. Wilma's guilty prize 135
   5.6   Reflections 137

6   Landscapes of fighting, feeling and hoping: place as material culture   139

   6.1   Hostile landscapes and the vernacular of terror 139
   6.2   The making of places: opportunity and consolation 143

6.3 *The unmaking of places 149*
    6.3.1   Home, falling apart 151
    6.3.2   The unlikely comfort of the uplands 155
6.4 *Searching for invisibility: stealth and secrecy in everyday materialities 156*
6.5 *The marginality of bodies, the liminality of the river 159*
6.6 *Going back 160*

7 The conclusion of a journey through regions of silence   163

By way of foreword 163
7.1 *Compassionate scholarship: using affect and postmemory towards a recognition of the uncanniness of civil war 164*
    7.1.1   An intermission: Levi, the partisan 165
7.2 *Making place for a future 166*
7.3 *Engaging with the poetics of conflict experience 170*
    7.3.1   The poetics of violence 170
    7.3.2   The poetics of exclusion 174
7.4 *A past we can know 177*
7.5 *Engaging humanely with the materialities of others 179*

Appendix	183
Bibliography	190
Index	205

Figures

I.1	The killing of Armando Baldini by Garibaldi Brigade partisans. Vittorio Veneto, 30 April 1945.	1
I.2	The killing of Baldini.	3
I.3	A wall plaque commemorating the loss of lives in partisan Division Nino Nannetti.	9
I.4	Gufo Nero (Black Owl) Brigade composed of Allied soldiers and German, Austrian and Polish deserters.	13
1.1	In a town near Rome, people celebrate Italy's Armistice with the Allies.	19
1.2	A witness and a friend.	23
1.3	Cesare Pozzi and a friend laugh at a Fascist draft poster, Montù (Pavia), Lombardy, 18 April 1944.	32
1.4	Sesto San Giovanni (Milan), Lombardy: factory workers strike in 1944.	37
2.1	Bundesarchiv picture_101I-316–1181–11: Benito Mussolini with an Italian soldier.	41
2.2	A spy to the Germans is paraded through a crowd in Belluno, May 1945.	62
2.3	1944. Montanes, where Nino De Marchi was betrayed by someone he thought a friend.	64
3.1	A melancholy scene: the body of one dead partisan in a wintry landscape.	67
3.2	The Buss de la Lum and the Silentes Loquimur memorial.	89
3.3	'No trace of "*infoibati*" inside Buss de la Lum': a 1966 headline.	91
5.1	The infamous castle of Conegliano.	117
5.2	Dead partisans Mario Cappelli, Luigi Nicolò and Adelio Pagliarani, 1945, Rimini.	126
5.3	The poem, Page One.	132
6.1	Piazza Campitello/Piazza Martiri, Belluno.	140

6.2	The remains of a church where the SS slaughtered the civilians of Marzabotto, south of Florence, between 5 and 9 October 1944.	152
6.3	Destroyed German vehicles in Monte Cassino, May 1944.	161
7.1	The River Sile, Veneto. On its shores a bitter civil war was fought by partisans vs. Fascists, whose memory still divides communities today (see section 6.4).	181
A.1	Schio (Vicenza), 1943. German poster declaring the establishment of martial law in the town and announcing a draft of Italian men into the forces of the Salo' Republican Army.	185
A.2	*News Chronicle*: Italy's unconditional surrender is big news.	186
A.3	Carpi (Modena). German-issued order to cut down maize fields as they can 'hide men'.	187
A.4	Poster inviting Italians to work in Germany.	188
A.5	Rome Open City proclaim.	189

Disclaimer

This book explicitly draws from the historical experience and events of the Italian civil war and resistance to German occupation as lived, experienced, witnessed and felt through the materiality of persons, communities and places directly implicated in the quotidian business of surviving. These persons do not include just the guerrilla-style partisans, but rather also civilians and German Wehrmacht soldiers inhabiting the same places and landscapes between autumn 1943 and spring 1945. I mostly use the term 'partisan' to refer to the Italian fighters, but also their helpers. The limited timeframe of inquiry warrants limited generalisation, although the underlying theoretical analysis might lend itself well to other war and conflict contexts.

Acknowledgements

I am extremely thankful to my research participants for their inspirational tales of bravery and duress – for better and for worse. Special thanks go to the Arts and Humanities Council UK, without whom much of this research would not be possible. I am indebted to the insights and support of colleague and mentor David Atkinson. I owe much to my colleagues at Istituto per la Storia della Resistenza e della Società Contemporanea del Vittoriese (ISREV) and Istituto Storico Bellunese della Resistenza e dell'Età Contemporanea (ISBREC) – in particular to Pier Paolo Brescacin, ISREV's Head of Research. I also thank Vittorino Pianca (ISREV) and Enrico Bacchetti and Agostino Amantia (ISBREC) for their inspirational collaboration and advice. I am grateful to Istituto per la Storia della Resistenza e Società Contemporanea della Marca Trevigiana for granting me use of one of their archival photographs for the book cover, and endlessly indebted to Sonia Residori for her support and precious information on the Vicenza region, Veneto. I also owe a huge thank you to the staff at the Archivio dei Diari, Pieve Santo Stefano, and to the staff at Tagebuchsarchiv, Emmendingen, for their kind assistance in my research. Many thanks go to the colleagues who read and provided useful feedback on early drafts of this manuscript, namely Mark Pearce, Divya Tolia-Kelly, Nick Saunders and Ruth Whitehouse. Lastly, I am eternally indebted to the wonderful individuals who kindly crowdfunded my research trip to Freiburg at a time when I was not formally employed by an institution: they are, in alphabetical order, Céline Ammeux, Lee Buss, Susanna Harris, Erik Jälevik, Sudeep Menon, Robert Monk, Gabriel Moshenska, Neeme Oja, David O'Reilly, Hilary Orange, Alessandra Salvin and three anonymous pledgers.

Introduction
A poetics of civil war and resistance

> Memories of the outside world will never have the same tonality as those of home and, by recalling these memories, we add to our store of dreams.
>
> Gaston Bachelard, *The Poetics of Space* (1958: 6)

Figure I.1 The killing of Armando Baldini by Garibaldi Brigade partisans. Vittorio Veneto, 30 April 1945.

Baldini dies in the end: journey through a world at war

Hastily scribbled 'field' diaries, hidden and forgotten as the resistance fighters moved on or died but then retrieved, typed up and circulated; cups of coffee and mugs of home-brewed beer drunk at oral history interviews; words full of hate and neo-Nazi slogans defacing the monuments to the resistance movement and its martyrs; yellowing letters written to worried parents at home; sketchbooks and sketches; bullet holes and bullet wounds; military draft posters calling the youth of the fatherland; love poems; scarves, lockets and other belongings of the dead; the resentful anti-memorials to the Fascist victims of the civil war; abandoned, burned out or destroyed villages and streets, haunting in their melancholy materiality; mass graves and their memories; the bodies of those telling stories about the war; and the tears shed for those who did not make it – these are the bread-and-butter of Second World War materiality past and present.

Italy joined the war on Germany's side in 1940 under the aegis of Mussolini's Fascist regime. Eventually the Prime Minister was ousted on 25 July 1943 and imprisoned; then on 8 September 1943, the Italian King stipulated an armistice with the Allies. The Italian capitulation to the Allies (better known as Armistice Day) precipitated civil war when Hitler freed Mussolini, who in turn established a new Fascist regime in the north. From then on, the Fascists, in tandem with the occupying German Wehrmacht, fought the Italian anti-Fascists. Supported by the Allies, slowly creeping up the peninsula, the resistance eventually succeeded in defeating both Fascists and Germans. Each chapter tells the story of a phase of this momentous event in recent European history framed within its quotidian, exceptional and unforgettable remains in memory, and in the physical world through a 'critical and historicized phenomenology' (Veder 2013: 8).

Look at Figures I.1 and I.2. What do you see in those two photographs? On 30 April 1945 in Vittorio Veneto, a town in northeast Italy (my hometown), a firing squad composed of anti-Fascist resistance fighters from the largely Communist Garibaldi Brigades executed a Lieutenant of the Guardia Nazionale Repubblicana (GNR henceforth): Armando Baldini. Baldini was not local to this area: he came from the Marche region of central Italy and had found himself deployed in the Danilo Mercuri Division of Mussolini's army in the northeast; here he would meet his end. We know exactly how Baldini was captured thanks to contemporary written sources (Brescacin 2013); we do not, however, know exactly who he *was* in the wider context of the civil war, nor do we know why he had to die. In the frantic and often bloody weeks following the Allied liberation of Italy on 25 April 1945, such killings were not rare (Neri Sernieri 1995; Mammone 2006). But was Baldini even a Fascist? Many apologists of Fascism have been quick to discredit the cause of the resistance movement precisely because of the summary violence bloodying city streets all over the country in the immediate aftermath of the war (see Pansa's 2003 revisionist best seller).

In any case, there are several interpretations for Baldini's execution. Many Vittorio Veneto residents claim that Baldini was executed here to avenge the killing of a young partisan on the self-same spot in the spring of 1944. My colleague and fellow Vittorio Veneto native Pier Paolo Brescacin has conjectured that perhaps the Danilo Mercuri Division had been accused of perpetrating violence against

Figure I.2 The killing of Baldini.

the populace (2012: 13), and Baldini himself had been identified as the instigator. Brescacin, however, does wonder if perhaps Baldini was simply guilty of wearing the wrong uniform.

Still, we do not know exactly why Armando Baldini had to die. But we know what the moments immediately before his demise looked like thanks to two photographs taken by an unknown person at the site of his execution. The expression on the condemned man's face is indecipherable, but we should probe behind the ambiguity of the photographic façade. We want to satisfy our 'curiosities about the dead' (de Certeau 1988: 10), excavate the materiality of the event stratified and congealed, but emanating from, an archetypal object of material culture – the photographs.

When I held the photographs in my hand, they felt small, fragile and inconsequential, yet alive somehow. They were a paper epitaph to a condemned man. After engaging with this 'dense' historicity, I felt the need to carry out a photographic ethnography to better understand what had happened, and who Baldini really was in the context of the Italian civil war. The photographic autopsy of Baldini's demise does not imply any victimisation of an individual representative (perhaps despite himself) of gratuitous Fascist violence and Colonial dehumanisation and repression. Rather, I want to think how we could reconstruct Baldini's world at the point of death, and to consider his role in a world inhabited by himself, his executioners and a myriad other elements leading to his death. The photographic 'trace' invites me to try to 'get to' the sensations experienced by this particular human being at the point where other human beings were about to end his life. Even though the moment is on a printed page, I still feel close, vicariously, to that world.

Recent warfare and political events' corporeality and multivocality are being heralded across disciplines ranging from sociology to conflict resolution studies, not forgetting anthropology and cultural geography (Curti 2008; Anderson 2010; Henig 2012; Sylvester 2012; Wool 2013; Cobb 2013; Cornish and Saunders 2014; Cole 2015; McSorley 2012b). Cobb defines 'conflict' as a situation given by markers such as violence, exclusion and displacement (2013: 7) which are all embodied, material practices. Still, attention to the perceptual multivocality of the political in World War Two narratives is inadequate; it is as if mainstream narratives, still largely dominated by the 'Nazis vs. the rest of the world' model, should not be questioned. Historical perspectives on the war have seldom attended to what de Certeau calls the 'making' and 'doing' inherent in historiography as a practice embedded in the human condition (1988). While this volume deconstructs and problematises precisely that kind of dichotomous (and disembodied) thinking, it also scaffolds a broad theory of conflict experience that handles identity and materiality as one and the same, and then contextualises it in the historical setting of the Italian civil war of 1943–45 in order to untangle its more elusive mechanisms of othering, exclusion, alienation and violence.

Identities, then, are central to this argument. A key idea is that our embodied materialities allow or enable us to communicate, or not, with others. Materiality is the self-aware baggage we carry within us and skin deep, and something acts as a sort of 'passport' inscribed in the flesh, in the colouring of our eyes or the smell of our skin as much as our gait, dialect, sexual orientation and personal histories (Ingold 2000; Tolia-Kelly 2004, 2006). Even when anthropologists have tackled the issue of the *materiality of behaviour*, some (i.e. Schiffer 1999) have tended to speculate in the abstract, often by deploying terminology and theories directly borrowed from the natural sciences. While endeavouring to investigate the materiality of everyday communication and behaviour, the emphasis has been on building models and categories. These studies have often overlooked the workings of emotion and affect as catalysts and/or precipitates of political events. On the other hand, anthropological and cultural historical studies concerned with the identity and emotions of historical actors have often completely ignored the materiality of experience (both historical and historiographical) and any substantial discussion of emplacement (what it meant to be in place) from the final text (e.g. Thelen 1990; Reddy 2001; Woolf 2005; Rosenwein 2006, but see Riley and Harvey 2005). Other ethnographies of war (Cappelletto 2003; van Boeschoten 2005; Focardi 2013) exclude entirely the materiality of the everyday and the material catalysts of memory from their accounts.

Moreover, the affective and non-representational turn in geography (Thrift 2000, 2004; Rose 2002; Sedgwick Kosofsky 2003; Lorimer 2005; Whatmore 2006; Anderson and Harrison 2010; Simonsen 2010; Jones 2011) have produced highly intellectualised studies on the workings of the sensing body and its networked environment, but these works come across as strangely abstracted, almost wary of the run-of-the-mill materiality of the meaningful assemblages and lifeworlds they theorise (but see Stewart 2007).

A shift from human actors to non-human agency and places – *contra* the primacy of human experience advocated by classical phenomenology – has further sharpened the awareness of lived experience and memory as a colourful ensemble of moods, imaginations and intimations in which human and non-human actors interact in meaningful ways (Bendix 2000; Brennan 2004; Ahmed 2004b; DeSilvey 2006; Henare et al. 2007; Anderson and McFarlane 2011; Barad 2013; Crouch 2015 et al.). Wetherell (2013: 3) conceives of affect as embodied meaning-making; Ahmed posits that affects stick to people and objects, too (2010). Affects, we are told, have the potential to be a transformative experience (Witcomb 2010). Moreover, affects are something that affective communities *do* (Walkerdine 2009, 2010). Affects, then, it may be argued, similarly permeate mnemonic communities such as war veterans, too. Thrift (2000: 36 ff.) makes the case for affect as 'embodied dispositions', that is to say, potential emotions and perceptions-to-be. Various methodologies have been employed in an attempt to explore the materiality of affect and perception, although historical studies have been peculiarly reluctant to adopt this theoretical approach.

However, affect-centred research has mostly neglected the historical dimension of the lived world: a significant lacuna that needs rectifying. This separation of lifeworld, time, person and object does not make sense – cross-culturally (see also Hoskins 1998; Dant 1999; Olsen 2003; Turkle 2007; Edwards et al. 2006; Henare et al. 2007; Dudley 2009; Wetherell 2013). Treating objects, their biographies and places as peripheral to the foregrounded human action and interaction occludes an in-depth understanding of the moods, motivations and atmospheres influencing human actors to behave the way they did towards one another and towards their environing lifeworlds – their *Umwelt*, as it were (von Uexküll 1926; Ingold 2000; Agamben 2002). In biology, the idea of Umwelt purports that each living being is only able to perceive so many stimuli and signals from their environment, which is necessarily limited, and that different creatures experience different, and often incompatible, *Umwelten*.

This book takes the stance that virtually everything to do with identity, human interaction and perception involved a materiality of some kind. Materiality *makes* our Umwelt and acts as a bridge between our different versions and declinations of that perceptible world (Taussig 1991; Pink 2009) and between different times (Seremetakis 1994). The experience of civil war and occupation deeply affected the lives and identities of all actors in the conflict, but also, and perhaps most importantly, their materialities. This volume takes 8 September 1943, capitulation day,[1] as the affective 'event in action' that changed lives, imaginations and experiential worlds in wartime Italy. The day marks the shift in allegiance from Germany to the Allies, and the start of the military invasion and reprisals by the Reich against Italians suspected to be implicated in resistance activities. The date 8 September 1943 is a temporal but also a spatial benchmark, dividing two worlds and two experiential realms: the uncanny from the known and familiar. After capitulation, we can begin to trace the emergence of novel practices and experiences, 'new categories of person or types of object' made up of 'intersecting processes, entities, and forces in ways that might be unexpected, unforeseen, and unplanned' (Fowler 2013: 27).

Fleshly, sensorially saturated and precarious material worlds had to be learnt anew, adapted, or imagined in order to cope with the sudden uncanniness of the everyday. New sensory modes had to be assimilated in changing circumstances (Classen 1993). After an out-of-the-blue, life-changing event such as the Armistice, with its subsequent sudden change of sides in the conflict, 'a new experiential knowledge about the vulnerability of solid objects, like bodies [. . .] and buildings, has transformed their experience of seeing, feeling, and moving in the world' (Wool 2013: 421). Now, Baldini's demise is a portal (for want of a better word) to an understanding of the vulnerability that permeated the events of the resistance and civil war.

This book assembles a syntax of sensory geographies, affective histories and bodily anthropologies of conflict and occupation. Indeed, the stories in this book progressively trace the *heteroglossia* (after Bakhtin 1981) or speaking at cross-purposes characterising the events of the civil war. This process is important, but not altogether irreversible: in the final chapter, I suggest that heteroglossia is responsible for the misunderstandings and divided memory of the conflict, and propose that we engage with and report others' stories with imagination and sympathy (Ricoeur 1996) as the only way to reach out to others humanely and fairly. Cobb also warns us that

> agency itself is all too often a casualty of conflict. In order to 'get on', people must be able to tell a story in which they are positioned as agents, able to describe and account for their own victimization, able to *respond humanely* to the stories of others'.
>
> (Cobb 2013: 8, my emphasis)

The notion that we should respond humanely to the stories of others even when we do not understand them greatly appeals to me, and I strongly believe that responding humanely and attempting to accept and understand the materialities of others could be a step towards a resolution of the painful memories of decade-long conflicts.

The importance of embodying conflict experience cannot be overstated (Curti 2008; Sylvester 2012; Wool 2013; McSorley 2014). A growing literature on the body-in-conflict in sociology and international relations studies is expanding our expectations of how war affects corporeal experience, but there are limitations; namely, we lack critical geographical discourses on how this wartime embodiment occurs in place, and on the materiality of other agents in a world at war. So, for instance, Sylvester proposed to 'pull the bodies and experiences of war out of entombments created by theories operating at higher levels of analysis and into the open as crucial elements of war' (2012: 503). Being physically in conflict is a paramount aspect of all war experience: all bodies from the activist to the child become involved in it. In thinking about embodiment as a way of knowing the world at war, here I use embodiment as a 'mode of presence and engagement in the world' (Csordas 1994: 12). The expression 'mode of presence' underlies the whole spectrum of wartime experience, but not only the mode of presence (or absence) we live by has long-reaching consequences. Society – now as then – is constituted by the agencies and bodies of many, who create worlds through their corporeal existence and movement across locales (see also Munn 1996, 2013). No story, witness account or war testimony is devoid of a fundamental ingredient: a meaningful setting in which and through which stories and materialities unfolded, intermingled and produced understandings of the world.

The Italian war experience lends itself to a rich 'hands-on' ethnography of the entanglement of place, thing, person, event and conflict dynamics – what Witmore calls a 'mediation': 'the multiple ways humans and non-humans swap properties in the process of moving towards a goal, a possibility, an outcome' (2007: 552). Through the photographic evidence of Baldini's doom, we can trace the goals and possibilities that that event created in its unfolding: what would have happened if a high-ranking Allied officer's intervention had stopped Baldini's execution? What would have happened to him then? What if there had been a different kind of intervention? Baldini's protestation that he was not a true Fascist? What if he had attempted to run away? White raises some interesting methodological questions: 'What are the canons of evidence for what is untrue?' she asks, and 'what's the historical method for things that never happened?' (2000: 13).

Here I consider conflict materiality as an all-encompassing quality permeating and often determining what happened to identities, bodies, perceptions and interactions. Materiality can be thought of as an overarching story mapping out the entanglement of human beings, other species, things, places, events, stories, trajectories, imaginations and memories – and so much more besides. Materiality, then, also encompasses the ephemeral and the imaginary: from the fleeting instants before the execution of a man wearing the wrong uniform to the partisans' long night watches spent whittling at a piece of wood to pass the time and conquer fear. Places are imbued with memories of our own creation, whether we like it or not (Bachelard 1958 [1969]). War mementoes and relics, the affective sites of feeling and memory, similarly disclose and channel waves of hope, despair, love and hatred in non-linear stories. Multiple stories of occupation, use, discard, attachment and rejection live in 'evocative objects' (Turkle 2007). Participation in a resistance movement can be understood as the enactment and transformation of identities and possibilities: so Baldini's photographs act as a bridge between our world and his, charged with affective energy in a continuity that excites, disorients and moves us.

I have an ulterior motive for wanting to bring these issues to the fore: this fraught history is my own, or rather, it owns *me*. This book is a homage to my ancestors and my homeland, and my authorship a carrier and transmitter of many of the haunting stories within it. It is my attempt at 'gathering [. . .] a historical narrative into the presence of a thing' (Levinas 1998: 163). This volume serves as a 'road map' tracing the presences and absences of conflict experiences – a travelogue through the poetics of war perceived by multiple actors on multiple, shifting experiential planes. After all, absence and presence are modes of givenness of the same reality (Ricoeur 1991: 120).

In order to deploy a broad spectrum of experience in this volume, I review Italian, British and German sources, although German material is not as readily available. I have attempted to integrate competing voices and discordant outlooks whenever possible in an attempt to demonstrate how experience and the senses unify all actors in a conflict that deprived many of their identities, lives, homes and livelihoods. Anti-Fascist voices figure in it as prominently as German and Fascist perspectives. The German memories haunting these pages recall the experiences of Wehrmacht soldiers who fought in Italy between 1943 and 1945 and who left behind interviews, diaries and letters recounting their experience. An inclusivity of perspectives is of paramount importance in our understanding of the war – any war. So with the exception of Chapter 2 that 'picks apart' the main protagonists of these chapters and tells their collective stories ordered into separate sections, I have put competing voices into a mutual conversation. So, rather than treating Germans, Italian Fascists and anti-Fascists, civilians and the Allies separately in relation to a theme (such as material culture, place, storytelling), I weave together their multiple perspectives in the same story.

In attempting to draft an ethnography of these competing perspectives, I am fully aware that, as an Italian partisan's grandchild, I cannot speak for the memories and actions of Germans and Fascists: with the exception of a great-uncle I have never met (see next chapter), the Blackshirts' stories do not concern me, and their perspective is not part of my identity in the same intimate way as the resistance. As a

Figure I.3 A wall plaque commemorating the loss of lives in partisan Division Nino Nannetti.
Photo: Sarah De Nardi

whole, the book's central narrative does not in any way attempt an apology of Fascism or German military invasion, but neither does it overtly critique their moral compass. Instead, multiple actors' voices enter in a dialogue guided by themes and experiences in each chapter, irrespective of nationality and political beliefs. Although this approach will no doubt irk and disturb some, I believe this *intermingling* is 'closer to life' in the world of conflict in which enemies and bystanders dwelled; an ongoing connection of memories and affects serves to bring to life the complex, ambiguous and messy nature of war.

The photographs of Baldini's killing speak of the human condition, the desperate futility of civil war, and the injustice of conflict in general. Beyond the military-historical framework of the greater war, Baldini's fate (and the photographic mementoes of his demise) is but one fragment of a social, cultural and historical world delineated and atomized by the vagaries of violence, displacement and divided memory. The killing of Baldini constitutes an ethnographic-place-as-event (Pink 2009: 49), part of a brutal internecine struggle responsible for the fracturing and division of communities that still scars the nation.

Armchair strategists vs. affective archives

> Academic scholars and armchair strategists should try to figure out step by step *how action takes place*.
>
> (Max Salvadori quoted in Tudor 2004: 21, my emphasis)

How action takes place. As I flipped through Tudor's slender booklet, a compendium of British Special Operations Executive (SOE)-related memories of the Italian resistance, this phrase stuck insistently in my mind. How action takes place. How about how action *makes* place? What of the materiality of historical events? When do battles, events and people become or generate their own material culture? We might begin answering these methodological questions by considering approaches that do not take into account or allow for the materiality and emplacement of events. Historical writings sometimes come across as very abstract; they tend to neglect the human and material side of life as it is lived in practice – in places, surrounded by other beings caught up in their own stories and emotions (see also Stewart 2007; Watson 2007). 'The stories that people tell about place can be both stories that they tell about themselves and others and also a way of telling those stories' (Cole 2015: 2). I agree that this synergy is essential to any project seeking to understand conflict experience.

Law (2004: 84–85) maintains that things possess one of three qualities: presence, manifest absence and otherness. While presence might be commonly understood to refer to the 'being-in-the-world' of an object and its personhood, manifest absence is an 'in your face', blatant absence of something that very much feels as though it should be there. Otherness, Law's third category, refers to absent things that are not manifest and the expression or embodiment of things like routine, insignificance and repression (2004: 85). These three tiers of 'thereness' offer an interesting approach to three of the case studies explored in this study: a mass grave 'othered' in memory and elided with Yugoslavian *foibe* mass graves (Chapter 3); a fabled assemblage of stolen gold and currency that civilians looted in the wake of a bombed-out retreating German column (Chapter 4); and mementoes, or 'sites of feeling' enmeshed in the affective process of storytelling in Chapter 5. Following this line of reasoning leads us to encompass the spatiality and materiality of 'absent things' as well: in one case, the mass grave speaks of the bodies that still haunt the gravesite long after their removal; in another, a robbery perpetrated in 1945 embodies the lingering materiality of an invisible and imagined assemblage of precious objects; in yet another case, local people remembered the display of corpses on a river as the end of days – an act that witnessed the loss or absence of values and human compassion (Chapter 6).

Time and space are interwoven in the materiality of experience – an entanglement of which human lives are but a part (Dant 1999; Gibson 2004; Miller 2008; Miller and Parrot 2009). And that experience is anything but linear. In the context of civil war and military occupation, where every day might be the last – not only for those on the frontline of civil disobedience and armed resistance, but also for anyone deemed culpable of collusion with the 'rebels' – each day took on a particularly intense quality. The temporality of the everyday is closely interlinked with the materiality of the war in the sense that in the midst of confusion and precariousness of conflict objects, things and places tend to act as landmarks, beacons that guide (if not shape) people's actions, projects, thoughts and desires. After all, we should consider that sabotages, ambushes, raids, desertions and executions did not take place as abstract log or diary entries – as we have come to learn about them in the archives. Rather, these were real-life, distressing events involving tense bodies in the battlefield of city streets, hillsides, remote villages and treacherous woodland (Curti 2008). Wartime lives depended on coping mechanisms and strategies which they learnt by going along in the world, by perception which is not the encoding of nature by the senses but rather a process of learning (Ingold 2000: 79). The battles, clashes and reprisals were events, actions affecting friends, neighbours, foreigners and spies, all of whom were implicated in the tense and confusing daily process of fighting and striving to survive; survival did not include an instruction manual, nor did it entail a plan of action beyond the next few hours (see Secchia and Nizza 1968; Behan 2009).

Learning about place and the revelation of the environment to us as we engage with it are paramount. After all, learning and gaining experience represent ways in which we frequently cope with our surroundings and make sense of them; moving around in a landscape and engaging with other actors unmasks the lifeworld's concealment, bringing its aspects and qualities to explicit attention – with particular focus on the concept of *dwelling* (Ingold 2000). In coming to terms with the present and haunting materiality of the invisible or absent past, affect acts as the powerful bond between worlds, between what we can grasp and feel and discuss and suffer, and the traces of things and people gone, but not forgotten. This tension is already an affect even when not explicitly understood as such, whereby materiality and immateriality are parts of a 'spectrum of engagements and entrapments' (Meskell 2010: 212).

Despite the fact that the events in this volume occurred in a different time and place (for non-Italian readers, anyway), their stories are present in the here and now (here being a site of their retelling – this volume; see also van Alphen 1997: 93–94). We feel close to this absent past because although the lifeworlds and realities in this book have passed, and people who have since passed away inhabited and interacted with the places we come across, they all left behind potent and far-reaching traces. These traces are by no means self-explanatory, nor are the presences and absences of their materiality straightforward. In her extraordinary memoir, Magda Ceccarelli (2011: 244) commented that the self-appointed commentators speculating about the social situation on the radio, spinning sophisticated theories, did not know what it was like to live in the everyday, for people who have to eat every day somehow, and sleep, and clothe themselves, and live and take risks.

In Chapter 3, we will encounter messenger girl Rosetta Banchieri, who undertook dangerous missions to deliver food and intelligence to the partisans; the anticipation of a well-deserved meal and a cosy slumber under warm sheepskin rugs was a force pulling her on and giving her aching body the strength to conclude her mission as much as her ideals and loyalty to the freedom fighters. In the same chapter, English intelligence officer John Ross will recount his mortifying discovery of fleas. In Chapter 4, it is not physical objects that affect imaginations and identities – rather, the rumour of treasure illegally confiscated by civilians (and resistance activists) from retreating German lorries and subsequently hidden was to shape a community and change lives. In Chapter 5, Bruno Canella enacts through his wife's letter/poem the affects and lives of three individuals: Bruno, his very ill spouse and the partisan friend executed by the Germans in his prime. All these entanglements *matter*.

De Certeau (1988), Frisch (1990) and Darnton (1991), in particular, have argued that history is never linear, always entangled with the preoccupations of the historian and their publics, the 'webbings of conflicts, or plays of force' (de Certeau 1988: 48) unravelling in the everyday; Frisch's 'more history' approach also seeks to encompass the exuberance of past lives from the perspective of the grassroots and the ethnographic. Darnton situated himself as an ethnographic historian who studies the way ordinary people made sense of the world. 'He [sic] attempts to uncover their cosmology, to show how they organized reality in their minds, and expressed it in their behaviour' (Darnton 1991: 11). In our engagement with the history of the resistance and occupation in Italy, we can reclaim Darnton's statement in a cultural, affective and non-Cartesian manner, in an attempt to explore the way in which 'non-ordinary' people made sense of their worlds from an experiential point of view. In this way we may posit the self, identity and materiality as essential to our understanding of historical phenomena. Indeed, we will be able to 'sense' that the open-endedness of history is at its most vivid and vibrant in the stories told by witnesses among the pages that follow.

Which brings us to a crucial theme in this volume: storytelling as a form of material culture. The practice of storytelling co-produces history and shapes the material world through the actions and interactions of storyteller, listener, reader and their surroundings (de Certeau 1988; Ricoeur 1996; Jackson 2002). The material life of storytelling weaves around the seams and joins of everyday life, bringing history to life. Using affective storytelling to frame historical events frees up and foregrounds the unrealized potentialities of the historical past. Affect can highlight what is deemed important in historical narratives (see Watson 2007) and relevant today, creating (or co-creating) inclusive and relevant histories. That is also a way to understand affect as a forward-pulling diachronic amalgam of impulses and energies precipitating in resistance movements in Europe: hearsay and rumours (Chapter 4).

> To understand the full significance of the mid-war crises in Germany, we need to think more about the uncensorable forms of public opinion which were voiced in the form of rumour and humour, and we need to explore the wartime crises in Nazi Germany often profoundly dissonant qualities of individual subjectivity.
> (Stargardt 2011: 201–202)

Figure I.4 Gufo Nero (Black Owl) Brigade composed of Allied soldiers and German, Austrian and Polish deserters.

Source: Wikicommons

The materialities of absence

This book also interrogates the spatiality, materiality and agency of absence. Chapters 3, 4 and 5 devote special attention to the ambivalent and often messy nature of entities, things, people and events implicated in the occurrences happening in Italy between 1943 and 1945, considering them as simultaneously present and absent, embodied and intangible. We might infer that materiality represents not only things and artefacts, but also include 'elements which are not directly "observable" (. . .): desires, ideas etc.' (Fowler 2013: 23). When we think of Baldini's killing, the elements which are not directly observable are the agency and purpose of the photographer, the temperature, weather conditions and atmosphere on that square, and the impression the execution left on the bystanders. What was going on off frame? What dramas unravelled out of shot?

As a historical context redolent of traces in memory, in social customs and in political legacies, the occupation, resistance and civil war constitute the quintessential 'absent present' (Domanska 2006). I have faced the challenge to represent the vibrant and haunting qualities of the lives, stories and places that were at the centre of the lifeworlds of the characters and communities presented in this book. 'Although, strictly speaking, absence is a thing without matter, absence is ordered, remembered, evoked and made discussable and sufferable through materialities' (Meyer 2012: 109). Working with a materiality of absence reveals the challenges posed on social scientists and historians seeking to disentangle the ambiguous borders between what is present and what is literally no longer there (Hallam and Hockey 1991; Buchli 2015). In my interactions with the witness community, in my visits to gravesites and veterans' living rooms, I have experienced precisely that tension: the dissonance between present traces and lost persons, places, emotions and bodies. I have grappled with the materiality of that absence, which I try to conjure up through my autobiographical entanglements in the story. When I think of Baldini's killing, his lost body is at the centre of a human drama unfolding in places that have also changed beyond recognition. I was walking across that very square in the spring of 2015, and the place looked peaceful and serene – the church's forecourt empty save for a few cars. All material traces of the killing ritual have disappeared (Baldini's blood, the shell casings, the priest's prayer book), as have the remnants of the execution of the young partisan on the spot. The accoutrements of both deaths have disappeared, but a lingering memory of this absence remains. Their materiality lives on, emerging not only through places and buildings, but through the process of ethnographic enquiry as well – in the actions and perceptions of researchers.

Stoller 1997: xvi reminds us that a focus on embodiment need not concern the social sciences alone: 'memory and history are an embodied phenomenon'. I use the term 'embodiment', after Csordas (1994), to express the concept of the human body as a channel of interaction with the world, both in experience and in memory.

There are, of course, histories 'from above', constituted by historical texts that are read, reread, interpreted, and re-interpreted. There are, as well, 'histories "from below" that are embodied in objects, song, movement and the body' (Stoller 1997: xvi). The endeavour of understanding bodily and emotional practices, then, should be allowed to inform history as well. This endeavour resonates with de Certeau's approach, subsequently taken up by the so-called historians of emotions (Reddy 2001; Rosenwein 2006, among others). Reddy's study of 'emotional communities' (2001) centres around the socio-political dimension of historical emotion. Echoing social psychology's focus on the dynamics of emotional ingroups and outgroups (Leyens et al. 2000), Reddy contends that every stage of human development is characterised by emotional regimes dictating what emotions become legitimated or excluded, which leads to emotional suffering (see also Kivimäki and Tepora 2009). Are these not manifestations of affect? Could the poetics of such regimes also be understood as 'collective remembrance' and even counter-memory (Lipsitz 1990)?

In the chapters that follow, I use excerpts of interviews and memoirs to unravel events taking place between 1943 and 1945. I also map out the affective underbelly of the war by using affects as a sort of connective tissue between the myriad versions of events, discordant memories, feelings and 'truths' existing in parallel. Affects in these stories express the interconnectedness of events, people, places, things and meaningful worlds resonating within the stories, memories and narratives shaping the material culture(s) of the Italian war and resistance. In the following chapters, archival and oral sources will be interrogated through four interconnected themes: the construction of identities through emplacement and materiality, the problematic materiality of the body-at-war, the affective materiality of 'things' and objects in understanding war experience, and the interplay between person and place. Together, these strands serve to disentangle identity formation processes and socio-cultural politics and poetics of inclusion and exclusion.

In turn, these ideas consider the overarching role of the materiality and 'a-whereness' of embodied feelings and 'gut' instincts and imaginations to unravel the modes of production of geographies of conflict. This thick, embodied geography consists in multiple and entangled senses of place. In other words: how did people fabricate and cope with the idea of the enemy, and how did the Other's foreignness or alterity act to destabilise their worlds? As a whole, an experiential approach offers a hands-on contribution to ongoing debate in the cultural-historic, anthropological and cultural-geographical disciplines. It will provide a case study-based and historically grounded debate on issues of embodiment and emplacement, whilst offering the reader an opportunity to get acquainted with the complex phenomenon of the Italian resistance through the dual lens of the spatial and sensory. The stories in this book will take us on a journey through and in memory alongside the actors in the resistance and occupation, as we follow their emotions, preoccupations and plans.

Chapter 1 positions Italy in the wider European war context and takes as a starting point a momentous date — Italy's capitulation and Armistice with the Allies on 8 September 1943 — to introduce the idea of conflict materiality. Here I also explore the extent to which the 1943 Armistice has not only a temporal dimension but also 'acts' as liminal space in the imaginary and poetics of the whole Italian war. Chapter 2 devotes attention to the complex interplay of identities in the war and during the start of the German occupation in September and October 1943 by maintaining that competing/alien materialities contributed to processes of hostility, exclusion and othering. Chapter 3 focuses on the materiality of the body in the turbulent months of late 1943 and mid-war, in 1944. Chapter 4 explores the affectivity of stories as 'intangible' material culture from the Armistice until Liberation. Chapter 5 focuses on the materiality of wartime mementoes and 'evocative objects' (after Turkle 2007), such as a poem and photographs, as 'sites of feeling' born, collected and shared in the last days of war and in its aftermath. Chapter 6 engages with the related notion that places and spaces of resistance and conflict constitute material culture insofar as actors in the war made, learnt about and unmade place: the momentous last days of the war orientate the spatial stories within. The final chapter does not so much conclude but rather complicates the 'story' woven through these pages by opening up problems rather than offering closure. The last chapter tries to reconcile the troubled 'forever-remnant trace of a beginning that is as impossible to recover as to forget' (de Certeau 1988: 47). In so doing, it makes a case for compassion and humane engagement with our own and others' stories and mutual materialities as a way to reconcile painful memories of war and conflict.

The interview process

'You never know with these interviews', said my mother. She sometimes drove me to the interviews, as she personally knew many of my research participants, who had been her father's partisan friends. After interviews, on the drive home, we would often comment together on what had happened. Mum would get animated, comparing the experiences of the person or people we had just met with her recollections of her father's resistance stories. 'You know, I think *Nonno [my Grandad Domenico 'Memi' Favero]* said something different about that attack on the Barracks in June 1944', she once said. Was she trying to tell me that the person we had just talked with had *lied*? Once she parked the car before one of our 'encounters' with a sweet elderly lady whom neither of us knew. Her name and address I had found scouring through an old Associazione Nazionale Partigiani d' Italia (ANPI) partisan directory and the local phonebook. Mother went on, 'Do you ever get the feeling that you are their guest, or even a friend, but not a researcher?' What I now assume my mother was trying to say is that, to her untrained eye, my encounters with the research participants seemed too unofficial, too cosy and too intimate to constitute 'proper' scholarship. Her comment made me think. Not only was her input in my research priceless – *she* is a partisan's daughter – but her participation in the research and analysis process has been so substantial that I wonder if she should appear as co-author of some of my work. My point is this: auto-ethnographic fieldwork is challenging due to the difficulty in separating the natural, mundane everyday encounters with members of one's own cultural and affective group from the research 'data' to be used in scholarship. Much of the ethnographic data I use in this monograph is the outcome of what, to my mother, looked like informal chats over coffee or a glass of wine. The fact that I wrote this book based on insights gained in sitting rooms, gardens and front yards over refreshments and gossip and then wove them together with theoretical abstractions fascinated her. My grandmother Maria was of a different opinion: she was unable to understand why on earth I would bother digging around when everyone around her, she claimed, was trying to forget and move on. Her story, told in the next chapter, may go some way towards explaining her feelings.

Note

1 Capitulation Day, 8 September 1943, saw the surrender of Italy to the Western Allies after months of secret negotiations between the Italian King and Marshal Badoglio and the Anglo-Americans.

1   8 September 1943, 'end of days'
Italy's capitulation and its dystopian aftermath

> My father and I walk together across the courtyard, eyeing his late Uncle Franco's house as we approach. He is telling me the story of Franco's improbable adventures during the war – except that those rocambolesque adventures did not take place in exotic battlefields or in the heat of gunfire up in the hills – it happened right there in that yard. I listen, amused, as Dad speaks with a tone that is imbued with a curious kind of pride about his uncle's inventiveness. An almost Ulyssean cunning (I am thinking, sharpened by fear) led Uncle Franco to dodge the persistent, ominous German and Fascists' drafts by constructing a bunker under the chicken coops in the yard. It is a story, my Dad says with a chuckle, that Uncle Franco was fond of telling over Sunday supper when Dad and my aunt visited. The story was told in the epic tone of a great exotic adventure a' la Jules Verne. After the narration was over, Uncle would inevitably take them to the spot. Now I was being led to that same spot, a witness implicated in a bizarre, yet moving, postmemory of the conflict. Good old Uncle Franco.

Italy's capitulation or Armistice Day, 8 September 1943, is an event traditionally studied as a political and strategic landmark for the Italian war, although it meant much more than simply a change in allegiance (Ginsborg 1990). The caption to the photograph in Figure 1.1 refers to a 'party all over Italy' because at the time, people thought that that was it: Italy would finally be at peace. Not so. That day signified the rise of a dangerous new reality made of shifting identities and roles; the switch to the Allied side created the uneasy identities of spies and collaborators, and pushed dissident lives underground. It was an event whose antecedents were inadequate to fully explain its emergence; as an event, 'its settlement, when under way, is uncertain; and it makes a real difference in the world, for good or ill' (Connolly 2013: 404). Taking 8 September 1943 as a paradigm for change, this volume

Figure 1.1 In a town near Rome, people celebrate Italy's Armistice with the Allies.
Source: Agenzia Nazionale Stampa Associata (ANSA)

attempts a phenomenological exploration of the unstable and often ephemeral new practices and materialities it precipitated. An attention to the perceptual shift in circumstances caused by Italy's capitulation on that day illuminates several paramount factors of the war: sensing the new world order engendered by the shift can lead us to better understand why some persons were implicitly or explicitly biased against others; how places and things were situated and experienced; how identities were constructed and how communities and individuals remember, evoke and share the memory of conflict events today. For Antze and Lambek, then, identities work through a 'dialectical, ceaseless activity of remembering and forgetting, assimilating and discarding' (1996: xxix). This volume attempts to release the differences and potentialities in conflict events, and in so doing to unlock 'the silent power of the possible' (Heidegger 1996: 360) as a viable research topic.

'Guerrilla warfare is even more cruel than conventional war, the chances of surviving slimmer. Whoever joined a patriot or partisan band . . . signed his or her death warrant. "It had to be seen to be believed", was said later. It was the atonement for Fascist crimes' (Max Salvadori quoted in Tudor 2004: 24). With hindsight, significance was attached to the events, but what about the messiness of their unfolding? What about actions, reactions and consequences in shaping the identities of those who witnessed and participated in the events of resistance, collaboration and occupation? I disagree with Antze and Lambek (1996: xii) that the idea of memory has become entangled with the study of trauma, 'memory worth remembering . . . is memory of trauma'(1996: xii). Wartime memory encompasses so much more: the mundane, the everyday and the quietly uncanny, as well as the traumatic and the disruptive. Memory also defines how we define ourselves. As human beings, we tend to identify with and enact those memories we choose or are able to foster and cherish (see also Radstone 2007), but as Hirsch (2008) noted, we might also come to inhabit others' memories as if they were our own, like my father recounting Uncle Franco's adventures in his yard bunker. Indeed, the everyday was the arena in which the occupation and resistance were experienced. Hill (2013: 392) has argued that 'repetition is crucial to the reproduction and evocation of memory; the repetition of stories told, objects used, and paths walked'. We might infer that, as an affectual event, a resistance movement to Nazism and Fascism would take an energetic, emphatic and proactive form – but this is not necessarily so. A widespread sentiment, compassion towards those in active combat, could take place and exist in distinct separation from the heat of the fight. Not all resistance was armed, as Semelin justly pointed out. He proposed the concept of civilian resistance, defined as 'the spontaneous process of resistance by civilian society using unarmed means, and mobilizing either its principal institutions or its people – or both at the same time' (1993: 2). Was Uncle Franco a civilian resistance activist? My father's proud recollections of his deeds would seem to suggest that is the case in family memory.

Let us use the killing of Baldini as an example of selective memory. Any Fascist sympathisers who look at these photographs might condemn and inhabit a discourse that renders the resistance movement impure and unjust. When a resistance veteran looks at the same images, they might get a sense that the killing was a 'job that had to be done' in the context of the civil war. Much literature speculating on the meanings and memories of the Italian civil war draws on oral history accounts and memoirs left by the protagonists of the events (Cooke 1997 ed.; Portelli 1997; Morgan 2009, among many others). The uniqueness of personal memories, Morgan argues, seems to fragment historical reality so much that it renders the scholarly obligation to generalise, to explain and to interpret almost impossible (2009). This sentiment seemingly follows the pronouncement that historiography, the act of writing historical facts and events, severs its present time from a past (de Certeau 1988: 3). The foreignness of the past, more complex than chronological distance alone (see Lowenthal 1985), seems to have long affected the way professionals study the past. Yet something has changed: a greater attention to the lived element of the struggle has slowly started to infiltrate scholarly publications, informing our current understanding of the political and social reverberations of the civil war (see, for example, Focardi 2013). Yet we still undertheorize the everyday experience of persons and communities implicated in resistance movements and subjected to German occupation. Rubbed out places, unlikely enemies, contradictory stories and imagined objects: a constellation of 'things' irreducible to documents and data, and exceeding the discursive and representational, populates the lore and memory of the Italian war.

The first purpose of the present chapter is to 'set the scene' by introducing the historical foundation of the workings of competing materialities and identities suddenly taking shape and spiralling out of control after Armistice Day. It is a reflection on the multiple ways in which competing materialities feature in wartime interactions.

Here, the ineradicable conjunction between individuals, things and place in conflict cannot be understated: from plaques on the wall to the beloved yellowing relics of private museums, materiality is paramount to any understanding of conflict experience and its poetics. The writing of the present manuscript relies on precisely that kind of materiality; the act of writing, remembering and conceptualising in the present day relies on the constellation of artefacts, stories, people and places I have come across in my research and the fact that they all *mattered* to me and to one another. Building on this perspective, I explore the everyday dimension of materiality inbuilt in the narratives developed in the coming chapters. The narratives, or stories, will develop of their own accord as is the way in real life: once told, they will beg to be remembered.

1.1 My family history as a story of the resistance

A discussion bringing to the fore the maelstrom of identities and materialities of a historical event of this import would sound hollow without an elucidation of my subjective and autobiographical investment in this research. I recognise that, as a native of an area crucial to the development of the resistance, I somewhat unsteadily position myself within that same cultural history. After six years of meeting and interviewing partisans and their families I am coming to terms with my own 'place' within the research process and its lively materiality. Indeed, as I worked on the anti-Nazi and anti-Fascist resistance movement in my hometown, Vittorio Veneto, and conducted fieldwork in the Treviso, Belluno, Vicenza and Pordenone provinces, I actively and critically scrutinised an emotional heritage deeply rooted in my own family history and cultural background: in this chapter I call this dense entanglement 'autobiographical materiality', a habitus (after Bourdieu 1986) or set of cultural and emotional meanings and perceptions that you are born in and carry with you.

To an extent, the present book is an autoethnography of my family and my native community. My project reflects and is shaped by the relationship of my affective background to the research I 'do', and in fact my family illustrates the rich spectrum of lived experience throughout the resistance episode: here is how. On the one hand, my maternal grandmother Maria had an older brother in the Fascist 'Brigate Nere' who died in a partisan ambush in 1945, aged only twenty. After he was killed, his mother (my great-grandmother) swore that she would never tolerate the sight of a partisan: her only son had been taken from her by the murdering 'bandits'. However, after the war Maria went on to marry my grandfather Domenico, an ex-partisan. I am not exactly sure how my great-grandmother saw this fact, but they all seemed to get along well enough. There was never any talk of great-grandmother's attempt to challenge Maria's decision to marry Domenico, at any rate. My granny assures us that she only accepted my grandfather's courtship because he had been one of the *good* partisans – a humane patriot who had openly shunned gratuitous violence.

In contrast to Nonno Domenico's 'good' resistance, my grandmother's older sister had another experience. Widowed in her forties, Palmira remarried a former member of the local Communist Garibaldi brigades. My grandfather Domenico never liked his brother-in-law; when explicitly quizzed about this antipathy, he would answer that this chap, a butcher by trade, had also been known as a butcher of men in his partisan days. Without going into detail, my Nonno explained that he had known his brother-in-law back then, when he was not squeamish in meting out punishment on enemy hostages and suspected spies. On my father's side, meanwhile, while his father Giuseppe languished rather comfortably in a British prison camp in North Africa, his Uncle Franco spent the best part of the mid-1940s hiding out underneath one of the family's chicken coops to evade Fascist and Nazi drafts. Apparently he just could not make his mind up about what to do, had no clear political conscience and wanted to stay out of trouble. This colourful cast of characters is not only in my DNA, but also constitutes the very backbone of Italian emotional memories of the years 1943–45.

The memory of a great-uncle I never met, the young Fascist killed by partisans, haunts my consciousness in ways that exceed the writing and researching for this book. The legacy of this young man, a stranger to me, is a conflicting particle of my heritage, at odds with the partisan identity defining my mother's side of the family. How do I reconcile the two 'heritages'?

I am related to a Fascist, an anti-Fascist, a prisoner of war and an absconding draft-dodger – all of whom belonged to the same extended family living in the same area. This complexity of identities and motives is one of the reasons why I became interested in the dynamics between places, people, what people did in the war and where they came from. I wanted to find out how the different characters in such a complex lived history experienced their sensory environment, negotiating the paths of their own individual destinies through dangerous environments. I am curious to discover how different actors assimilated and metabolised their political or existential choices through their bodies and emotions. The dramatically intense memories of the veterans cast long shadows onto the present, and I believe their reconstruction to be fundamental to any understanding of the resistance and its arch-nemesis, Fascism. An emphasis on storytelling (Chapter 4) as a manifestation of materiality is crucial here. There are still many stories to tell, and some will remain untold because they belong to the defeated.

Moreover, the ageing storytellers are passing one after one: their stories – and their coterminous materialities – may indeed be too many to record. The nature of the old timers' stories is so disparate and subjective that weaving a coherent, all-encompassing story out of all the hearsay, memories, recriminations, hiding places, accusations, penal procedures, keepsakes, rumours and pride proves undeniably challenging. This book is what I made of it.

Figure 1.2 A witness and a friend.

Photo: Sarah De Nardi

1.2 The genesis of civil war and German occupation

The Italian resistance movement of 1943–45 was an iconic episode. Its mythical and material legacy has had a profound impact on political and intellectual discourse in the post-war period and is still the topic of heated debate today. The resistance movement originated amid the chaos of the Second World War and the collapse of Italy's Fascist regime. Benito Mussolini had risen to power in 1922 in an endeavour to reinstate the power of Italy in the world as the rightful heir of the Roman Empire of old (Lepre 1995). By the end of 1926, all opposition parties had been banned by Mussolini in Italy (Battaglia 1957: 20) and discontent was rife. In 1929, brothers Carlo and Nello Rosselli founded the underground movement Giustizia e Libertà, and several of its members were subsequently exiled for life to the Lipari Islands. In 1937, the OVRA (the Fascist secret police) managed to assassinate the brothers, but in 1942 the old members of the Giustizia e Libertà instituted a political party proper, the Partito d'Azione (The Action Party).

The development of the resistance in Italy was unique to that country, and as such it shaped a uniquely Italian materiality of conflict. The events, imaginaries and occurrences of the conflict in Italy would not have developed without Italy's experience in the First World War – for many, the point of origin of their own materiality enacted during the subsequent conflict. As can be imagined, the symbolic importance of the resistance was decisive for Italians during the war but especially afterwards, as well as representing an important protraction of interwar politics and mirroring First World War grudges against German-speaking foes.

Italy joined the war on the German side on 10 June 1940 as the southern end of the Berlin-Rome Axis. After a disastrous war effort where the German allies often prevaricated, ignored or exploited their Italian comrades, the King and Mussolini's (outlawed) opposition parties decided to put an end to the war travesty. More importantly, the non-Fascist Italian populace acutely felt the desire to surrender from a conflict fought on a side they despised. 'The undermining of Italian morale by radio broadcasts, leaflets, and the spreading of false rumours met with some success as Italian forces faced defeats abroad and conditions for civilians deteriorated at home' (Tudor 2004: 1). And the propaganda worked. British and American forces had first landed in Sicily between 9 and 10 July 1943 (Operation Husky). Mussolini was dismissed from office as Prime Minister on 25 July 1943 by King Emmanuel III amid the dissolving Italian war effort by a coalition of ministers and the monarchy, and was subsequently imprisoned. Yet Mussolini's ousting gave rise to further chaos. During the momentous 'Forty-five Days' following Mussolini's arrest, an anti-Fascist Committee of Opposition met in Milan and effectively dissolved the Fascist party. Despite the population's relief, the war went on and all hell broke loose in Germany: by the end of July 1943, there was a 100,000-strong German presence in Italy (Ginsborg 1990; Behan 2009). Then came D-Day for Italy. On 8 September 1943, a radio announcement reached every wireless in every Italian home which possessed one. King Emmanuel III proclaimed the following:

> The Italian government, having recognized the impossibility of continuing the unequal struggle against the overwhelming power of the opponent, and in order to prevent more and more serious disasters to the nation, has pleaded for an armistice with General Eisenhower, supreme commander of allied Anglo-American forces. The request was granted. Consequently, any act of hostility against the Anglo-American forces must cease by the Italian forces everywhere. However, they will react to attacks from any other source.

The 'allusion' to other parties referred to the Germans who were now, predictably, furious about the ultimate betrayal on the part of the Italians: they had become mortal enemies overnight. A myriad of households in Italy held their breath at that moment, but especially those of families who lived in close proximity to a German barracks or Headquarters. The materiality of the Armistice announcement must have constituted something unprecedented, sly and all-pervasive at the same time. We might imagine the incredulity of a topsy-turvy reality, the uneasy materiality of sweat, bulging eyes, dropped glasses, the crackling static of the wireless radio. The Armistice entailed the as-yet-unknown materiality of a new reality in the making that enveloped everyone and everything: Italians, Fascists, anti-Fascists, Germans, and the Allied prisoners of war stranded in camps whose gates soon hung off their hinges in the haste of escape. With southern Italy in Allied hands, the collapse of the Fascist regime created a political vacuum in the north and centre. Confusion was almost palpable. After the shock to the system of the Armistice, Marshal Badoglio and the King fled from Rome in a panic, fearing German retaliation. It all came about rather suddenly. To most, Armistice Day was to become the only memorable event orientating, shaping and organising one's placelessness or spatial bearings in the aftermath of the conflict.

On 16 February 1985, the *Economist* described the plight of British intelligence officers who were parachuted into Italy after the Armistice of September 1943 as follows: 'men and women (. . .) deep inside enemy-held territory, giving aid to the indigenous resistance movements, and nearly always on the run'. As Tudor observes, Allied officers and agents endured loneliness and hunger, and they had to 'find their way around an unfamiliar maze' (2004: 21). Mainstream academic scholarship has too long neglected these emotional and often raw historical experiences in favour of tidier and more linear narratives of the war and resistance. We might consider what this excerpt tells us about how British intelligence officers felt once they were catapulted onto a warzone. Bodies were sent to perform certain tasks and make place in their wake – places of safety for the resistance and the Allies. Tudor mentions sensations and feelings (loneliness) but also actions (navigate), and states (hunger) that, when combined, they make up the mesh of affect. We might, then, attempt to frame wartime experiences such as the above as so many affects generated by feeling at home (or not), homesickness, loneliness and a sense of alienation in a foreign place.

In Emanuele Artom's partisan diary (Artom and Schwarz 2008: 57), we read that:

> 10 September 1943. A terrible day. Yesterday the Germans stormed Turin and the craziest rumours are going around; they say the Germans cut off people's hands to get their watches, etc. The English radio screams Churchill's and Roosevelt's orders to Badoglio. They talk about the King's abdication. They say that Farinacci is in Turin, that Mussolini has been freed, and that the Fascists have joined forces with the Germans. What is the truth in all this? Only that half of Italy is now German, half is English, and there is no longer an Italian Italy.

As Artom asked in his diary, what was real and what was made-up hysteria? We shall see in Chapter 4 how significant to a materiality of the conflict the power of rumours and hearsay was – how central to the fabrication and enactments of stories about the war and identities in the everyday. The craziest rumours of violence and chaos were going around in the days following Italy's capitulation. Danger was all too real, however. What to do in the near future? Escape, join the resistance, or surrender?

Civilians were also affected by the spatio-temporal shift in political allegiance. Partisan leader Renato De Zordo (a native of Perarolo in the German-occupied and administered Belluno section of the Alpenvorland region) left a brief diary before his capture, torture and death at the hands of the SS on 15 February 1945. Writing about the Armistice, he said:

> All of us we are lost, we feel around blindly in the dark while gunshots echo in our streets. The village lanes resonate with hidden bullets aiming for the backs of those wearing a scarlet band on their uniform sleeve. They are the apparent cause of our ruin. People are dying everywhere, there's a sense of Italian energy dying out, and in every heart you will find the pain and shame of defeat.
> (De Zordo quoted in Amantia and Svaluto Moreolo 2004: 191; original document ISBREC Accession no. RV/B/122)

The thick materiality of the war is powerfully conjured up in these brief lines. The soundscape of sudden ambushes, the rich red band of the Fascist uniforms and the seeping energy of a people are evoked in a vignette that speaks of much more than shifting ideological and political happenings; it speaks of everyday moods embroiled in a complex quotidian sensorium, ordinary and extraordinary at the same time. In an interview, Aida Tiso Olivero (Lotto 2008: 185) shared with her interlocutor the desolate feeling of being dispossessed within her own village. German officers and their Alsatian dogs 'relentlessly' stalked the partisans in the Santa Giustina Bellunese area as early as October 1943. She concluded that 'the province of Belluno had been annexed to Germany: it was no longer Italy'. Aida referred to the fact that the Belluno province of northern Veneto had been declared an operation zone that was part of the greater Reich: Alpenvorland on 10 September 1943 (Gentile 2012) and administered by German-speaking High Commissioner (*Gauleiter*) Franz Hofer (Vendramini 1993). The administrative shift in a mixed-language part of Italy was to have enduring consequences for Italian speakers and German speakers alike, as it fragmented identities more than ever in the far north of the country.

But what of the Allied prisoners of war in Italian camps in the wake of the Armistice? Ian Bell recalled the confusion and displacement following the rather sudden change of tide. When asked what Armistice Day had meant to him, Bell responded:

> Freedom! It was ours at last. But where would we go? We're on our own, sort of. We had to use our common sense and not feel that we are being looked after in the sense that when you're a prisoner of war you're a little bit secure.
> (Bell, Imperial War Museum [IWM]
> Accession no. 19875; Bell 1999)

Leaving behind the relative safety and security of the camp where they had been held, Bell and others escaped into the unknown. They lay low for a few days in a valley, sheltering among the vine trees, until the Italians told them it was safe to leave. By this point, the Germans were carrying out extensive searches within peasant farmhouses to capture escaped POWs. Bell and his fellow escapees were moved from one farmhouse to the next, where they 'dug themselves in the hay and slept in the cowshed. "The Ferraris looked after us wonderfully well" ' (IWM Accession no. 19875; Bell 1999).

Another Allied prisoner of war recalled the moments before the final announcement (Tudor 2004: 8):

> I had only been in the camps for nine weeks when Italy capitulated . . . We knew something was happening. There were rumours galore and we were waiting for an announcement. [. . .] When the armistice was official the compound concert band would play our national anthem. Meanwhile, the Regiment Sergeant Major suggested that we carry on as usual, and nobody moved. Some of the men shouted for the gates to be open straight away, but he told us that this would not happen until he was sure he was right.

On Armistice Day, Sonia Ciapetti was a thirteen-year-old living in Florence with her family. In her diary she commented on the terrified atmosphere in a city square that day. She had got off a bus and was trying to cross the square to go home, but the crowd around her were petrified, silent, listening to a menacing guttural voice addressing them from a German military vehicle. Sonia had never liked the Germans much but now wondered how come 'their allies were behaving like enemies' (Ciapetti 2007: 40). Meanwhile, on 9 September, German Wehrmacht soldier Otto A. commented on the big shake-up thus:

> Something incredible has happened: Italy has betrayed us for the second time. Already on the 3rd they asked for a ceasefire with the Anglo-Americans and now they got it. Since last night at 00:00 we have had a state of alarm. In the middle of the night we packed everything up, which upset some *Kameraden*. We felt around in the dark and bid farewell to our beautiful quarters. We now have to wait and see what will become of us. This is ample proof of the falsity of that whole ancient Roman-Pope loving lot. First Mussolini had to go and then there was no one in charge, then this lot turn their coats in a perfect show of falsehood, letting us believe that they want to stay on our side. Then this! But do you know what – we will win this war no matter what.
> (Otto A., Tagebuchsarchiv Accession no. 802/II, 1–7)

Englishwoman Iris Origo's war diary tells a bottom-up story of occupation and civilian resistance, lending powerful insights into emotional lives during wartime: we learn that on 1 April 1943 (2000: 33), the following change was noted:

> Since January a marked change has come over [Italian] public opinion. The active resentment and dismay which followed upon the Allies' landing in North Africa and the bombing of Italian cities has given place to a despairing apathy. The whole country is sunk under its leaden weight.

Iris' words evoke Reddy's emotional regimes as much as they resonate with Rosenwein's idea of emotional communities. In this case, Italy as a country constituted an emotional community united in their suffering: resentment, dismay, apathy – what better ways to describe affectual states, events and practices? The materiality of the body politics of social discontent is embedded in Iris' choice of words: 'leaden weight'. One gets a feel for the slugging, onerous business of living day after day in political apathy which is not quite 'becoming' expectation or action. For Connolly (2013: 400), '(p)olitics (. . .) is experimental action extending into the element of mystery of the future'. And yet, as well as manifesting itself in apparently 'passive' or static mundane events, affect has the power to make a change. It is dynamic and political. 'Typically, sharp bursts of affect are action-oriented. They constitute a strong push to do something' (Wetherell 2013: 29).

I would like to suggest that the very decision to rebel against the repressive social, cultural and political Fascist-Nazi alliance would precipitate one of the most powerful and iconic affectual events in history – the anti-Fascist armed resistance. Indeed, in the midst of the unprecedented chaos, all the anti-Fascist parties who had been persecuted and driven underground by Fascism were suddenly free to return to the political scene. After the Armistice announcement, political parties and non-politically affiliated patriots established the Comitato di Liberazione Nazionale (CLN), with an HQ in Milan (Behan 2009) and with regional CLNs set up all over the country. The situation was complicated. The Wehrmacht occupied northern Italy as early as 9 September, the day after Allied Armistice Day. On 12 September, when specialist SS forces launched Operation Eiche and sprung Mussolini from captivity, Hitler installed him as head of the Italian Social Republic (RSI, or Salò Republic) on the shores of Lake Garda in the occupied north.

Mainstream discourses on the resistance have tended to privilege a homogenous canonical image of the patriotic guerrilla fighters, known as the partisans, as jointly striving towards the same goal: putting an end to Fascism once and for all and driving out the Nazis from Italy (Battaglia 1953; Ginsborg 1990). The different groups that constituted the resistance – and particularly the armed bands – struggled against the occupation of northern and central Italy by German Nazi forces and their allies, the Salò Republic, the puppet regime led by Mussolini and the remnants of the Fascist dictatorship. The resistance was truly significant in both military and political terms. Numbers pertaining to its success vary, but journalist and ex-partisan Giorgio Bocca estimates that 300,000 Italians were involved in direct action against the Nazi-Fascist Salò regime by April 1945. Many more supported the partisans with food, provisions, intelligence, shelter and other everyday necessities. SOE Special Forces expert Lawrence Lewis claims that up to 70,000 of the armed partisans were killed and a further 40,000 wounded (1985: 23). The rank and file of the resistance grew substantially through to 1945. From a base of around 9,000 in late 1943 and 20,000–30,000 in the spring of 1944, Paul Ginsborg (1990) estimates there was an average of 100,000 partisans before their recruitment accelerated and their numbers exploded in the final months of the war. This rapid rise in the resistance numbers was due to more and more ex-Fascists and Wehrmacht deserters joining partisan bands. Bocca, using the most stringent of criteria, claims that 300,000 active partisans existed by April 1945. Of these, Bocca estimates 35,000 fatalities. This staggering figure is backed by the findings of Italian historian and former partisan Claudio Pavone, who offers precise figures of 44,720 dead and 9,980 killed in reprisals (1991).

Emanuele Artom, a doomed Jewish resistance fighter in the mountains of Piemonte and Val d'Aosta in northwest Italy, described the state of affairs of the partisan life in his compelling and moving war diary (Artom and Schwarz 2008). In an entry dated mid-November 1943 (Artom and Schwarz 2008: 61), he observed:

> The life of a bandit is very complicated and endless accidents happen. . . . [I will recount] two episodes: a drunken partisan fights with a policeman and

is taken away for a few hours, then released; another impregnates a girl. You have to write these facts, because in a few years a neopatriotic or pseudo liberal rhetoric must not idealize our formations as bands of immaculate heroes; who we are: a group of individuals, some without ulterior motives and in good faith, some of us political careerists, some of us displaced soldiers who fear being deported to Germany.

The question of choice in joining (or not) the resistance movement has been the topic of heated debate for decades, and I do not wish to add to it, although the issue of personal choice influenced, and was influenced by, the individual's autobiographical identity and to an extent, materiality. The workings of materiality and identity are two reasons, I argue, why, the resistance worked.

I was on my bike, looking for answers, worried about Carlo, about the lads who had been arrested, and I had lost any notion of time. I just pedalled. At moments such as this one thinks, is it worth it, this dog's life, this suffering, these discomforts, this disaster . . . When you're in deep, in something like that, you cannot be reflexive and lucid on certain things. You are living in a *nightmare*, and that's that.

(Marcella D., interview 20 December 2010)

In light of (or rather, in the shadow of) the traumatic episode of the underlying Italian civil war that framed these events, it is not surprising that the resistance tradition should play such a significant role in subsequent Italian memory.

The resistance was fractured into different versions and seldom meant the same thing to its participants – let alone to all Italians. It was constituted by a shifting mixture of men and women from different Italian regions, plus Allied officers from overseas, entangled in a web of competing materialities, emplacements and perceptions. The first wave of armed resistance erupted in the northern Italian regions after the Armistice of 8 September 1943, and immediately targeted the Nazis and the mixture of convinced followers and conscripts mobilised by the Salò Republic. The resistance activists soon started forming small, mobile units and often based themselves in the higher, less accessible mountains. The partisans employed guerrilla tactics in their daily fighting. These strategies included the sabotage of power lines and power stations, and the destruction of bridges and roadways used by the Germans to transfer livestock and other war necessities to Germany. Ambushes took the enemy by surprise and led to the capture of soldiers or foodstuffs, followed by a retreat back to hidden mountain bases. In moderate Fascist Emilio Cimberle's diary (2004), we read:

The partisans used guerrilla tactics against us which I thought were sly and unfair as they caught you unaware when you were crossing the road or mounting guard. They hit you in the back in the dark. They were utterly invisible.

Furthermore, in order to be able to provide the populace with goods looted from German and Fascist convoys, some partisans were based within local communities and liaised with the civilians. Community-based partisans did not usually take part in active fighting, but rather sought to further the cause of the resistance by disrupting normal life and spreading propaganda – pro-Allied material in the case of the moderate and Catholic partisans, or pro-Communist material in the case of the Garibaldi brigades.

Class and political divisions differentiated the brigades: whereas Communist Garibaldi formations constituted the majority in most regions, liberal and Catholic units also existed; most brigades established their own territories. The partisans belonging to different 'tribes' profoundly influenced the way they acted towards one another and towards their enemies. Not all agreed with Levinas' proposition that '[t]here is no arguing about tastes! In the differences between persons and between dispersed collectivities – matter, or nature, or being, reveals or expresses or celebrates, according to Merleau-Ponty, its soul' (1996: 183). As can be expected, inter-partisan feuds could prove bloody on occasion: one such event was the massacre of Catholic Osoppo partisans by the Communist Garibaldini on 7 February 1945 (the 'Porzus bloodshed').

The continuous cat-and-mouse game between Fascists and partisans would grow deadlier and inexorable. In her diary, young Fascist Zelmira Marazio (2004: 38) commented on the start of the civil war. It had unleashed fratricidal violence where she had hoped that a new Fascism would bring peace and stability to the community and the country at large. Who had fired the first shot, she asked? What side had the first dead? No one knew, she concluded bitterly. Mario, a member of the Communist 18th Garibaldi brigade in Forlì (central Italy) recalled:

> The thought that it was enough to wear a uniform to turn your neighbour into your tormentor is still hard to accept. We [the partisans] were dying of hunger, typhus and fear. They [the Fascists] were laughing and enjoying themselves. I still remember the face of a little guy, half my size, who was hitting me while I was tied to a chair. If only I could move I would have beaten him to death. Their laughter was the worst torture, like when they lined us up against the wall and told us it was our final hour and then a shooter fired blanks only to terrorize us. Our hearts jumped out of our chests.
> (Mario quoted in Faure, Liparoto and Papi 2012: 103)

The potency of that statement, and its implications for the wider significance of war and resistance, stands out from the printed page as 'compelling, sensorily laden, psychically charged' (Hancock 2009: 114). Attention to an autobiographical materiality of the people and things involved in the conflict and its aftermath helps us consider the meanings of events from a quite different perspective. Autobiographical materiality is a useful concept to understand why, when individuals from the most disparate backgrounds and social classes came together in the partisan bands and the Fascist formations, all sorts of misunderstandings and even hostilities arose. We will take a closer look at how identities

Figure 1.3 Cesare Pozzi and a friend laugh at a Fascist draft poster, Montù (Pavia), Lombardy, 18 April 1944.

Source: Wikicommons

were constructed, perceived and embodied in the following chapters, but one episode should suffice to 'set the scene' here. I talked with a resistance veteran who was a native of Vittorio Veneto but had spent the years before the war as a film actor in Rome's prestigious Cinecittà, working with glamorous actresses of the time. After Italy switched sides, in late September 1943, he returned to his northern hometown and became part of a local resistance band. Giuseppe, however, was not popular with some of the local lads in light of his exotic and glamorous materiality: his movie-star clothes and his hairstyle. 'When I joined the Revine partisans I was well received except by a man they called Weasel [*Donnola*]. He hated me because I had worked in the pictures, and *I came from* Rome' (G. Taffarel interview, 11 August 2010).

1.3 Materiality and memory

Much has been said and written about the experience and process of 'doing' oral history interviews with war veterans and their families. We routinely reflect on the 'need' to remember, to unburden oneself for a tape recorder (Thompson 2000). In the midst of much scholarship on the reflexivity of interviewing and research, we turn to the experience of witnesses and non-witnesses to frame the past in ways that make sense to us in the present. But we have learnt to live with the absence of memory, too. A significant amount of research has also been dedicated to the silence of those who choose, won't, or can't remember or talk about their experiences (Radstone 2007). Here I point out that some of the impressive research into trans-generational memory-making (such as Cappelletto 2003; Kidron 2012) has neglected the materiality of the interview process: the interpersonal poetics of affect (but see Tolia-Kelly 2004; Pink 2009). The sensorium of interviews cannot be simply 'coded' to reflect themes, research questions and narratives, but must, I contend, be considered part and parcel of something greater, deeper – and more meaningful. Here I explore the non-verbal, sensory aspects of what I call autobiographical materiality.

Respondents, participants and any object they choose to bring to an interview shape its materiality – for instance, a well-thumbed map or letter; or a favourite item of clothing; a good luck charm; the favourite coffee cup; the family pet; the battered and scribbled sheets of paper on which the interviewer jots down insights as the interview progresses (see Pink 2009 for a sensory-ethnographic approach to community interviews). Although not all of these interview elements will possess a self-aware autobiography, the overall effect/affect exercised by them will decide how, and what, is said. The affective moods created by the unique variables in an interview will shape the unravelling of events. I have personally experienced this when two or more interviews with the same subject turned out very differently when the setting was changed even slightly, like when someone opened a window, or sat in a different armchair or at a different place at the table. The mood changes.

So when you ask someone to recount, or rather to relive their experiences during the war, the way they will choose to talk or keep silent depends on many unique variables. An interest in this unpredictable combination of effects was the impetus behind much of my ethnographic interviews with veterans, activists, their families and their friends. This shared materiality is constantly negotiated, in the sense that we share (or not) each other's memories, expectations, demands and fears in compatible or incompatible ways. Autobiographical materiality grows out of our conscious and subconscious communication, from our (sometimes coercive) inter-relatedness. Ultimately this co-materiality is the result of our desire to connect, to reach out for the other(s) through words, gestures and meaningful 'things'. Not only does autobiographical materiality shape and power the interview, exploring the memories of those who witnessed facts and events, but I contend it also affects the protagonists of those past events. An instinctive web of communications, expectations, fears, affections, material cultures and power relations moved the activists, the Fascists, the Germans and the civilians to feel and act as they did. An autobiographical materiality led to persons being and becoming who they were and what they became, for better or for worse.

Contrary to a frequent cliché, not all Fascists were political fanatics. 'The grave moment of choice' is the expression with which Renato Fucini framed the decision to join either side in the civil war. Renato's (2008) diary tells a story of half-conviction which, I am sure, was common to many boys. He commented on the fact that his father, a First World War veteran, had joined the RSI out of soldierly principle, and that joining the new-born Fascist army was a matter of honour and a way to keep promises broken by the King and Badoglio. In early October 1943, Renato also enlisted in the RSI, although he was still a seventeen-year-old schoolboy with no clear political identity. He was neither passionate about his choice nor troubled by it – rather, he was devoted to his family, so he chose to follow his father's path. On the other hand, Friuli-born Emilio Cimberle (2004) embodied the kind of reflexive and self-critical Fascist that problematizes and unpacks the neat dichotomies of good vs. bad present in much traditional Italian wartime narrative. Twenty-seven years old at the time of the Armistice, Emilio left behind a thoughtful war diary in which he questioned, time and again, the futility and unfairness of civil war. Thus, when ordered by his superiors to carry out a *rastrellamento*, an anti-partisan reconnaissance, he wrote: 'They had promised us that we would not have to shoot to kill other Italians. They lied' (Cimberle, E. 1998, *Il Passaggio*, Archivio dei Diari di Pieve Santo Stefano, Accession no. MG/04). As he reluctantly readied himself for confrontation, he pondered, 'We were sent off to hunt for partisans: were they really there? Who were they? Would we meet them?' In a later passage, Emilio developed his anti-civil war sentiment, 'we called the partisans delinquents, lawless bandits, but they were Italians against whom we had to turn out German-issued rifles'.

The archives resonate with autobiographical materiality as well. The Diary Archive at Pieve Santo Stefano in Tuscany collects hundreds of diaries and journals, many of which hark from the war. Among these is Corrado Di Pompeo's diary and published memoir (2009). His words convey the melancholy materiality of the everyday. His wife and young sons had left Rome for the safety of the countryside, whereas Di Pompeo had stayed behind, continuing his job in a minor administrative capacity for Mussolini's Fascist regime. He felt so lonely that he turned to carpentry and to making things to kill time and fill his wretched solitude. On 22 November 1943 (2009: 48), he described a redundant furniture unit he was planning for the family kitchen: a place to store all rags, bleach, cleaning products and so on. Di Pompeo readily admitted that the desire to make their home functional and beautiful for when they would return was all he had got left (2009: 49). When his carpentry supplies ran out and he found himself unable to construct anything else, Di Pompeo turned to cookery (2009: 72) and started experimenting with what little food he could get to while away boredom and anguish – to trick time, in his own words.

London's Imperial War Museum holds a vast library of oral history interviews with British veterans in Western Europe, many of whom spent at least some time in Italy. Their recollections represent a gold mine for my research, as through their memories I can grasp a perspective on conflict experience that is not dictated or shaped by ideological or political beliefs. More to the point, many of the interviews illuminate the corporeal and material culture of the war. George Stephens recalled how one of his comrades went 'crazy':

Q: *Did anyone in your company go bomb happy at Cassino?*
   No.

Q: *You all stuck it out.*
   No. The only time I seen someone go . . . it was one time before going on patrol. He started whooping and hollering. He always carried a bottle of rum when you went down on patrol so we got hold of him and we knocked him out. We picked him up on our way back. He was in a hell of a state. There had been no warning that he was going to go like that. No, just . . . when guns started firing left right and centre and that were it.

The trembling flesh, the bottle of rum, the shouting, and the gunfire. The sensorium and intense assemblage of things, places and bodies shaping this story and evoked by this single quote alone seems to justify the unnamed man's panic attack and his subsequent restraining. Similarly, during my research at the Diary Archive in Emmendingen, Germany, I enjoyed reading about Wehrmacht officers' experiences in Italy, entrusted to pages oozing corporeal memories and embodied understandings of war and conflict. One fascinating source was the brief diary of Munich native, Peter G., who was in Italy from June 1943 until the 8 September Armistice. Speaking of his life in the Italian south in late June of 1943, Peter recorded:

> I only have my old school-time Italian phrase book to learn the language [. . .] but it's something. Later, in Naples, I learnt from experience that here kids are known to empty their bladders freely from the balconies down onto the street three floors down. You can imagine the stench, like all the backstreets of Arabia concentrated into one narrow lane. I also see a lot of naked kids everywhere. On Sundays the local people sit down in front of houses and entertain themselves, filling their bellies with chatter. The only thing I like about this place are the pitch-black eyes of the girls. Their hair would also be as shiny as blackest mahogany if it was not matted with filth.

Here, the utterly Other materiality of the Neapolitans made sense for Peter (in the ontological realm of his materiality and lifeworld) not as a series of rational thoughts or observation, but as a series of thick vignettes on the body and impacting on the body. His own autobiographical materiality and dwelling practices, imbued with the sensory memory of tidy and elegant northern cities, clashed with the more instinctive, earthier way of living of the southern Other. Sadly, Peter would die in action in 1944, far away from home, and so he never had a chance to reflect retrospectively on his time in Italy. I would have liked to read more about his feelings, his thoughts and impressions of the faraway land where he would lose his life, far removed from familiar northern 'atmospheres'.

1.4 The poetics of storytelling: interviewing, imagining, mapping

The geographical distribution of resistance activities varied, but in the north especially, armed formations operated and hid in uplands and forests. The materiality of shelter and hiddenness in the forest milieux resonates in the memory and consciousness of veteran partisans due to its liminality. Aside from the spatial specificity of forests and uplands, the armed resistance was primarily a northern phenomenon, and this is one reason why it is remembered and celebrated so differently in different parts of the country. Various books, articles and films routinely locate the resistance in upland areas, and the otherwise precise and detailed resistance literature often notes the frequent 'retreat to the hills'. The mountain-dwelling partisans have become almost romantic figureheads of the wider movement, portrayed as heroic bodies hiding in primaeval forests and attacking the noxious foreigners occupying the cities and plains down below. This widespread mythology represents the partisans as militarily, politically and geographically separate from the occupied, perhaps compromised, lowland areas, and from the Italians enlisted in the Salò Republic's forces. The mountain partisans convey a vision of a resistance unspoiled by the necessities of compromise, co-existence and even collaboration that made up the everyday realities for Italians in the more easily occupied urban and lowland areas (David Atkinson, pers. comm.).

The differences between these operational zones during the civil war became apparent in the differential autobiographical materialities enacted by fighters on both sides, their associates, friends and foes in the battle zones, in the towns and cities, and in the home, as we shall see in the following chapters. Resistance also unfolded in urban centres, where it acquired momentum through the actions of mobilised workers, Francs-tireurs and political and intellectual groups. Turin and Milan were hotbeds of armed and unarmed resistance (Behan 2009) (see Figure 1.4).

Figure 1.4 Sesto San Giovanni (Milan), Lombardy: factory workers strike in 1944.

Source: Wikicommons

The paths of experience weaving in and thorough the resistance stories echo the paths in which the fighters and their helpers moved, the same paths that German and Fascist patrols endlessly stalked. These paths are the ones veterans and eyewitnesses revisit and re-trace today when they engage with memory – and here I argue that storytelling weaves a tapestry or draws a map through the materiality of the 'journey' (see de Certeau 1984; Ingold 2011) rather than tracing linear narrative lines. Perceptions, materiality and cultural imagination are paths leading to an experiential world: these paths jump out at you from the story, asking you to pay attention and to follow them to indeterminate destinations. Mapping memory shares a deep affectual materiality with storytelling: one might say that the two are one and the same, only differently explored and conceptualised. They spin, re-elaborate, upend, join up, and (as I argue in Chapter 7) they separate worlds. Mapping can delineate not only the presences of memory but also the 'silencings, violent endings, (. . .) cultural losses and erasures' (Tolia-Kelly, in press).

Mapping powerfully encapsulates the mutual discourse between orality, places and the open-ended materiality of memory in the everyday. During my ethnographic fieldwork, I progressively became aware that places and objects were deeply and mutually entrenched in the sensory embrace of remembrance. I elected to let these elements and phenomena speak for themselves, to illuminate themselves rather than trying to apply theoretical labels and understanding to them as they unravelled. I can still recall my delight when, at the very start of our interview, resistance activist Marcella Dallan (2010) invited me directly into the materiality of her mementoes – original documents, maps and letters. The printed word cannot do justice to the excitement in this lady's voice as she uttered the following words:

> Look, I'll show you on the map the places that I will mention, as and when the story of my experience takes me to these locations. Bear in mind that most of these places have changed! Also, as I tell my story I'll show you the documents. Those over there are photocopies, and you *must* take them home – I insist. I always carry the original documents and copies with me when I give a talk in schools or speak to the public. You got to have the original documents handy, because the spoken word, as you know, is empty. One could say whatever they want, as it happens. Survivors told what they wanted. Sometimes people talk about things that they have not experienced. Then it all happened so long ago, and memory fades, even with the best intentions. What you have to do, is tell a story starting from the written documents and the maps. I wanted to give you a picture . . . you asked me about the places, and about the emotions that they inspired in me. I will start, then, from places. Then I will continue to tell the story as it developed through different places. Many of these are no longer there, however, so bear with me. OK then, this map . . . [rustling paper] we start from places. Really, I think special places have auras. Places have a soul, a personality, like people.

It's true. I think it matters a lot, a lot, where one finds himself. It makes a big difference, being in a town, or in the countryside, rather than another. For me space and time are two things that go together . . . I strongly believe, look here, I second the belief of the ancient Romans that there are genius loci, the spirits of place . . . but yes, let's look at the map now.

Marcella's tale began unfolding as she led me across the battered map on her travels and adventures across the landscape, risking big in delivering supplies and intelligence to the partisans of the Castelfranco Veneto area of northeast Italy. She would point to things and places that were no longer there or had changed beyond recognition. This engagement is what I would call autobiographical materiality writ large. In the next chapter, I turn to the issue of identities – the building blocks of conflict materiality.

2 Unsettling identities

> 'Non sono Tedesco' – I am not German. Those were the words with which the young Englishman broke the ice upon entering the coffee bar in a remote Tuscan town in the late 1960s. An archaeologist doing fieldwork in central Italy, he spoke good Italian but his fair looks had obviously triggered something of a negative reaction in the residents of this small town, still mourning ghastly German civilian massacres perpetrated in nearby Civitella and Sant'Anna di Stazzema in 1944 and 1945. Many years later, my friend told this anecdote and I found it revealing of how 'embodied' identity might still be 'a big deal' in Italy.

In one of my favourite passages of Pavone's *A Civil War*, Pavone reports an almost Homeric moment of Weltschmerz in which the love for one's mother unites two Italian boys fighting on opposite sides. In this anecdote, a young Fascist officer carried a moribund partisan he had shot in self-defence (or so we are told) to the roadside to die. In a letter the Fascist later wrote to his mother, he told her:

> He asked me if I was going to hurt his *mamma* too, and, albeit incredulous when I said no, he asked me about you, Mummy, and if I received any letters from you at all – then he asked me to show him a photograph of you. He had none of his Mother and he wanted to see the face of his *mamma* in your face one last time.
> (Pavone 1991: 58)

Over and above this story's historical accuracy, we can reflect on Pavone's story of the dying partisan and his executioner through the prism of affect and haunting presence. The victim and perpetrator reach out to one another in a profoundly affective event. The two, separated by politics and ideology, act as if they were responsible for each other, in a way. As an event, this story feels hauntingly present, and it stays in the memory of the reader long after the storytelling is over. Beyond the rhetoric of politics and the ontology of conflict, similar 'lived' episodes and their moods seem to frame, better than any elaborate theoretical argument, the impossibility of constructing the Italian war as a dichotomous and clear-cut affair.

Figure 2.1 Bundesarchiv picture_101I-316–1181–11: Benito Mussolini with an Italian soldier.

Humanity got in the way, all the way through. Stories such as this reach out to us and make us care about the war, one way or another. They muddy the waters, and defy our expectations of what it was like to be in the conflict – or they confuse us about the way that people acted and felt.

In this chapter, I explore degrees of intercorporeality and perception in the identities at play during the civil war and occupation by examining some of the things which may or may not have been 'good'. Without an attention to materiality in its relation with identity or loss of identity (alienation), we are in no position to fully comprehend the impact of the conflict on wider society, then and now. Here I consider the materiality of the narratives of inclusion/exclusion that haunt the memory of the conflict; materiality, I argue, demarcates the boundaries of belonging, citizenship and community itself (Wodak 2006).

1944

Throughout Europe, the Second World War was devastating, and Italy's experience was traumatic for the population at large: Italians of the centre and north found themselves surrounded by warring foreign armies as the Allies fought their way northwards and Nazi-Fascist forces sometimes applied a scorched-earth policy as they retreated. While German troops (with enlisted Italians) and Salò-Fascist forces battled with the partisans, Italians often found themselves fighting each other through conviction or coercion. Finally, civilians faced demands for supplies and support from all sides in the conflict, and many non-combatants were subject to random violence – be it Allied bombing or several infamous massacres by retreating SS troops, such as Civitella and Sant'Anna di Stazzema in Tuscany and Marzabotto in Emilia-Romagna (Klinkhammer 1996; Gentile 2012).

In 1944, the resistance movement was growing stronger and better organised. The cause of the resistance was winning the support of the populace through affective and social-political mechanisms as more and more Italians identified with, or supported, the partisan struggle. Contemporary German sources illuminate the progress of the anti-German and anti-Fascist sentiment in the country. The report on the situation in Italy between 19 May and 19 June 1944 conceded that 'every German and every Italian' knew very well by then that the Duce and his government commanded no respect or authority whatsoever (Bundesarchiv Freiburg, Accession no. RH/31/VI/09). It had become clear that the Salo' Republic was utterly powerless – merely an empty administrative vessel. All drafts for the military and work forces of the regime were thoroughly ignored. Furthermore, a contemporary German-issued document (Bundesarchiv Freiburg, Accession no. RH_31_VI) continued; Italians appeared to be strongly opposed to every single aspect of the war and to be increasing their passive resistance, week after week. The report suggested that Italians were by that point convinced of the superiority of the Anglo-Americans and aware of the insufficient presence of the Luftwaffe in Italy. The Italians' fear of Germany, and the repulsion and anxiety inspired by the idea of deportation to work camps, was known to the Germans. The same report purported that, for the most part, Italians lived in a 'panic terror' (*panische Angst*) of being recruited and shipped off to the Reich to work. Interestingly, the document records some extreme attempts to evade this fate as men made for 'grotesque flights' (*groteske Flucht*), especially from administrative units and departments whence there might be a chance of a transfer to the Reich.

The fear of shipment to Germany was helping the cause of the resistance in no small measure. For the most part, people helped each other avoid that dreaded fate. Generally, all scholars agree that fighters relied on extensive support networks. One estimate argues that each partisan in the field (or mountain) needed ten to fifteen civilian supporters to sustain their efforts via food, shelter, supplies and information (Behan 2009). These large support networks also increased risks, however: shifting ideological allegiances and the coercion of individuals to feed the partisans meant that betrayals and reprisals were frequent between Fascists and non-Fascists. The relationship between the resistance and the civilians was not always rosy, either. A German military report (Bundesarchiv Freiburg, Accession no. RW_31_VI) records that on 11 June 1944 in Lesegno (Piemonte), the partisans killed a civilian and took ten prisoners. Were these spies or collaborators? In this case, the documents alone cannot tell the whole story.

2.1 Identities and the uneasy materiality of conflict

Remembrance narratives of the civil war convey a sense of nightmarish confusion perceived by many as the difficulty of navigating and dwelling in places, landscapes, towns and neighbourhoods where suddenly, danger lurked everywhere. Around each corner, behind each window, there could be an enemy, watching and waiting. In any civil war or conflict where a population is subjected to foreign occupation, a focus on embodied identities and interpersonal interactions represents a way to untangle the emotional and affective mayhem of everyday life. Further, multivocality is central to the 'embodying' project positioning its lens on the materiality and interrelatedness of identity. A proper focus on the materiality or experience of that very multiple web of interrelations is missing from the current attention to multivocality, however. While landscape historians are ever more aware of the central role of embodiment to the experience of place and the interrelatedness of emplacement, this knowledge is still underplayed in military history. Thus, 'contingencies of place, time, and economics – such as the habits of diet, . . . access to varied clothing and conveyances . . . and previous experiences of built and natural environments' contribute to 'physical postures, gestures, and modes of comportment' in space (Veder 2013: 17).

Aside from an interactive embodiment (see the following chapter), material culture is another medium enabling the interchange of human interaction and socialisation (Hoskins 1998; Henare et al. 2007; Fahlander and Oestigaard 2014: 10) and undeniably entangled with historicity, at least in the sense that phenomenologists conceive of it: interactional, self-projecting and immersive (Heidegger 1953). Therefore, it makes sense to attend to materiality in considering the modes of interaction of individuals caught up in a conflict that brought together people from different parts of the world, each with their own backstory of material culture(s), names for things, eating habits and dress sense. I develop this point further by looking at how Italian anti-Fascists, Fascists, Germans and civilians defined, perceived and enacted the materiality of their respective (and competing) identities.

When Operation Eiche sprung Mussolini from prison on 12 September 1943 and proceeded to appoint him as head of the spurious Salò Republic in northern Italy, the resurrected Fascists and anti-Fascists started fighting each other to the death; the resistance struggle was exacerbated by the numerous German troops deployed on Italian soil – which became Italy's arch-enemy literally overnight in the wake of the Armistice with the Anglo-Americans. What did dwelling in a world at war feel like? Who was fighting whom? The nature of the partisans' enemies – and the construction of these enemies – require attention. My worry is that broad categories of identity and dichotomist partisan factions have been unquestioningly accepted by scholarship based on the common-sense assumption that 'that's the way things were'. Instead, I have spoken to, listened to and read about the lives and practices of Communist-hating resistance fighters, humane Fascists, duplicitous

Allied officers and compassionate Germans. The variety of human experience means that conflict materiality is as unique as every individual and place touched by and engaged in occupation, resistance and fighting. A focus on identity helps to 'flesh out' the material impact of the war, and the enduring and haunting legacy of a conflict with its multiple histories and stories.

We have all too readily accepted notions of the enemy and enemy factions, while questions of how the enemy was constructed, situated and perceived have not been asked. Attending to the materiality of the conflict can answer many unresolved issues and lead to reconciliation, as will become clear by pointing the way to a greater mutual understanding of embodied identities and affects, and their coterminous cultural perceptions.

2.2 Materialities and the uncanny

The agency and identity of actors in the conflict tearing Italian communities apart in 1943–45 have so far been approached in loose cultural historical terms, but not in terms of lived experience (Focardi 2005). Leyens (2009: 808) notes how '(m)ost of the time, lacking degrees of humanity are 'animalized' . . . A non-human group might be compared to wild (e.g. ape) or domesticated (e.g. donkeys) animals'. The latter concept is particularly interesting here as the Germans' favourite term to discredit the Italian Other was *Schwein* (pig). Moreover, Leyens goes on, 'people infrahumanize the groups they would not like or want to belong to' (2009: 813). This latter assertion certainly makes sense in the case of the major actors in the Italian conflict. The degrees of humanity inferred by the infrahumanisation predicate a multiplicity of worlds, perceptions and realities for different people, environments and affects.

Passerini (2005) argues that wartime enemies become all too readily reduced to singular stereotypes, noting how Italian histories of the resistance persistently conflate 'Nazis' with 'Germans', and how differences *even within* the German forces require attention. A parallel strategy in much resistance literature conflates categories by linking 'Nazis' with 'Fascists' – commonly through the portmanteau *Nazi-Fascist*, which is used unproblematically in most *memorialistica* (memoirs produced by local and national bodies) (see also Morgan 2009). To bind 'Fascists' with 'Nazis' constructs the former as a new and separate category from 'Italians' when, of course, they were not (Foot 2009). By extension, this move negates some of the *Italian* responsibility for the conflict in the Salò Republic, because collaboration with the Nazis is hereby ascribed to a minority of 'Fascist' officials and sections of the military rather than other 'Italians' of varying degrees of conviction, motivation and coercion (Di Scala 1999; Behan 2009). In this sense, Jentsch's (1906) concept of uncanny is particularly useful: the conditions of uncanny affect are more or less the conditions of uncertainty. In identifying these conditions, Jentsch split the world into things old, known and familiar, and other things new, foreign and hostile (1906: 4–5). This idea is important to delineate the dynamics and poetics of things new, foreign and hostile happening to Italians during military occupation. The emergence of sensations of uncertainty precipitates a lack of orientation: to 'new/foreign/hostile' corresponded a disintegrating, no longer relevant 'old/known/familiar'! Ricoeur also observed that in our everyday experiences, we display a tendency to 'make our own' what is alien to us in order to understand it. This is a 'struggle between the otherness that transforms all spatial and temporal distance into cultural estrangement and the ownness by which all understanding aims at the extension of self-understanding' (1976: 43). It is a coping strategy, in other words.

In the context of the Italian resistance, lack of understanding or lack of dialogue between northern partisans and southern Italians who joined their rank and file expressed itself in the materiality of everyday contact and communication. Not speaking the local dialects, not knowing what food one was been offered, not being used (corporeally) to strong liquor *grappa*: these were just some facets of a mundane materiality separating and distancing individuals from each other. Archival and oral sources resonate with recent theories in social psychology (Leyens et al. 2000; Leyens 2009) that postulate that sense of identity, self and other is always emotionally constructed, and that persons and social groups differentiate between 'us' and 'them' based on a perceived capability to feel the full spectrum of secondary emotions. '[P]lacing people in the others category, or discriminating against them, results in denying them one or several of the typically human characteristics' (Leyens et al. 2000: 187). Infrahumanisation is different to dehumanisation in that the term 'infrahumanisation' indicates the co-existence and co-enactment of degrees of humanity (Leyens 2009).

It is thus fundamental to attend to perception and identity in understanding the experience of the fighters and civilians across the board. Even within broad categories such as Italian anti-Fascists, self-identity differed according to one's cultural and familial background. The resistance experience of Catholic fighters differed from that of Jewish or Communist activists. The resistance experience could not simply conform and enact previously embodied identities but also create novel ways of being and dwelling. In his poignant resistance memoir, Enrico 'Ico' Lowenthal commented on the fact that becoming a partisan meant that people would not tease him any longer – they could no longer call him a 'filthy Jew' (2015: 75) because he had become a go-getter, a paladin of Italian freedom. That same young man reacted indifferently to meeting other Jews once he had become part of the armed resistance movement; Enrico's encounter with American officer Singer – 'surely Jewish' (2015: 98) does not give rise to particular comment, whereas Emanuele Artom (Artom and Schwartz 2015: 67) embodied his Jewishness differently in a resistance context, resolutely challenging anti-Semitic views within his partisan band.

These examples illuminate in practice how the positioning of self and others worked in the context of civil war and resistance. We now agree that memory carries deep implications for personhood, accountability and identity (Antze and

46 *Unsettling identities*

Lambek 1996). The suggestion of 'selective' humanity might explain unpredictable modes of engagement with others and attitudes toward violence in the context of conflict and, specifically, with the civil war in Italy. More to the point, without a construction of and confrontation with the 'enemy', a political stance could not be taken. First, however, actors in the events of those portentous twenty months had to position themselves in relation to others and to the places and landscapes that they (and the inimical other) inhabited. The materiality and identities enacted during the conflict reveal perceptual mechanisms of othering, and their role in the subsequent creation of dystopian environments is understood as uncomfortable materialities that can destabilise interpersonal interactions.

An emphasis on the dehumanisation of the Fascists is found in Pavone's *A Civil War* (1991): here, the author – an ex-partisan – dissects the issues and motives leading to the establishment and events of the resistance into three overlapping categories of patriotic war, class war and civil war. An attempt to dehumanise the Fascists protected Italians from facing the unsavoury notion that even the affable, Catholic Italians were capable of betrayal, violence and persecution. It was much more convenient to paint the resistance as purely a struggle in which Italians attempted and succeeded in ejecting the 'Other' par excellence – Nazi Germans. It may also be that the memory of a war against a foreign enemy is not as hauntingly painful as the memory of people in the same village turning against each other. Further, and despite recent research on the notion of identity and ethnicity in war memories of the German occupation of Italy (Focardi 2005, 2013; Röhrs 2009), we still lack an analysis focusing on the embodied, perceptive dimension of experience and memory in everyday life. The clues are there, if one knows where to look. For instance, written sources give clues that many Germans perceived relations between themselves and Italians as stilted, to say the least. Here is an excerpt from Otto A.'s field diary detailing the situation:

> 5 November 1943: The Italians still don't like us. Whenever an Italian and a German soldier meet, two things can happen: either the Italian tries to get out of the situation, ignoring the German; or they boycott the conversation. Most of the time Italians just give us German(s) dirty looks.
> (Otto A., Tagebucharchiv Accession no. 802/II, 1–7)

The bombings provide another key aspect of experience. Even after the Armistice of 8 September 1943, the Allies were targeting train stations and transport hubs in city and town centres to thwart the German advance. In the process, they terrorised and alienated thousands of Italian civilians.

> And then on April 7, 1944, when I was still at school, the Allies threw bombs on Treviso. I used to go to school by train and one day, one afternoon, I boarded a Treviso-bound train to visit my aunt, and I found myself in the same

compartment with my future husband Carlo. Suddenly we witness the burning of Treviso. You could see a huge wall of fire and smoke that covered the entire sky, from the ground to the clouds, a sight not unlike Dante's Inferno. Then the train crashed on the rails. I was shocked, the train had stopped there, and it could go no further. I heard about the bombing, but I never imagined such a thing. I was so upset. Then we were told that the British were bombing Treviso. On that train I felt so bitter, because here were these famous Englishmen we had been waiting for day by day, minute by minute; now they had arrived and created this devastation. So disappointing.

(Marcella D., interview 20 December 2010)

With these bitter words, a witness recalls the confusing and contradictory experience of being violently attacked by the so-called Allies – the British saviours that Italians had been taught to respect, await and embrace when they pushed northwards. Who were the enemies in that specific instance? The categories of Self and Other, of Good and Bad Guys, were hopelessly blurred. In what follows, I offer some examples of how identities are embodied and performed, drawing upon oral history interviews and memoirs.

2.3 The partisan experience

According to the pervasive myth of the resistance, all Italian people were one hundred per cent behind the movement. This absurd exaggeration transpires from a myriad of sources: the mutual lack of understanding of urban and rural communities proved one of the most common causes of miscommunication, distrust and enmity between the populace and the fighters.

> Another factor making for improved morale was the slowly awakened sympathy of the peasants. The men in the formations were almost all from the towns, mainly Genoa. They had little knowledge of, or interest in, peasant ways and the peasants responded by resenting their intrusion and the additional dangers it meant for them. This lack of sympathy was occasionally acute. On the whole it seems to have decreased . . . and at the end there was even cordiality.
>
> (McMullen quoted in Tudor 2004: 75)

Not all partisans were heroic friends of the people. Sometimes they acted against the grain of the local 'dwelling perspectives' and disrupted local affective regimes by behaving in an inappropriate or chancy manner, which may have led to reprisals against the civilian populace. In German-speaking Süd-Tirol, clashes between Italian-speaking partisans and the locals reinforced the sense of mutual exclusion between the two cultural groups. Gehler (1996: 109) comments that historians have tended to be content with the dichotomy – 'Sud-Tyroler patriots: good; Belluno partisans: bad', but that the clashes between ethnic Italians and Sud-Tyroler civilians were not one-off, isolated incidents. Gehler (1996: 109) quotes an Austrian field report stating the occurrence of these incidents: 'arbitrary arrests, house searches, thefts and looting happen on a daily basis up here. Even the Americans, whose policy is to not become embroiled in local feuds, launched an investigation'. This tension suggests that acceptance or rejection took place along lines that touched on ethnic identity and territorial belonging as much as on political allegiance and beliefs. Meanwhile, Fascist Gio Batta Rossi's diary described the non-violent dynamics that led to the partisans' descent into the town as victors on Liberation. Gio Batta's Fascist division had always had a very hands-off relationship with local partisans . . . therefore the encounter only provoked some embarrassment on the part of Rossi's men. 'There was no dialogue between us, only some embarrassment on our part, but there were no signs of intolerance or hatred', he wrote (2007: 29). There was no overt hostility towards these Fascists on the part of the partisans because Gio Batta's division had behaved fairly towards civilians.

2.4 Understanding the Fascists

'Our readiness to die was authentic, as was our burning desire to live' wrote the Fascist Gustavo Tomsich (1995: 57). How has scholarship come to terms with the absolutist worldview of the Fascists? How might their worldview be woven into the wider experience of the war? The summer of 1944 was a time of great success on the part of the resistance forces: on 14 June, the Comitato Liberazione Nazionale Alta Italia (CLNAI), spokesperson for anti-Fascist Italy, circulated a statement stating that: 'The time has come for the people of Italy to rise against the German invaders and the Fascist traitors' (Battaglia 1957: 187). This statement encapsulated the feelings of many – the Zeitgeist of much of the collective imaginary of neutral and anti-Fascist Italians.

The Fascists always favoured a self-image aimed to destabilise democratic values: their identities are as varied as those of the anti-Fascists, but geared towards views, passions and beliefs that are occluded from the vast majority. The Fascists, in their most extreme incarnation, seem to have embodied a secret death cult, except that their gestalt was theatrical, boisterous and public; they are conceptualised as energetic and dynamic, yet morbid, brooding and inward-looking; as proud and militaristic, yet also intrinsically fatalist. The most useful way to understand Fascists is through their interactions with the *other* – the Germans, the anti-Fascists, apolitical elements and the Allies. One particular category of Fascist alterity, as is often encountered in northern Italian resistance narratives, is exemplified by the difficulty of their relations with the wider population. Scholars of wartime Italy observe the northern Italian civilians' inborn hostility towards other Italians, namely Fascists from the South. The worst stereotypes and attributes of a southern Other populate Roncade's stories, too:

The composition of the Brigate Nere was . . . varied. You could have local career-hungry officers, young recruits from the South, and, often, elements from organized crime in the south, and they all wore the same uniform. With a few exceptions, we were dealing with unscrupulous riff-raff, noisy and instinctive rabble, who did not even attempt to positively impress the German allies.
(Favero 2003: 71)

Civilians in the north regarded the (predominantly) southern Fascists as bullies who, in turn, were terrified by their far superior German counterparts. One of Favero's sources, PS, synthetically voiced the opinion of many: 'In our area the worst elements were definitely the Fascists. The Germans, at least, had their code of conduct – the Fascists were psychopaths' (interview with Gianni Favero, 6 April 2012). When a group of female Ausiliarie (female volunteers in Mussolini's Army) was dispatched to Teresa's village (1987: 76), they paraded around town dressed like soldiers, walking up and down the main road singing anti-Badoglio songs. They were joined in their rounds by German soldiers singing 'Rosamunde' and male Fascists singing songs of victory. When Teresa's sister Neri befriended one of the Ausiliarie and decided to enlist as well, ostensibly to defend her fatherland, their mortified mother told her off for joining those 'fanatic idiots'. Civil war had come to Teresa's home, divested in grotesque and scary performances and unprecedented views, sounds and materialities (such as the women dressed like soldiers).

For Pezzino, 'rather than admitting that the conflict involved members of the same community, the adversary was denied the status of an enemy once the civil war was over, and degraded to the level of traitor and lackey of the foreigner' (2005: 397). While the image of the Fascist comes across as Pezzino describes, as Other, one might observe that, from the perspective of narrative representations and the materiality of memory, friends and foes overlapped in unpredictable ways: the Wehrmacht officer could be good, whereas a partisan could be bad. In Morgan's words, the often 'ambiguous triangular relationship' between Germans, partisans and local people comes across in Favero's stories as somewhat flattened and, paradoxically, two-dimensional, but this is due to the obvious lack of first-hand witness accounts by either German Wehrmacht, SS or Fascist officers active in the area at the time (2003: 229). Not all partisans failed to see the instability of the situation: an aversion to the killing of Fascist prisoners affected those who were 'supposed' to want nothing more than the obliteration of the abject 'category'. Jewish partisan Emanuele Artom reflected on the cruelty required to kill a man in cold blood. He recounted the moment when fellow partisans captured a Fascist:

They had taken a prisoner in a public toilet. I saw him get off the truck between two of our men; slight, silent, demoralized, tied up. This abject being got up this morning with the intention of hunting down young men who are against the idea of fighting against Italy; he got up and didn't think it would be the last time. Yet, the idea he might be killed troubles me. I am so happy I didn't capture him myself! Just thinking about his possible end, I would have let him go. To kill in battle, but not in cold blood. Maybe he is not guilty of being who he is, because life is a terrible mystery: and who would destroy a mystery without understanding it first?

(Artom and Schwartz 2015: 103–104)

The notion of understanding and mercy inspired by the ultimate 'shared lot' of life's terrible mystery strikes us as highly sophisticated and noble; knowing that the Fascists, later on, would not hesitate to enact unspeakable tortures on the body of Emanuele Artom upon his capture serves to make his story, in all its cosmic humanity, even more heart-rending.

For their own part, the Fascists were aware of the difference between their way of operating and the partisans. Both the content and form of a radio message (Pavone 1991: 237) broadcast by Alessandro Pavolini, charismatic founder of the Fascist *Camicie Nere* and secretary of the Fascist Party (PFI), on 25 July 1944 are revealing in this sense:

> The Italians are not afraid of fighting. [. . .] They, however, do not like being cooped up in a barrack, ordered around, homologated. . . . The Partisan movement is successful because the fighter in the Partisan ranks has the impression of being a free man [sic]. He is proud of his doings for he acts independently, and develops actions according to his individual personality. We, therefore, need to institute an anti-Partisan movement guided by the same attitudes, and using the same tactics.

The Fascists were aware of differences and prepared to bridge the chasm to their advantage. The perception of the partisans as 'free' was certainly appealing to the population, but perhaps also to several less-than-devoted Fascist militia men, too. The Fascists' lack of popularity was due to their almost anachronistic rigidity, their stiff military ways, and the fact that they failed to positively 'connect' with the population. More to the point, at a time before mass economic migration from the south to the industrialised north, the Fascists, who were often deployed from other regions to the northern fringes beyond the Gothic Line, stood out like sore thumbs due to their different embodiment and their southern materiality. Blonde, fair-skinned northern resistance fighters and their parent communities often eyed with suspicion and distaste the olive-skinned, black-moustached and aggressive southern Fascists. The embodiment of men who looked different, spoke different and often 'smelled' different – due to different diets and eating habits – contributed to distance them in emotional, material and cultural terms from the populations of the northern regions. Their materiality, in the sense of their embodiment and engagement with the material world, was incompatible with the Italians. While commenting on the abject poverty of the Milanese populace, Magda Ceccarelli (2011: 288) wrote that the citizens were having to fell public park trees to keep warm in their homes, whereas not a day went by without the odious boasts and showing off of wealth on the part of the Fascist scum, who even indulged in manicures and pedicures before going off with their harlots.

2.5 Who were the Germans, and what did they want?

Here I explore some of the ways in which Italians perceived and engaged with German soldiers. Sometimes civilians and Italian partisans drew a clear-cut distinction between German Wehrmacht and the SS; at other times, Italians lumped all Germans together in a hostile category of otherness. All the stories and accounts I have examined in researching this book tell a different story to this regard.

2.5.1 Germans ... or Austrians?

In his book of memoirs, Enrico Lowenthal (2015: 139) published the copy of a letter written by Bavarian Wehrmacht deserters Seiwald and Wissner, dated January 1945, in which they exhorted their comrades to desert the army, capitulate and entrust themselves to the partisans, who would then ensure safe passage to Switzerland and freedom. The main interest of this document, beside the fact that it bears witness to the unwillingness of some Wehrmacht men to fight the war until the bitter end, lies in the fact that the authors claimed to be Austrian. They had introduced themselves to Enrico 'Ico' as Austrians. They declare themselves Austrian in the letter. The fiction they had established was, presumably, aiming to save their skin. Austrians feature in many resistance accounts as the German German Nazi's good cousins. As Italy's Catholic neighbours, the Austrians appeared less scary to the civilian populace.[1]

In their compelling book on the secret surveillance tapes of German prisoners of war, Neitzel and Welzer reflect on the nature of the Wehrmacht soldiers caught on tape. Hence, we learn that:

> Most of the soldiers are scarcely interested in ideology, politics, world orders, and anything of that nature. They wage war not out of conviction, but because they are soldiers, and fighting is their job. Many of them are anti-Semites, but that is not identical with being 'Nazis'. Nor does anti-Semitism have anything to do with willingness to kill. A substantial number of soldiers hate 'the Jews' but are shocked at the mass executions by firing squad. Some are clear 'anti-Nazis' but support the anti-Jewish policies of Hitler's regime. [. . .] Some complain that the Germans are too 'humane' and then tell in the same breath and in great detail how they mowed down entire villages.
>
> (Neitzel and Welzer 2013: 7)

52 *Unsettling identities*

Further in the book, the authors speculate on the Wehrmacht's willingness to perpetrate atrocities even when the soldiers, taken individually, would profess to abhor violence:

> Total institutions . . . say, for instance, the Wehrmacht or the SS – claim total dispensation over the individual. Individuals are given uniforms and special haircuts and thereby lose control over the enactment of their own identities. They no longer do with their time as they see fit but are constantly subjected to external compulsion, drills, harassment, and draconian punishment for violating rules. Total institutions function as hermetically sealed worlds of a special sort, directed towards producing a finished result. The soldiers do not just learn how to use weapons and negotiate various types of terrain. They are taught to obey, to subjugate themselves to hierarchy, and to act on command at a moment's notice.
>
> (Neitzel and Welzer 2013: 21–22)

I am interested in how the insights gleaned from Neitzel and Welzer's masterful study apply to the Italian context. How did Italians relate to their former allies/occupiers?

Among the testimonies collected by Veneto historian Favero, we come across fond memories of the German lads inhabiting the local fields and living in the villages along the river banks: some locals started perceiving the inoffensive presence of certain Germans, namely the orderlies, the ones keeping themselves to themselves, as naturalised, and the locals almost integrate them into the local social and affective fabric. Hence:

> We never saw that many Germans here . . . there were always few in Roncade and between them and the partisan there was – more or less accidentally – a mutually advantageous relationship. [. . .] The *'ribelli'*, on their end, had the good sense to leave the stranger alone, so that, as many recount, Wehrmacht patrols could often eat lunch in peace with local farmers in Bagaggiolo and Ca' Tron, even allowing themselves the courting of local young ladies. They pretended to ignore that, in the next room, there was at least one deserter German brother who could do nothing but wait, silently, for the Kraut to clear off and return to his motorcycle. Harming a German – everyone knew this – implied an immediate reprisal.
>
> (Favero 2003: 76)

The fraternising of Germans with local women, however, could lead to trouble. In his memoirs, Raimondo Zanolin recalled the following:

> We had a small Beretta gun and used it to disarm a German in Budoia [a village in Friuli-Venezia Giulia]. It was Sunday and the German was strolling, holding

a woman close. We noticed the large pistol he wore in his holster, a Stayr it was, and wanted to get it off him. We pointed our gun at him and took his without doing him any harm. He started barking something in German as we ran away.
(Zanolin and Brescacin 2013: 10)

A potential resistance focus had to be nipped in the bud, or so the German logic prescribed. In *Soldaten*, we read that:

Although this approach proved ineffective, in some regions the German struggle to put down resistance movements led to an unprecedented spiral of violence. Before long the killing of hostages and innocent victims, and the razing of whole villages, was part of *everyday routine*.
(Neitzel and Welzer 2013: 80, my emphasis)

In Langhardt-Söntgen's memoir (2011: 73), a northern Italian lawyer whose house is requisitioned by the Germans did not show hostility towards his Wehrmacht guests. The professional man frankly admitted that he by far preferred to open his home to German soldiers than to refugees from the South, adding that 'with the Germans, I know I can rest easy in the knowledge that you won't damage my things'. This insight provoked hearty laughter in the Commander in charge.

In Teresa Sartorelli's diary, we learn that, as the German defeats grew more hopeless, their relations with all Italians, even the Fascists and the innocent populace, turned sour (1987: 87). Meanwhile, Teresa's mother became more and more supportive of the Germans ('*filo-tedesca*') and found increasingly more improbable and vehement excuses for German brutalities. She kept saying, 'They have orders, they have to obey . . . They are never the first to act – the partisans make them do it. If left alone, the Germans are the best, kindest people in the world'. And yet the Germans did, on occasion, behave in a chivalrous manner towards civilians in occupied Italy.

In Teresa's diary, we also find ample evidence for the empathetic attitude of some German soldiers towards her family. She recalls how a party of German soldiers and Fascists came looking for her brother Gigino (1987: 69–70). Gigino was a partisan, and he was due home any minute after his missions, but Teresa's mother was so genuinely distraught about her other son Beppino, deported to Germany without a trace, that she bawled her eyes out. She pretended that Gigino had also been sent to Germany. She cried so bitterly about her son about whom she knew nothing that the German soldiers took pity on her and soothed her with 'Bona mama, bona mama . . .' while the grim-faced Fascists took to searching the entire house room by room. Although armed to the teeth, the Germans gathered around the hearth waiting for the hot coffee to brew. It looked like they were not in a hurry, and the heady aroma of the coffee had brought a shy smile to their 'young faces'. When her father was finally taken away for interrogation, Teresa's mother started crying once more, and once again the Germans soothed her by murmuring, 'Bona mama, bona mama'.

Anna Lotto (2008) interviewed several resistance messengers who had been young girls at the time. In the words of Rosina Paris,

> In the morning . . . the Fascists wanted to confiscate our sacks of flour, instead the Germans helped us push the cart with the sack on it, seeing as we were in their jurisdiction. In other words, the Italians gave us grief, whereas the Germans helped us.
>
> (Paris quoted in Lotto 2008: 122)

Rosalia Peterle similarly recalled:

> When we got to Vittorio Veneto we convinced the Germans to let us through, but only for the night; then we spent the night in the open, under a chestnut tree. On another occasion the Germans tied our carts that were heavy and full of food to their trucks and pulled them along. Once we got to the Fadalto, the Fascists made us untie them and make our own way back [uphill] to Alpago unaided. God bless the Italians, isn't that what they say?
>
> (Peterle quoted in Lotto 2008: 123)

The issue of German deserters is still under-researched. Matthias Röhrs (2009) has devoted a whole book to the experiences of Italian partisans who fought alongside Germans. In the Friuli, partisan Raimondo Zanolin recalled one German soldier with fondness in his memoir:

> Among the German soldiers on duty at the prison there was a man called Paolo [sic]. He was a music teacher and played the saxophone. He was a sensitive person and certainly not convinced of the war. Sometimes I saw him cry. Given the ways in which the Germans treated their prisoners, I risked being shot overnight. I plucked up the courage to ask Paolo for a gun. He did not give it to me. Since that time I did not sleep more at night for fear of Paolo's betrayal. I would end up in the hands of the 'butcher' Donnenburg, who would cut me into pieces. Fortunately he did not. At the end of the war, when the Germans retreated and went to Roveredo, Paul defected from the German army. The partisans of the 'Osoppo' captured him in Maniago. To save himself, he said he knew a partisan named 'Lupo' [me], who had escaped from prison, and who would recognize him. 'Danilo' came from Maniago to look for me:
>
> — Come with me- there is a German who will not shut up about it, he asking after you.
>
> I went to Maniago, where Paolo was, and I told the partisans who held him prisoner about the gun incident: Paolo had been loyal and not handed me over

to the 'butcher'. So they let him go and he stayed on in Roveredo. Since then, he came to see me every day by bike, until I went to work in Belgium.

(Zanolin and Brescacin 2013: 130)

The otherness of violence resonates in many of the stories, and it is something that happens 'to' the peaceful local communities of the Sile plains. As is the case in Civitella's memories and mourning community, violence is not recognised as a 'domestic element, embedded in the local relations. Locally the source of violence is conceived as something external, different from "the ingroup", and membership in the mnemonic community is characterised by the status of victim of violence, not of perpetrator of violence' (Cappelletto 2003: 246). Violence was an expression of the noxious otherness of foreign types. Otherness permeates the whole lifeworld of local communities, including, disturbingly, the river Sile, once a source of local livelihood (fishing, transportation), and transformed into a noxious receptacle of death almost overnight. Once familiar landscapes became a theatre of the macabre, and the town of Roncade's memories rather pointedly convey this dizziness and disorienting displacement (see Chapter 6).

Yet Germans and German sympathisers were often lumped together in the partisans' perception.

> In spring we were located under the Lagorai, located just beyond the western province of Belluno – on the Trentino side. Those were hard times for us, because that was Reich territory and the Germans were particularly ferocious on their turf – worse than in Veneto, I think out of principle and out of propaganda reasons. Some of those areas, people spoke German, but in the Cadore too. When we moved out into Trentino we were very close to the border with Veneto, thank god. We had a strong emotional bond with the Veneto people; even if we were not local, we came from Bologna, well, we were still Italians. We came from a different culture but kind of the same. We found it *extremely hard to relate* to the German-loving South-Tyrolese in any way.
>
> (Giorgio Vicchi, interview 20 December 2010, my emphasis)

The Fascist relationship with Germans was one fraught with difficulty and humiliations: the general sense one gets from memoirs and diaries is that the Germans systematically underestimated and exploited their lesser allies in the Axis. Danilo Durando's diary (2007) reflected on the ambiguous nature of the political-military alliance in eloquent terms: 'I felt a distinct antipathy towards our German "allies", but when taken individually they were often decent chaps, proving to be in a bond to follow orders'. When Danilo told a German soldier that he was tired of the war, the chap replied that he too had had enough of that life, and many of his Wehrmacht comrades felt the same. Danilo then asked the German soldier why they should not '*subvert the order of things*, disobey, or desert' (my emphasis). The German calmly and resignedly answered that he would not do so because he cared about the well-being of his family. I have emphasised Danilo's use of words here to underline the root of all conflict experience: deserting and running away constituted subversion, a toppling of fate and an upending of events; to resist, to rebel, destabilised the system, and the German was afraid of just that subversion in case it affected the safety of his loved ones. Danilo would later shed the Fascist uniform and join a partisan band in the Piedmont mountains under the battle name of 'Moro'. Former internee Lieutenant Francesco Celentano recalled the confusing amalgam of motivations and serendipitous circumstances leading his enlisting in the Fascist Republican Army while a military prisoner of war in Germany, aged twenty-two:

> The propaganda spun by Italian officers who had come up from Italy found us primed for obedience; we had seen the end of our Army on the Greek front [where Francesco had been captured by the Germans on Armistice Day], witnessed the shameful flight of the King and Badoglio, we had felt the betrayal towards the German allies, and we carried within us the bleak and demoralizing notion that we had seen the inside of a concentration camp: these were the reasons why we enlisted in the RSI. My colleagues enlisted en masse. We did it not because we were keen to fight more but for Italy's honour and to revive the kudos of our Army.
> (Celentano, F., n.d., *Burro: 1943–1945,* Archivio dei Diari di Pieve Santo Stefano, Accession no. DG/06, unpublished diary)

An Allied perspective to the interactions with Germans is given to us by Private Whatmore, who recalled his proximity with Germans:

> *Q: What do you remember about being in Anzio?*
> I remember being in trenches all the while. The fighting was pretty static then. It was all living in trenches with the Germans being as far away as possibly those houses over there – a few dozen yards. If you kept quiet you could hear them talking. German stretcher bearers came out just before daylight with a white flag on the stretcher to collect the dead and wounded. Once in a while one would look over at you. There was a chap in my Unit who was a bit overenthusiastic and trigger happy. He wanted to take a pop at one of them but I discouraged him (Whatmore, IWM Accession no. 2703).

An Allied source mentioned a German atrocity against civilians in their interview with the Imperial War Museum. Thus, Peter Douglas-Taylor recalled desertions and violence in the rank and file of an infamous German infantry division:

> Once in Italy we came across the 715 Big Wheel Division, a German infantry division, it was composed of 32 different kinds of Europeans recruited from

satellite countries, Croats, Slovenes, Poles, Checks, Russians, Finns, etc. either been forced to enlist or coerced. They weren't particularly good solders; they would fight up to a point, then when it got to beyond that point they would pack in. Of course the desertion rate was very high. Very high in that period when we were in north Italy. And of course this 715 Division had been responsible for an atrocity. I think five or six Italian civilians had been killed and hidden, and they were found by one of our Companies. [. . .] What happened to that Division after that I do not know. They were taken out of that line . . . they disappeared from our front anyway.

(Douglas-Taylor, IWM Accession no. 10484)

Was the 715 Division removed in the aftermath of that atrocity or for another reason? The ruthlessness of certain components of the German armed forces made them fearsome to the Allies and the civilians. Thus, George Stephens recalls:

We got mixed up quite a lot with the Panzer and the SS all the way through the war. If you got mixed up with the Germans . . . you see they always say they were two different races, the SS and the paratroopers – and the ordinary Germans. If you got mixed up with them they would walk away, they would take no prisoners. But not the SS.

(Stephens, IWM Accession no. 24630)

Q: *Did you think they were more fearsome, the SS? Were they better soldiers?*
Well they were trained, I mean, the ordinary soldiers that we took prisoner was [sic] the same as we. And . . . a lot of them could speak English and a lot of them would tell you that they didn't want to fight, they had to fight just like we did. And . . . but the SS Panzers they were hellish, they were (Stephens, IWM Accession no. 24630).

2.5.2 *German self-reflections*

The Germans recorded their own experiences in Italy with admirable diligence. Some of their observations surpass Italian and Allied sources in their depth of reflection. In a letter to his wife dated 1 November 1943, Helmut K. wrote that so far they had not experienced enemy disturbances (*Fremdberührung*), but there was no telling when things might change. He complained, however, that the relationship with the Italian people was not good [*natürlich nicht gut*] because they had to requisition cattle and because of the occasional attacks against the civilians by some *Truppenteil* (division) or other. Helmut proceeded to state that he was very sorry about this state of affairs, as he had thus far established a very good relationship with his Italian neighbours and was beginning to understand spoken Italian rather well.

Bernhard P. told of the everyday experience of fighting a double enemy – the Allies and the partisans:

> We have now moved to a rural area near Campagnatico and set up camp in an abandoned hut. There are partisans in the area, so our men are uneasy. [*Partisanengefahr* is the term Bernhard uses]. I truly hope that we will have nothing to do [no experiences with] with these subjects.
>
> (Bernhard P. n.d., Tagebuchsarchiv Accession no. 3310)

A separate entry in the diary talks about a situation in the field: '*vor uns der Feind, hinter uns Partisanen*' – in front of us the enemy, and behind us the partisans. His choice of words leads me to believe that this German did not really view the partisans as the enemy proper. The partisans had blown up a bridge that would have ensured a speedy escape from an area where the Americans had advanced. They still managed to break through but had to leave a lot of stuff behind.

From Karl Wolff's interview, we learn that the SS were recruited mainly in the northern German agricultural district, farmers' sons in particular, and they had to be tall and strong and blond. Elsewhere, they were recruited based on performance (*Leistung*) and personality. They had to be loyal and possess German virtues (*Germanische Tugenden*). Wolff then goes on to talk about how he found it difficult to relate to the Catholic population of Italy.

Others were suspicious of Italians on principle, and reacted to denunciations against men suspected of being partisans with an attitude of 'we will check it out, but where there is smoke, there is fire', an adage of German wisdom according to Langhardt-Söntgen (2011: 73). Unsurprisingly, many Germans understood the lunacy of the operation the Wehrmacht was carrying out in occupied Italy. Blaas, a translator deployed with German troops in occupied Italy, expressed outrage at the way in which Wehrmacht soldiers treated the civilian population:

> At Barletta they called the population together and told them that they were going to distribute food and then they fired into them with machine guns. Those were the sort of things they did. And they snatched watches and rings off people in the street, like bandits. Our soldiers themselves told us how they carried on. They simply entered a village and if there was anything they didn't like, they just shot down a few people, just like that. They told us about it as though it were the natural thing to do. One man boasted of how they broke into a church and put on the priest's vestments and committed sacrilege in the church. They behaved like Bolshevists there and then they were surprised when the people turned against them.
>
> (Neitzel and Welzer 2013: 152)

2.6 Why weren't the Allies more helpful?

On 28 July 1943, Fascist teenager Eufemia F. had complained about the *English* invasion of her homeland. In her diary (1972), she claimed that she would do anything to stop the advance of the Anglo-Saxons. She was so obsessed by their invasion that she dedicated a whole diary entry to them on 14 August 1943. On 26 August of the same year, we read of her chagrin over the 'fall' of Sicily, as she reminisced about the year and a half she lived in Taormina. There used to be, she mused, many Germans and English holiday-makers there, and already at the time, the Sicilians did not take too kindly to the English. Eufemia wondered what suffering the local people would have to endure now that the British were the 'bosses' (*i padroni*). She was positively terrified of the possibility where they would land on the mainland. On 30 October 1944, the Milanese Magda Ceccarelli commented on the fact that the Anglo-Americans kept on bombing suburban trams: but why? she asked. She concluded that that behaviour was only so much fodder for Fascist propaganda (Ceccarelli 2011: 286). I agree on this point. A native of Perarolo (Beluno) in the Alpenvorland occupied area (the (Alpine foothills), Renato De Zardo, in considering the bitter aftermath of Italian capitulation, mused 'No dreams of glory for Italy now then. We are at the mercy of the enemy, whether Anglophone or German-speaking. . . . Our land has become someone else's battlefield' (Amantia and Svaluto Moreolo 2004: 191).

Finally, the Allies had an ambivalent relationship with Italy and Italians: the populace begrudged the carpet bombing of the time before the Armistice while harbouring hopes for a speedy end of the war afterwards, and greeting the Anglo-American as saviours. This was especially true in the liberated south, where Germans had behaved the worst before the switch in allegiance – presumably due to an innate German mistrust of southern peasant types, considered by most as base, lazy, backward and duplicitous. Even Allied officers collaborating with the resistance found it difficult to communicate with the locals, however. This difficulty was not always dictated by a linguistic barrier, but also by obvious cultural and religious differences between the reserved, formal British officers and ambitious WASP American types on the one side, and the emotional, highly strung Italian Catholics on the other; the Italian-Americans were the exception and had an altogether different relationship with the local populace, as most could speak the language and were Catholic. Thus, Alfredo Bernacchi, a native of San Francisco, when asked how the living conditions were in Naples, answered sympathetically:

> The living, of course, the – streets were always loaded with beggars. You walked out and the streets were – Naples had been bombed – the Port of Naples had been bombed very heavily during World War II.
>
> (Library of Congress, interview with S. Khan on 26 February 2007)

On the whole, sources suggest that the Allies were greeted like heroes in southern Italy after the Armistice. Veteran John Donnelly recalled their welcome in the Salerno countryside:

> I didn't see many civilians about. We didn't see many civilians at all. The people were . . . the villages we passed through were empty. People were . . . There were just plenty Germans. Then people would start throwing grapes at you in the tank, and the grapes would stick to the tank and you could not see for flies because of the juice.
>
> (Donnelly, IWM Accession no. 19799)

They had to ask the civilians they did see not to throw grapes at the tanks. 'We didn't speak Italian of course, but we said, "No grapes!" They meant well but the grapes were bursting on the tanks' (Donnelly, IWM Accession no. 19799). Dusty Rhodes mentioned an incident that alludes to the alienating experience of being a Briton in a foreign land. His battalion wanted to steal a train in order to rescue British escapees from Italian POW camps post-capitulation. According to Dusty, these chaps were 'running around on the hills, utterly at a loss'. The battalion managed to take charge of a train thanks to the expertise of a chap who used to work in the railways back in the UK, but unfortunately they derailed. The unfortunate turn of events was possibly due to the damaged condition of the rail tracks. The train went off the tracks and they couldn't get it back on the tracks again so they abandoned it; although, Dusty commented, the train would have been very convenient to speed up the rescue of some hundred stranded British men (Rhodes, IWM Accession no. 18176).

Others, in the north, were not so lucky. Nedda Zanfranceschi, a young teenager in 1944, commented:

> After the bombardments the people of Treviso lived in terror. Even the school was in ruins, you know, and the station . . . the whole city centre, up in smoke. Everyone down in the shelters! Something like the Twin Towers. But so pointless. How cruel the English were- how ferocious, bombing us like that. Why, asked everyone? Couldn't they leave the partisans to blow up trains and factories?
>
> (Interview 13 October 2010)

'We Italians wait anxiously for the Allies, our liberators today are yesterday's enemies. But *still* they keep bombing us to death' wrote Renato Da Zordo (Amantia and Svaluto Moreolo 2004: 191). His words intimate that, on the ground, in the everyday life of civilians, the Allies were still harbingers of destruction, and that not much had changed since the Armistice!

The Allies sensed the immense pressure to advance and win. Many soldiers found the strain unbearable, and, predictably, sometimes things went wrong in the heat of the moment. George Stephens recalled his accidental killing of two British soldiers. One morning, just after dawn, George led his company and moved towards a farmhouse on a hilltop to make it the battalion HQ. On the hill path leading to the farmhouse, he bumped into two artillery officers, one after the other, who both failed to provide the password (it had been changed from Jackal to 'Bread and Butter' overnight).

George: A bloke, he come running down, he had a heavy coat on and he had a revolver. Like that.

Q: Pointed at you?
Yeah. I gave him the password, Bread, and he never answered. What did I do? Fired. Before he hit the ground another one come down. So I shouted [clears throat] Bread! He never answered. And down he went. And we went on.

Q: So you shot them?
Shot the pair of them. Well you had to in those . . .

Q: Were they British?

The two turned out to be officers of the same artillery who had wandered off behind enemy lines up on the hills and were trying to rejoin the rank and file. 'Well, that's the point that upset everybody. [. . .] I never knew who they were'.

When quizzed by the interviewer whether the two men had shouted anything at him even though they had not been aware of the new, changed password, he said that no, they hadn't said a thing.

George: When they don't answer straight away, bang bang and that's it.

Q: It was night, was it?
No, this was in the early morning. Yeah, it was light.

'Of course, they nicknamed me *killer* for a long time'. Stephens continued, 'At the time I didn't feel that strongly about it, I thought it was just one of these things. A British soldier killing other British soldiers in the line of duty: this knowledge seems to have troubled George's companions more than it did him, because in his worldview, and in his perception, that is what one came to war, to defend themselves at all costs' (Stephens, IWM Accession no. 24630).

As for the British and the Italians, accounts vary wildly. Their materiality and dwelling practices were utterly different: in an almost comical vignette, Italian partisans inside a hut, huddled in blankets and shivering, watched incredulously as the Englishman Tilman washed in a semi-frozen stream (interview, Nino De Marchi).

2.7 Spies: the ultimate uncanny element

In addition to warring political factions, an insidious danger plagued local communities and made partisans' lives hell – spies. Spies had to be local elements as they needed the resistance members' trust in order to obtain information that they could then sell to the Nazi or Fascist authorities in exchange for remuneration, extra food, and so on. Spies were insidious precisely because they masqueraded as friends, confidants and allies. They hid in plain sight. Published memoirs and official speeches appear reticent to mention these aberrant 'citizens', but they play an important role in veteran remembrance. When memoirs explicitly mention spies, such as Lowenthal's book, spies become or are interpreted as outsiders from elsewhere.

> The priest had been bullied by the Fascists to warn anyone harbouring a 'rebel' – a Partisan, that they would have their house torched. That evening my friend, a fugitive, came to seek shelter in our home. My mother was terrified . . . but felt sorry for him, and let him stay, only at midnight she crept to my room and said, in the *smallest* voice 'Fascists at the door, what *are* we going to do'. Someone, an ex-Partisan of all people- informed the Blackshirts. That was our sorry life. This was May 6th, 1944.
>
> (Gildo Perin, interview 16 July 2011)

Figure 2.2 A spy to the Germans is paraded through a crowd in Belluno, May 1945.

Source: John Ross's private archive

Another partisan recalls how someone in a community of friends betrayed them to the Germans in a hurt, still incredulous tone.

> I arrived in Alpago after the winter [of 1944] and in the village everyone knew me and greeted me warmly. I told them about my adventures up in the mountains! They asked, where are you going tonight? I answered, 'I sleep in a real bed tonight, up in Montanes!' I was naive. After months of loneliness, up in the woods, I was so happy to be among people I knew and loved. Their warm welcome was so moving . . . I just didn't think there may be someone who would alert the Germans. [Voice breaks] And yet someone did. The next day Montanes was surrounded by 300 Germans. I couldn't believe it. I still can't. I thought those people were my friends, and I loved them dearly.
> (Nino De Marchi, interview 10 October 2009)

This is a story about a mistake. In recounting his disbelief in the friendly locals' betrayal, Nino's story incarnates the uneasy realm of the uncanny. Things should not have gone that way, yet they did, and in doing so they destabilised Nino's understanding of his affective world.

> Academic scholars and armchair strategists should try to figure out step by step how action takes place. It was not easy to cross a battlefront, whatever the means employed. A wireless set was not a bundle one could put under one's coat. In enemy territory it was not easy to find the people one was looking for, to find localities where supplies could be landed or dropped. It is easy to talk about destroying an enemy ammunition dump or bridge; it was difficult to do it. It was not easy to avoid the enemy, his collaborators and informers, to be aware of the duplicity of turncoats more interested in their factional goals than in winning the war, to recognise spies and double agents . . .
> (Max Salvadori quoted in Tudor 2004: 21)

In his autobiographical work *The Periodic Table*, the eminent Holocaust theorist, novelist and poet laureate Primo Levi described his torturer and captor thus:

> Cagni was the spy who had led to our capture: a pure spy in every gram of his flesh, spy by nature and temperament rather than out of Fascist conviction or interest: a spy for the sake of hurting, for the thrill of the hunt, the way a poacher takes down free-ranging game.
> (Levi 1975: 136–137)

I return to Levi's wartime experience in Chapter 7. Meanwhile, I note that summary violence was by no means the exclusive behaviour of Fascists or partisans. Even the Allies did not hesitate to eliminate civilians whom they suspected of

64 *Unsettling identities*

consorting with the Germans. This is how George Stephens recalls the shooting of three Italian civilians:

> Oh yes you used to see the civilians quite often, I remember once we were up at the observation post, and two of the blokes there came up and Colonel Mackenzie wanted to check out a thing, so we had to go to the Observation Post and here he says, 'What are those Italians doing over there, look! They been a long time' he said 'They aren't ploughing up. They are making signs to the Germans'. The Colonel said, 'Put a bullet in each of them', and he took the rifle away from one of us, a sniper rifle it was, and with that he shot all three of them. Because they were making signs to the Germans. He didn't mess about, he just come up and killed all of them, and they were men.
>
> (Stephens, IWM Accession no. 24630)

'They were men': what did Stephens mean by these concluding words? Partisan Aldo Azzalini recalled the shock of witnessing the execution of a spy:[2]

> I was *much* shaken when I had to witness the execution of a spy outside Vittorio Veneto Town Hall – Lanza, his name was. It was dreadful. All of his hair stood on end – I think out of sheer terror – as did mine. I am a sensitive kind of guy, always been. Violence shook me up real bad.
>
> (Interview 23 December 2010, my emphasis)

Figure 2.3 1944. Montanes, where Nino De Marchi was betrayed by someone he thought a friend.
Photo: Nino De Marchi

In conclusion, the otherness of personhood transpires in sets of encounters between differential material-cultured individuals and the clash of their (often) incompatible corporeality (see also Katz and Csordas 2003: 278). The reflexive practice of generating historical narratives increasingly positions past events (and their affect/effect on the present) as open-ended and apt to create dizziness rather than closure. One of the core aims of this book, besides investigating the competing materialities shaping social lives in conflict, is to foreground everyday practices and experiences, 'new categories of person or types of object, from a series of intersecting processes, entities, and forces in ways that might be unexpected, unforeseen, and unplanned' (Fowler 2013: 27). Let us think of the German soldiers' spatial and embodied alienation in strange southern landscapes, or the ambiguity inhabited by Italian spies, trapped between perceptual worlds and the irreconcilable identities of same and other, and of Italians and enemies. A reciprocal diffidence could evolve in mutual empathy in the face of death and violence; for instance, I am thinking of Aldo Azzalini's anathema in the face of a spy's execution, mirrored in Emanuele Artom's abhorrence of the cold-blooded killing of a Fascist. In the next chapter, I situate the material culture of the body and its multiple incarnations in the world at war as civil strife took a more sinister turn.

Notes

1 Among my research participants, Lavinia Frescura, Nino De Marchi, Domenico Favero, Aldo De Bin and Giuseppe Giust testify to that fact.
2 I attempted to locate this Lanza person, to no avail.

3 The lost bodies of the Italian resistance and civil war

> One hot August evening in 2008, like a bolt out of the blue, something happened. I was at the seaside resort on the Veneto Adriatic coast where my family spent our summer holidays. The resort is very popular with Austrians and Germans, as it is nearer (and a better value than) the trendier beaches further down the Adriatic coast, such as Rimini and Cattolica. In the Veneto, we are not as swamped with tourists. That night, my grandmother and I are taking a pleasant walk after dinner. In the street, people stroll with their ice creams and sunburns. All of a sudden, Grandma has a jolt. She elbows me slightly, pointing at two youths walking some four metres in front of us. They are tall, young, blond – possibly German, or eastern European. My Grandma whispers, 'You know, seeing those two gave me a start. Déjà vu, they call it, don't they? I have seen two lads just like that once before – blond, tall, walking in step, all tall and lanky and pink skinned. Only that time they had just raided my neighbour's house and set it on fire, and were walking away. I saw their square backs, their broad shoulders like that. They were wearing uniforms. They were hunting partisans'.

3.1 Bodies in the snow

Look at the photograph in Figure 3.1: does it drive home the corporeal reality of the civil war? To me, the scene is deeply melancholy, with frozen ground and barren trees visible in the background, forever framing the figure of the dead man. It was the winter of 1944 (or possibly 1945), before hope of liberation seized Italian hearts, giving them the strength to endure the horrors of war and occupation. We do not know who this unfortunate is. We do not know where the photograph was taken, or by whom. In contrast with the pictures depicting the last moments of Armando Baldini, this is a lonely scene – the photographer included the background of frozen ground and skeletal trees as if (I am thinking) to frame the tragedy of violent death,

Figure 3.1 A melancholy scene: the body of one dead partisan in a wintry landscape.
Source: Liviano Proia, private archive

choosing not to put the dead body at the centre of the picture. Perhaps your gaze is drawn from the lifeless body to the bleak frozen wintry landscape behind him; this man has been hanged on a sort of trough, a livestock farming implement that served as an improvised gallows, macabre in the mundane – if a touch gloomy – backdrop. The picture seems to intimate that spring will never come for the dead youth. Engaging with this haunting photograph triggers our bodily understanding of suffering, our sense of our own mortality and of our bodies' fragile nature.

Yet to me the picture evokes another sense of something missing. The literature on the Italian war does not pay sufficient attention to the experience of the conflict through the living body: wounded, healthy, in motion, hiding, starving, and so on. When some degree of anthropological attention is devoted to embodiment, it is to the defilement of corpses (Portelli 1997: 321) or to the concealment or ritual forgetting of *dead* bodies (Cappelletto 2005: 106). Portelli's work on embodied memories makes reference to oral history work with Vietnam (1997: 175) and Spanish Civil War veterans (1997: 161) rather than to Italian partisans and Fascists, whose experience he examines from the point of view of collective memory and political consciousness. The body-at-war looms large in memoirs and remembrance, and yet it has seldom been subjected to critical academic scrutiny. Our sensing bodies are the medium through which we explore and measure every encounter (Merleau-Ponty 1996; Csordas 1994). 'It is uncertain whether *any* experience can truly be told' Portelli muses (1997: 143). Here I suggest that the presence of the remembering body fills the void of the unspeakable left by narrative storytelling through the body's position in the present, reaching out to others. The body does so by orientating and placing perceptions of self and others through the senses of smell, sight and touch in particular (see Smith 2007).

In this chapter, I turn to embodiment as the intersection where materiality and identity form, shift shape, punish, corrupt and position persons with/in a world at war. The body is a site, or a place, of knowledge (c.f. Csordas 1994; Munn 1996). Embodiment is an integral process of the relationship between human animals and their environment (Pink 2009: 27): our bodies develop dwelling practices, physical habits and tendencies linking them (us) to places and other beings. I argue that the body at war, specifically, possesses its own worldviews, often independent of our conscious thought, shaping everything we do and how we engage with others through mutually implicated sensory experiences, memories and ways of imagining. For instance, veterans recall how they tried not to feel prejudiced against someone, but that they had a gut feeling that told them to distrust them. They might have known, rationally, that they should go to a place (e.g. to accomplish a mission), but somehow the thought made their flesh creep.

The memory of the body can be conceptualised in two ways; first, there is the memory triggered by bodily stimuli and by the senses – as in my grandmother's case. Seeing two young, tall blond boys walking in front of us on a pavement in 2008 reminded her of seeing two young Wehrmacht soldiers walking away from the scene of a crime perpetrated against civilians (or partisans) in Conegliano. Then there is the memory of the body – the recall of one's own body and the recall of others' bodies (Bourdieu 1986; Connerton 1989). The senses do not only trigger the latter kind of memory but also define the body as the focus of memory and as the object of its attention. The senses are fundamental to contemporary notions of selfhood and otherness (Smith 2007: 65).

Affect creates bodies as much as it circulates through them. As a long tradition of phenomenologists have postulated, we exist via the medium of our sentient bodies. Langer helpfully summarised this point (1989: 41), arguing that our awareness of the body is 'inseparable from the world of [its] perception . . . I perceive always in reference to my body'. In what follows, I want to propose ways in which affect and materiality shaped and socialised the bodies of the main actors in the conflict unravelling in Italy, but with implications for much wider and later wartime contexts. In my research on the sensory memory of the war, the informal context of the interview has afforded Second World War veterans an opportunity to engage with bodily and perceptual memory emotions (violence, hunger, fear, grief), a topic which they would avoid in any public talks and in the writing of memoirs. Talking of the body makes one feel exposed (see also Thompson 2000). Further, a private interview enables respondents to speak their native dialect and respond more openly to questions specifically to do with the body in wartime landscapes. My sample of veterans certainly responded well, after an initial surprise about my explicit request to share their memories of the senses rather than of the mind ('no one had asked me about that before!' protested Lorenzo Altoè) (De Nardi 2014). In historical scholarship especially, doubtlessly due to a predominant (and legitimate) privileging of objective, quantifiable fact, the body has often been hidden, drowning invisibly in the rivers of ink filling scholarly tomes of resistance narratives. Could we not start from here instead, and build our stories from the violated site of the body at war? Might we acknowledge the physical memories of hiding and fearing one's own demise as an aspect of historical experience?

Over and above the experience of the body in conflict (see Curti 2008; McSorley 2012b), our bodies remain the vehicles through which affects are engendered, shared and emanated. Ahmed conceives of affect as the key to the 'messiness of the experiential, the unfolding of bodies into worlds, and the drama of contingency' (2010: 30). Embodied affects determine how we are 'touched by what we are near' (2010: 30). I agree that affects touch bodies and set them up in an ongoing dialogue with other bodies, places and materialities. It is through our embodied 'autobiographical' materiality that we experience the world and the other under any given circumstances. Through the senses we go through life, and become conduits of perceptions and judgements on others (Merleau-Ponty 1996; Leyens et al. 2000). Through our sensing bodies, we may include or exclude others (Paladino et al. 2002). If I dislike you skin deep, I might give you a wide berth. Maybe you don't 'smell right'. Smell, argues Smith (2007: 59), 'more than any other sense perhaps, served to create and mark the 'other' '. Maybe you walk or stand too close behind me, and you scare me. Maybe your hair is too blond – your body too lank and tall. You look different from me. Do these sentiments *feel* familiar? This is how infrahumanisation works (Leyens et al. 2000; Haslam et al. 2005). Towards the end of the chapter, I turn to questions of how the body remembers, stores, *stories* and communicates embodied and material traces and memories of conflict.

3.2 The body of the fighter

> In march 1944 I ended up in Valsalega, with the brigade led by Renato Pizzol. They [the local partisans] look me up and down; they are studying me. Then Ieia (a local helper girl) offers me *puina*. I hesitated, because I did not know what it was.
>
> (Liviano Proia, interview 6 August 2011)

Thus, Umbria native partisan Liviano 'Gimmi' Proia narrated his first meeting with the northern partisans of the Cansiglio forest in the province of Belluno. The local lads looked him up and down, appraising his dark colouring and exotic accent. The danger of the enemy posing as a partisan was ever present, and they mostly came from elsewhere in central and southern Italy. Then the partisans offered Liviano food which he didn't know and whose name he didn't understand. When they produced a piece of soft ricotta cheese, everyone smiled at Liviano's relief. He was different; there is no doubt about that. They would grow to love him dearly, but his first impression was one of disorientation. His materiality was, at first, incompatible with theirs.

The embodiment of soldiers, whether Fascist, German or anti-Fascist guerrilla fighters, remains an overlooked variable in the messy formula of the civil war and occupation. Here I aim to contextualise the materiality of fighting bodies in the everyday. We know, for example, that the canonical embodiment of German Wehrmacht soldiers was one of belligerent masculinity. 'It was taboo, within the masculine culture of the military, to admit that one had wet one's pants, or vomited in fear' (Neitzel and Welzer 2013: 55). Their militarised bodies were deployed to the front with the sole purpose of maintaining order and killing whenever necessary. German sources reveal that Wehrmacht soldiers were not encouraged to fraternise with civilians, and that at any rate this was not always an option. Thus, Holewa recalled his interactions with Italians in Lazio (central Italy) in mid-1944:

> We didn't get in touch with the Italian civilians. They were particularly hostile towards us at that particular time, because I remember we were stationed at a winery, a vineyard actually, and the doors needed shutting and fastening, so I helped while I could. I still remember this man, went down to the wine cellar and brought back up a bottle covered in dust and cobwebs, cleaned it up and poured us a glass. It was good stuff! I can still taste it.
>
> (Holewa, IWM Accession no. 12340)

Holewa's memory of the body, the evocation triggered by the senses ('I can still taste it') takes precedence over the memory of the Italians' reticence to relate to the soldiers stationed in the area. Alcohol constitutes a comforting theme in Germans' memories of the front. German paratrooper Robert Frettlohr posited that

> You existed, you didn't live. You existed as a soldier. We had plenty whisky, well, farmer's whisky, schnapps really, and it gave you . . . well. We used to be pretty much sozzled, if you were wounded you didn't feel it. I can assure you, I didn't [he chuckles] and it creates a false courage, the alcohol, you see. Most of the heroes were either stupid or drunken ones . . . they say you fight for your country, but I tell you . . . in one case it is true but in the other case . . . you fight for self-survival. You want to get out in one piece if at all possible.
> (Frettlohr, IWM Accession no. 19590)

Creature comforts were hard to come by for the civilians, but even more so for the fighters. Briton George Stephens recalled a pivotal moment in the materiality of the war – the day he was offered a hot cup of tea. 'We had our first hot cup of tea since getting to Cassino in the Salvation Army canteen – nearly four months after we got sent there. There had been tea before but 'It was cold tea – everything was cold' (Stephens, IWM Accession no. 24630).

Stephens went on to say that he had been so grateful for the cup of hot tea the Salvation Army (SA) had given him when he was so very weary, that in later life every time he saw a SA girl down the street, he would always give her a pound in gratitude for 'that lovely cuppa' (Stephens, IWM Accession no. 24630). One can only imagine the bodily and psychological comfort that a weary Englishman in a foreign country embodied by a hot cup of steaming tea – a quasi-Proustian catalyst of blissful remembrance.

The daily comforts and habits that resistance fighters had before they took to the perilous life in the mountains and woods had to be abandoned. The stability of home, of regular meals and washes, had to be forsaken. Partisan Aldo Azzalini recalled:

> The main thing was being safe, feeling safe. We moved about continuously, there wasn't even enough time to grow attached to a place, to feel good in it, because we would have to move on as soon as it became dangerous. [. . .] There were discomforts, yes, even because I . . . my only need was . . . well, in the morning I needed milk. I really needed milk to start the day . . . and I had to learn to go without, often.
> (Interview 23 December 2010)

3.2.1 Sex

So, each fighter had a body. The fighter inhabited a gendered, sexualized body that had its needs. My Grandfather, framed it in unequivocal terms: 'What struck us the most, at the time, was ... What mattered the most at that age ... the blood boiled in your veins ... the snow was melting all around us ... without girls, without the opportunity for relations, all those months. ...'

(Domenico Favero, interview with S. Conte and C. Strazzer, 1 February 2002)

Artom (Artom and Schwarz 2008: 126) commented on the sexual starvation or enforced chastity of his comrades as a cruel but necessary condition, while also commenting on the presence, among them, of a homosexual man known only as L. (2008: 135).

In mid-1944, Wehrmacht soldier Arno commented on a somewhat desolate party for which, if we read between the lines, his superiors had lined up some prostitutes to relieve the young men's sexual needs. 'The Unteroffizierkorps 1 threw a "*grande festa*" [sic] with women from the town. The town seems to have offered us and the officers its "lowest creatures" '. Arno was so disappointed that he asked whatever happened to the pride of the Germans. The party turned progressively more desperate (*verkrampft*), and Arno felt increasingly uneasy (*unwohl*). But, he wrote, you had to pretend to be having a good time, not to stand out too much (*nicht zu sehr auffallen*). He only liked one young petite girl who held herself in a natural, cheerful way. She wore a modest green pullover. 'It is incredible', he observed, 'what the women in these parts must bear "on their heads" (*auf ihren Köpfen*)' – Arno compared the burden of the women to the burden of donkeys.

Bernhard, another German Wehrmacht soldier, recalled one particular Italian girl whom he had 'known well' before Italy switched sides. In July 1944, [they] 'returned to Marta on Lake Bolsena and here we met again some well-known faces [friendly locals]'. However, Bernhard discovered to his dismay that pretty Marcella ('*die Primadonna* of their former bathing parties'), who had (presumably) become intimate with them, was now possibly in Rome, 'fraternizing with Americans', mused Bernhard despondently (Bernhard P., n.d., Tagebucharchiv Accession no. 3310). Thus, the commingling of sexual longing and melancholy combined to make this German feel alienated, out of place, and ill at ease even in a town where he had rejoined friendly familiar faces. Sometimes German soldiers contented themselves with flirting with local girls without seeking to take things further. This 'consideration' still made women uncomfortable – especially if they were active in the resistance. One of my participants, Nedda Zanfranceschi, recalled her 'ordeal' with cat-calling thus:

> I'll tell you when I felt in danger. Down there, on the street, there is a large barracks. Just there, we had a German command, and there were always many German officers hanging around. I remember that whenever I went by on my bicycle they used to shout 'Stop by, *bella mora*' – pretty brunette. And I laughed

and was terrified. They were always shouting after me – and I was so afraid because they were Germans.

(Interview 13 October 2010)

The need to have sexual relations could effectively shape the way that Germans acted and interacted with the local women.

Sommer: (re: his 'Oberleutnant') In Italy too, wherever we arrived, he always said: 'Let's first bump a few people off!' I know Italian too and always had to carry out special tasks. He said: 'First of all we will kill twenty men in order to have peace here, to prevent them getting ideas!' [laughter] Then we put up a little notice saying: 'At the least sign of stubbornness fifty more will be killed!'
Bender: From what point of view did he pick them, just at random?
Sommer: Yes, just twenty men like that: 'Just come here'. They were all taken to the market-place and someone appeared with three MGs – rrr – and there they lay. That's how it was done. Then he said: 'Excellent! Swine!' You can't imagine how he loathed the Italians. There were a few pretty girls in the district where . . . he was quartered. He never touched any civilians there. He never hurt anyone where he lived, in principle.

(Neitzel and Welzer 2013: 86)

In the above exchange, we see two prisoners of war's boastful enjoyment of violence against civilians. Yet they also make reference to the strategic decision taken by their Oberleutnant, who took care not to jeopardise the chance for sexual encounters with local women by behaving brutally toward civilians. For his part, my ex-partisan respondent Giuseppe Giust was more bashful: he acknowledged that when they had a free afternoon, his comrades liked to seek out some local *señoritas* [sic], but that he was too shy to 'indulge'. Giuseppe's use of a foreign word to indicate young women who may or may not have been 'ladies' (he uses the Spanish *senorita*) suggests a certain embarrassment in talking about sexual conduct with a woman, even in the context of research. It feels as if, by using a foreign word to indicate an unpalatable fact of life, Giuseppe chose to negate any presence in the familiar surroundings of his Catholic hometown of the sexual appetite felt by his comrades – and very probably his own desires. Giuseppe framed prostitution and soliciting as facts external to his reality, literally *foreign* concepts that must be remembered, but in the right, proper way.

3.2.2 Bodily hygiene

'Ico' Lowenthal condemned the nomadic life of partisans for its many 'hygiene malfunctions' (2015: 122–123): 'It was rather embarrassing. I had to go long stretches without washing, I couldn't get a haircut and even medical attention was too much to ask'. The latter presumably refers to ailments such as nausea and diarrhoea, a regular plight of the fighters according to many respondents (Nino De Marchi and Liviano Proia inter alia). John Ross, an SOE man sent to the Veneto to aid the partisans in their operations, also remembered the duress of life under the resistance, and in particular the plight of fleas and parasites.

Partisan messenger Lavinia acknowledged the difficulties in having to do without a bath for days on end – and the risks some were willing to take in order to enjoy a fleeting moment of domesticity.

> Five days before his death [August 1944] my brother crept back into our family home to have a bath, and then fell asleep on the attic steps out of sheer exhaustion. He was so exhausted, he said, that he could not face going back outside. When he woke up, startled, it was 10 pm at night; he managed to flee down a woodland path behind the house. He did not want his partisan chief to know where he'd been.
>
> (Interview, 4 December 2010)

'Lupo' Zanolin remembered the hygienic conditions of his time in the resistance thus (Zanolin and Brescacin 2013: 25): 'There were so many fleas – plenty to go around. My friend used to pick whole handfuls off my back'. I also vividly recall my grandfather admitting that, after he had taken up the partisan life, he went back to his home in the northeastern village of Montaner as often as he could to take a bath and shave: he was proud of his Errol Flynn moustache, he claimed, and risked big in order to have a precious shave. All his comrades, he liked to joke, looked like cavemen with their long unkempt hair and beards. He did not wish to look like that. His friends teased him to no end about it – but he kept going back. Even his mother told him off. Then Nino De Marchi was reminded of the time when Major Tilman, the SOE man who was parachuted to train and guide partisan intelligence, came face to face with an English prisoner of war who, after escaping from a camp in Bologna, wanted to rejoin the Allies but had ended up in a partisan formation. The Italians watched with some trepidation as the two came closer, expecting a hug, a torrent of questions, or at any rate a manifestation of emotion. Not so: the first and only words Tilman spoke to the young soldier were 'For God's sake, man; have a shave!' The Englishman's reserve had surprised and amused the Italians.

It was not like that everywhere. The situation in Italy was extremely varied, and the liberated south of the country was abjectly poor, regardless of the fact that it did not suffer the blight of civil war. A British soldier, Private Whatmore, recalls in vivid tones his bodily repulsion towards the living conditions of Italians in the south, where he was parachuted. The materiality of the place, his words seem to say, was so utterly alien to him that it made him physically ill. Asked what the south of Italy was like, he answered:

> Oh, terrible. Worse than the Peak District in Derbyshire. The village people of southern Italy are you know, very crude. No toilets, no nothing. What I can remember is that the houses that they lived in, there was a bed in this corner and a couple of goats sleeping in that corner. A few fowls in this corner, and that would be it. The lanes leading out of the village were absolutely swarming with flies on human, what's the word, excreta. I never seen anything like it. There were never any toilets *anywhere*. So many of us got sick, some of us got malaria. I think that might have been why!
>
> (Whatmore, IWM Accession no. 2703)

The excited tones of his voice – sadly lost in transcription – poignantly conveys the dystopian sense of being displaced in a faraway village in a remote corner of the Italian south. The reference to the abject bodily practices of southerners – the lack of toilets, the excreta in public rights of way, the living in close proximity with animals – frames a discourse of otherness, alterity and disconnected embodiment. These words bear witness to the Other's incompatible materiality.

3.3 The female body

> I was preoccupied before meeting M. I had felt an uncharacteristic malaise, a feeling that I was unable to describe until the morning of the interview with this lady, and I realized I did not look forward to that particular interview. M. has been painted as a harsh, disillusioned woman, and my colleagues had warned me that she would be a tough nut to crack at interview. She had not given interviews to anyone apart from school children. The reasons for her selective engagement were soon to be revealed. M., as a female fighter who carried arms and fought in a Communist formation, I suspect, was the victim of sexual violence. A school child aged 12 or under would never probe into the body politics of the conflict. The Fascists called all female partisans whores.
>
> (Author's reflections on interview with M.)

Women's role in the resistance was paramount to the patriotic war effort. Even when they did not carry weapons, the importance of their local knowledge and their establishment and upkeep of local contacts were vital to the success of the resistance. Women had the vital role of maintaining local networks of communication, and took advantage of their extraordinary knowledge of the landscape and terrain to instruct and shape, manage and continuously update a crucial network of safe places for armed Partisan formations. Women's materiality included not only their handling and delivery of messages, supplies, and even weapons to the armed formations elsewhere, but it reflected their future materialities: their emancipation, their political consciousness, and their independence.

> I remember there was one time I had to make deliveries to the Corba house; there I would meet a certain girl with a bag made of cob leaves with a certain dress on . . . and give her these envelopes. I never knew what I was delivering, what I brought in my bag. They could be boots, weapons, print outs. I did not know.
>
> (Marcella D. interview 20 December 2010)

The above quote from my encounter with Marcella D. speaks volumes about the experience of women who chose to be activists for the resistance. During a conflict where guerrilla warfare is a part of the belligerents' tactics, the visibility of the women in a community corresponded to the invisibility of the men, hiding in the mountains since 8 September 1943, haunting the woods like ghosts. The materiality of women and men differed precisely because it was articulated by a presence/absence. The visible lives of women left behind traces that everyone could notice and engage with – the Fascists, the family, the Germans and the male partisans. Women's embodiment was obvious and present, active and dynamic, and it *made* history through its fleshly activism. In contrast, men's presence was absent – it bubbled under the surface, in caves and shelters, in cellars and under barns. Memory dictates that, especially when farms and households became deprived of the physical strength of male workers, men's embodiment emerged as a melancholy absence. Almost everyone was reminded of the absence of a male relative who had chosen to abscond in a million little ways, impinging on the everyday: from the lack of manpower in the fields to the vacant place at the kitchen table at mealtimes.

On the other hand, not all women were happy about their relatively marginal role in the war and resistance. In her beautifully honest memoir, Wilma De Paris wrote:

> If I had been a boy I would have gone to the war too. I wanted to be like them; I asked myself why they could serve their country and I couldn't. I so wanted to partake in their duress and sacrifices, so I slept on a plain blanket of the wooden floor without mattress or pillows. That made me feel closer to the men sacrificing their lives. To those who had become heroes after 8 September but never come home again.
>
> (De Paris 2005: 76)

Wanting to punish her inert female body, to feel the pain and discomfort of men called to the duty of serving their country, was an obsession for De Paris. She protested the inequality of the call to duty through her body – resisting through her flesh. Women's presence, their fleshly essence, was a hindrance and a bonus in their interaction with Fascists and Germans: their sexuality could be used to avert danger. Even a smile and a mild flirtation could make dangerous materials and clandestine leaflets go unobserved, as the men acknowledged a shapely leg, a rosy cheek or rounded bosom. However, the threat of sexual violence was ever present for women and girls involved in illegal acts of resistance. Nedda recalled the traumatic experience following her arrest by the Fascists in her hometown of Treviso:

> Among the Fascists was a woman – a woman! She started to tease me, humiliated me and then she undressed me. She exposed my figure to the men who competed to utter the worst depravities. They made obscene comments about my body, saying what they would do to me in bed. I nearly died of shame, and was so afraid.
>
> (Interview 13 October 2010)

Luckily, Nedda was not sexually assaulted and was able to return home.

Women's bodies had to adapt to a much more active lifestyle in close contact with nature, none more than Giovanna Zangrandi, partisan, novelist and teacher in Cortina D'Ampezzo – an Italian alpine town peopled with German-loving natives. In her extraordinary published diary, Giovanna poetically recalls her experience in the resistance; unmarried but not indifferent to men, she devoted herself, body and soul, to the fight for freedom. Her 'maternal' instinct turned to nature, perhaps to avoid uncomfortable reflections on her spinsterhood; her diary contains observation after observation on her relationship with 'harbouring' and 'sheltering' natural features in the landscape she has come to know so well. A native of the Emilia-Romagna plains, she had moved to the alpine town of Cortina to take up a teaching position. Her city-dwelling habits had already adapted to the harsh but homely ways of the mountains, but the resistance further tested her stamina and resilience.

> I hesitate to descend – this rock surface, this shrubbery . . . it's too much my own, too motherly.
>
> (Zangrandi 2001: 102)

> Here one can feel the maternal protection of the beech forest behind oneself, the safety of the trees.
>
> (Zangrandi 2001: 121)

Women risked their lives in order to protect the partisans and conceal their activities. And not only for Italians, but for foreigners too. The liminal worlds of those women and girls who made the decision to take up arms and join their boyfriends, brothers and even fathers up in the mountains is still under-researched. Wilma De Paris reflected on the danger of her resistance activities and her loneliness after her (despotic) father left to work in Germany for the Todt Association in the autumn of

1944. She missed him, in a way, but also enjoyed her freedom immensely. She was glad she no longer had to justify or explain herself, hide things, lie and pretend. She no longer had to make excuses for her nighttime absences when she was away on missions on behalf of the partisans of the Tollot Brigade (De Paris 2005: 81). Even though Wilma had felt unable to become a full-on arms-bearing partisan, contemporary sources clearly demonstrate that women were often welcomed in armed formations with the proviso that they would renounce their femininity and become 'one of the lads' (Residori 2008). But, I ask, how to deal with the discomfort of menstruation while on a dangerous stakeout or on a mission?

As anticipated, my encounter with M. turned out to be very tense. I had somewhat sensed the danger of interrogating her memory before our interview, suspecting that her traumatic experience might lead to an affective occlusion, a memory blockage, and a refusal to talk. There were also rumours of a love affair between her and an American pilot sent to lead an OSS mission (Brescacin, pers. comm.), but of course I was not going to ask her about that. The corporeality of women fighters' experience deserves much more complex and ample discussion than is afforded in a single chapter. I was not going to ask M. if she had indulged in romantic entanglements with fellow partisans and Allied officers. What worried me was the fact that she might have suffered sexual violence during her time in the resistance. With a forced smile, she reminded me time and again that she had only agreed to meet me because my Granddad had been a close friend during and after the war. She had, and I quote, 'No desire to remember at all'. M. also contextualised and situated her experience, perhaps in an attempt to make good her 'difference' and non-belonging in the masculine context of the guerrilla fighting through her profound know-how of the places of the resistance (the Cansiglio woods). 'I hid in the depth of the forest and stayed hidden. The Germans found my rucksack but I stood still until they left; after that, well, I was a local and could hide in plain sight'.

I found it extremely interesting that M. positioned herself very firmly in the affective and protective geography of the woods – her homeland – and yet distanced herself from the people, the 'friends and brothers' she had been fighting with after the war was over. In a way, she elected to be an exile from her own memories.

During the war, identities were rehearsed, made and rejected according to dwelling practices and materialities embedded in place. Place constituted not only an entanglement of identities and practices, but also a counter-current of destabilising energy: as we will see more specifically in Chapter 6, places were also 'unmade' through the actions and interactions and intersections of bodies and things. Destruction, destabilisation and alienation led to the unmaking of reality and the tearing asunder of communities' dwelling perspectives. Below, a ritual Fascist practice recounted in an interview carried out by Pavan[1] illustrates an attempt to destroy, to dehumanise women and, ultimately, to unmake place.

> They [the Fascists] arrived on a jeep. They . . . went into a restaurant during a party, grabbed the female guests and shaved their heads.

Q: *Why did they go into the inn?*
Eh, they never liked it when people partied and had fun.

Q: *Were they not rather looking for Partisans . . . ?*
No, they weren't looking for Partisans.

Q: *How long were they in the restaurant?*
An hour or so, then they left.

Q: *Did they eat and drink?*
No, they just shaved heads.

Remarkably, the partisans subjected women who 'went with' or simply entertained themselves with the Fascists and Germans to the same fate. The punishment of shaving a female head served, presumably, to de-feminize a woman and to chastise her immodesty. It can be noted that the double-edged objectification/abjectification served to make the aberrant woman 'less than' normal. The liminality of those melancholy shaved heads and the often scarred scalps, which the women clumsily concealed with head scarves, came to symbolise the gendered material culture of betrayal on both sides. Teresa Sartorelli's diary recalls this very public act of humiliation. One afternoon, the whole village gathered to witness the ritual shaving of those girls who had become friendly or intimate with the Germans. The culprits were shaved on the main square and paraded around the village; Teresa commented on how pathetic their small white heads looked (Sartorelli 1987: 103).

Finally, the experience of Fascist women and girls was as varied as can be expected. In Zelmira Marazio's diary, we learn that on Christmas Eve 1943, the Fascist party had organised social events for the German soldiers and the Fascist staff and soldiers to mingle. They sang German Christmas songs and drank wine and beer, sitting together at long tables. Zelmira commented that the Germans, ruddy and stocky lads, were much too 'friendly' (Marazio 2004: 59). One of the lads comically tried to convince her to spend the night with him, but she vehemently refused, explaining in broken German that she must leave 'abfahren' with the train or her mother will 'kaput' her. Aside from Zelmira, we know that several girls fraternised with German and Allied soldiers (Venohr 2002; Favero 2003; Mochmann and Larsen 2005; Von Widmann and Wiltenburg 2006). How do we situate these women's experience? There is no room here to fully explore the implications of romantic and sexual entanglements (and the much less visible male-on-male encounters taking place at the time), but their crucial place in memory must be acknowledged.

In one of his letters home to his wife in Hamburg, Helmut K. observed a likeness in countenance and behaviour between Germans and Englishmen with regards to local women (Tagebuchsarchiv, Accession no. 3261, 1 p. 40). He was clearly concerned about a possible Allied invasion of Hamburg but reassured his wife that she would be 'very unlikely to be raped by an Englishman if such an event was to happen', if the Brits were anything like the Allied soldiers stationed in his neck of the woods ('they leave the women alone'). Helmut claims soldiers should be 'correct but reserved' when dealing with the enemy, and, although not explicitly formulated, abstain from sexual violence. Women in southern Lazio were not as lucky. In the infamous rape epidemics of 19–30 May 1944, known as *Marocchinate*, the North African corps of the French Army (more specifically the French Expeditionary Corps (FEC)), commanded by General Alphonse Juins, spread terror, unwanted pregnancies and disease across a vast area south of Rome (Atkinson 2007: 556 ff.). The officers sexually violated over 2,000 women, men, children and elderly people, in an almost indiscriminate wave of violence. A reminder of the most fragile and vulnerable site of conflict – the human body. Violence and prejudice against the female body, and in particular against the aberrant females (spy, armed fighter, prostitute) map out a vernacular of terror on the body. Far from being inscribed onto the skin, the negative affects of war and conflict cling to the body, penetrate it and become one with women's personhood and experience.

3.4 The Jewish body in the resistance

Every body experienced the resistance and civil war differently, and it seems unnatural to artificially separate Jewish experience from a 'normalised' Italian perception of the events of the war. Schwarz (Artom and Schwarz 2008: 194) warns against any attempt to discriminate or unwittingly belittle individual Jewish resistance fighters' experience in light of their ethnicity and religion, and with reason. Yet, autobiographical materiality embodied by everyone dictated how one understood the world and the events around them. The import of embodied Jewish identity in the war is vast, but investigations into Jewishness in the Italian conflict have been comparatively scarce. Studies specifically exploring the sense of identity and place embodied by Italian Jews have looked at broader issues of political belonging, citizenship and the unspeakable loss of deportation and death.

We do have some testimonies of Jewish Italians who became involved in the resistance movement and stayed in Italy to fight the Fascists and Nazis, namely the experience of Emanuele Artom (Artom and Schwarz 2008), Enrico 'Ico' Lowenthal (Lowenthal 2015) and, to an extent, Primo Levi (1975). These memories provide a unique perspective from which to interpret and understand the significance of the resistance to occupation and Fascism after Italy's Allied armistice of 1943.

While we remain painfully aware of the plight and horrors of deportations initiated by the Fascists (Bosworth 2006), we know much less about the lives of those Jews who managed to remain in Italy as Italians and Jews, fighting or going underground for however long they were able to. One of my (Caucasian) Italian respondents told me a story which led me to reassess my assumption that Italians retaliated against the Nazis and Fascists because of the abysmal and inhuman treatment reserved to someone other than them – the European Jews. Lorenzo, a veteran partisan in the Veneto, commented:

> We were surrounded by Germans at some point. It was the summer 1944, I remember, at dawn, and one of us, Renato I think but I can't quite remember, he said, let's try to negotiate with them, and then Coledi got out his gun and said: 'Not me, I am going to . . . they're not going to get me alive!' And I realized, of course: Coledi was a Jew. He must have known about the atrocities perpetrated against his race in the extermination camps and would rather have killed himself.
> (Interview, 18 December 2011)

Renato, the other partisan present on that occasion, recalls his angle on the hair-rising event from which (obviously) all three men escaped unscathed.

> Coledi, Lorenzo and I were hiding under some hay and spent an uneasy night in this barn. In the morning, the first thing we hear are gunshots ringing very close – some fifty yards away. Oh my God. Then Coledi, who was Jewish, took his gun. Rather than being sent to a death camp, he said, I am going to kill myself.
> (Interview, 24 September 2011).

This episode, apparently just another one of many of Lorenzo's and Renato's anecdotes in the course of our lively, in-depth exchanges, framed the resistance experience in a new perspective. What if you were a fighter, a patriot, who had that much more baggage and that much greater an incentive to fight, and die, a hero? For instance, Artom, a highly politicised intellectual operating in Piemonte (Northwest), authored a diary/memoir recounting his subjective experience of the conflict in Italy (Artom and Schwarz 2008) as a Jewish intellectual.

The decision to position oneself as Jewish depended on a number of factors, of course: the eminent Primo Levi had been a partisan for four months before he was captured (see Chapter 7 for Levi's resistance experience). At first he was interrogated by a Fossa who had no interest in his identity.

> He considered me pathetic, a spoilt brat easily influenced by bad associations. In his deeply classist worldview he could not conceive of a university graduate

> being truly subversive. [. . .] His interrogation style was half-baked – he was a soldier, not a cop. He never asked embarrassing questions, nor did he ever ask me if I was Jewish.
>
> (Levi 1975: 136)

In contrast to the superficial questioning of his identity by a man full of pre-empted prejudice and rigid worldviews, Levi later commented on his interactions with another individual who had a different attitude towards his Jewishness:

> Cagni claimed (probably bluffing) that he knew I was a Jew, and that . . . I was *either a Jew or a partisan;* if partisan, I was in trouble; if a Jew, well, there was a collection camp in Carpi, he said, where they were not bloodthirsty, and I would stay there until the final victory. I admitted I was a Jew: in part out of sheer exhaustion, in part due to an irrational pride.
>
> (Levi 1975: 137, my emphasis)

Thus, in the worldview of that particular Fascist, one *could not* be a Jew and a partisan at the same time. Levi chose to be a Jew, and was deported to Auschwitz – certainly not to the idyllic work camp at Carpi he had been lured to believe in by his captors. Ico (Enrico Lowenthal) was not an overtly political young man, but the Racial Laws of 1943 and their dreadful implications for his family and loved ones obviously troubled him. Enrico reported that after Italy switched sides, a local Notary managed to get the whole family false identification papers declaring their Aryan Italian heritage (Lowenthal 2015: 69). Then he went on to comment that he couldn't wait to start fighting against the Germans: the omission of the Fascists in this instance could signify that in his mind, as an Italian Jew, the Nazis, not their Italian allies, symbolised the greatest and most urgent problem and preoccupation (Lowenthal 2015: 74). Then something else happens. In his memoir, we witness a significant shift in identity. He started identifying as 'one of them', an Italian, and no longer predominantly as Jewish. He wrote, 'Finally, I was like everyone else' (Lowenthal 2015: 75). The materiality of this shift is palpable through the pages of the partisan's memoir. First he recalled how the feel of the rifle and the ammunition in his hands changed his life (Lowenthal 2015: 74). He then returned to the theme of life-changing in the following pages where he described the joy he felt, upon entering a Communist Garibaldi partisan band, holding the shotgun that had changed his life (Lowenthal 2015: 76). Over and above the weapon, the possession of his new false identification card shifts his persona and his destiny. The new identification papers shape his new life, give him a new direction to follow. Enrico mentions the false papers again and again throughout the memoir – the material site of his salvation and resistance life as 'Ico', yet another partisan.

During this transformation, Ico gets a new body. His resistance is bodied not as a Jewish boy but as an Italian man. Ico now inhabits a body that fights, as opposed to the victimised, doomed body of a Jew. At any rate, Enrico was not a practising Jew: he eats pork whenever he is offered it and enjoys it (Lowenthal 2015: 98). Whether this dietary freedom was part of his new persona or not remains undisclosed.

3.5 Other bodies

Bodies that did not conform to the normative code of the resistance were, at the least, eyed with suspicion. By incarnating difference, the aberrant bodies instilled fear and anxiety in the normative residents of an area and disturbed the accepted way things were. The different bodies disrupted the status quo: were these individuals reliable, or a liability?

> We learn how to dodge German and Black Shirt patrols, and thus to fight against fear, tiredness, the cold, the fog. For a long time I have lingered on the memory of the relief when we reached the peak [where the Partisan HQ was located]; we often lost the way, missed the right path and our sense of direction owing to the fog . . . like in a nightmare, we could often hear voices but not figure out where they came from. I still remember the joyous welcome, the bread and butter and jam when we reached our destination, and then the well-deserved rest under warm sheepskin rugs, and early in the morning back down to the plains.
>
> (Rosetta Banchieri quoted in Sega 2008)

> Thus began a long and strenuous march . . . after 13 hours along the route, a violent blizzard catches us out . . . we carry on regardless in a long, exhausting march lasting all night. [. . .] The long, shattering march had some really difficult moments. The woods, and the snow, in places 1.5 metres tall, have hindered recognition of the right path. [. . .] Already prostrated by the long march in appalling weather, the Garibaldini are at the end of their tether. Our Guide, owing to bad visibility, led us on a course that lasted three hours when it should have taken one, and along difficult, perilous tracks, thus adding many more kilometers to the march.
>
> (Vicchi 1984: 494)

What stories did different, deviant autobiographical materialities tell in their intersection with others' embodied material cultures? Sometimes body language was the crucial factor to determine the outcome of an event or sequence of events. We find an extraordinary episode in Enrico Lowenthal's diary narrating his encounter with two German soldiers who surrendered to him and were given safe passage to Switzerland. The passage where Enrico describes his visit to one of the two soldiers after the war deserves to be reported in its entirety.

> After the war, in the Fifties, I went to visit Ludwig at his home in Berchtsgaden and asked him how it had been possible that they, war veterans in their thirties, would have so easily and readily surrendered to a young man like myself. Ludwig's answer was simple. 'You didn't just tell us *Hande hoch*, hands up. Instead you said, "*Hande hoch bitte*", hands up please'. He then went on to explain, as I looked confused. 'We were used to shoot first, ask for hands up later. We were so astonished by your polite "hands up please" in a good German accent that we realized you were a fighter and a gentleman, and that we could trust you' (Lowenthal 2015: 127). This trust was maintained in the hours that followed that bizarre encounter, when Ludwig and Arthur spent the night in the same hut as the partisans, sharing the hut floor with the partisans – 'on the floor, just like us'.
>
> (Lowenthal 2015: 127)

'Aberrant' German bodies also appear in the multitude of perceptions and transformations taking place in those fateful days of fighting. Elsewhere I make the case that more German officers than is realised actually defected and relied on local Italian friends and girlfriends in order to effect the transition (De Nardi 2015a, and see Röhrs 2009).

> Walter B. decided to defect. His Italian friends decided to help. They hid Walter B. in the apartment of an inn-keeper friend. Afterwards he was to spend a long time in those lodgings, regularly visited and supported by his sweetheart Giulia. She dyed his blond hair black and brought him civilian clothing.
>
> (Röhrs 2009: 102)

In the above passage, the bodily otherness of a defecting German is camouflaged. Neither 'properly' German nor Italian, Walter shed his Wehrmacht uniform and dyed his hair dark. He thus underwent a physical transformation intended to make him look Italian, to deceive the Wehrmacht, and to help him 'blend in'. Later on, his girlfriend would teach him Italian. However, when invited to join an armed partisan band later on, he declined, saying that he was not prepared to shoot against his former comrades. Walter's refusal may be seen as an emotional rejection of total desertion, insofar as German soldiers were still an ingroup rather than an outgroup, and violence against them was therefore still unthinkable (after Leyens et al. 2000).

Finally, the comparison to the animal kingdom could transform the body of the fighter into 'Other'. We find such inferences as '[y]ou understand that partisans become like animals in the mountains . . . ' (Portelli 1997: 138); again, both partisans *and* Fascists were described as 'half beasts', 'wolves', 'savages' . . . (1997: 139). Dehumanisation (or infrahumanisation) of the enemy served to distance, to alienate and to render the Other an easy target. In wartime storytelling, the use of non-human animal imagery in describing the enemy implied that what one did was the right thing to do. Comparing someone else to an animal of a different species ascribed the other to a realm 'beyond the pale of human and moral responsibility' (Portelli 1997: 175). 'Animal imagery is a pervasive metaphor of total difference, representing the loss humanity caused by the war' (Portelli 1997: 174).

3.6 Saved or dead: the body's tale

To enjoy the killing was the ultimate taboo. Wartime accounts express dark feelings, born of violence, and, sometimes, bringing about violence. The reluctance to admit to violence can engender 'the distortions, the symbols, the inventions: the unnecessary denials are the vehicle of the revelation' (Portelli 1997: 137). For the Germans, disposal of dead bodies was a central task and one from which, in the main, they did not seem to shy away.

> 'Taking care of partisans' was rationalized with the idea that they ambushed German soldiers. Revenge was a powerful motivator. Together with the execution of prisoners, the battle against partisans was the framework in which German soldiers most frequently committed war crimes.
>
> (Neitzel and Welzer 2013: 78)

International law seemed to furnish deeply ambiguous rules for dealing with guerrilla warfare. 'The 1907 Hague Convention was full of contradictions and open questions concerning the rights and responsibilities of an occupying force' (Neitzel and Welzer 2013: 78).

The taking and handling of prisoners, the engagement with human beings of opposite beliefs, where politics gave way to the necessary engagement with others' bodies, could be one of the most awkward and sensitive tasks the resistance bands had to perform. Ex-resistance fighter Domenico Favero thus recalls one incident involving a German prisoner, and his words vividly evoke the intensity of this man's embodied ordeal:

> We had captured a German aviation marshal on Mt St Boldo in autumn 1944. Despite the stifling summer heat, I remember he kept shivering and whimpering under three blankets. He trembled and sweated continuously, poor bastard. One of our Russian partisans had fun terrorizing him, he told him he would be killed, even if that wasn't our intention. One time they scared him so much, he

soiled himself. I felt so sorry for him. One time the chief asked him to go and collect wood, but he would not leave the hut, he hung on to it with legs and fists: he feared he would be really taken away and shot. He ended up joining our ranks instead – only he was later killed by his own German compatriots. A sad story, but there were many like this.

(Domenico Favero quoted in Conte and Strazzer 2003)

The body politics is encapsulated in this quote: the body of the German prisoner is the fleshy site of contestation and affect. Domenico Favero wonders what would have happened if the Wehrmacht had not killed the German marshal. I wonder what this German partisan experienced, during his brief time with the Italian 'Banditen'. How did his autobiographical materiality interact with theirs?

Serena Conte and Chiara Strazzer filmed an interview with my late partisan Grandfather Domenico, where they asked him about his experiences of 'the enemy'. A slight melancholy intermingled with his signature dry humour inflected his memories. Granddad had been fortunate; he claimed (and I believe him) to never having fired a single shot against anyone; he was proud not to have injured or killed anybody. On the contrary, Granddad felt an emotional and even embodied empathy towards the enemies of the resistance: Fascists and Germans. Below, he expressed his aversion towards wartime violence on the body by making an implicit case for mercy and forgiveness.

> When we were surrounded and had to run for it I hesitated. We had three German prisoners we'd captured in Alpago. They were forty, forty-five years old, not regular soldiers but servicemen, you know, cooks. Everyone was scattering, ready to flee. My comrade Coledi [*remember him?*] handed me a gun and told me: 'Look here, before you take off, shoot the Germans'. But my conscience was in turmoil . . . To look at them, we were very young, the German cooks looked to us like harmless old men [*veciòt*, a marvelous dialect expression conveying an affectionate note, dear old men] They had been with us for two months, they had cooked for our band, we partisans had started calling them by their name, Peter etc. How could I possibly? The three looked at me, as if to ask, what about us? No, no. I was with a friend, we both agreed. We gave them instructions, 'Follow that path, that way'. They looked ghastly. It was clear that they expected to die on that path- to be shot from the back. They set off down that path and when they got to a shrub I shot three times in the air. The three old men turned, white as sheets. They saw themselves alive. 'Go! Go!' we shouted.

(Domenico Favero quoted in Conte and Strazzer 2003)

What a wonderful heartwarming little tale. As I watched the tape over and over, I kept trying to figure out what went through the minds and bodies of those three befuddled *veciòt*, careering down a path towards the unknown, after the 'conscience' of two sympathetic partisans saved their lives. What makes me well up every time I think about that story, is that Domenico and his friend could not bring themselves to end the lives of three elderly people [affectionately referred to as *veciòt*] they had got to know well – so well that they started calling them by their names. The mention of the name that my Granddad still remembered – '*Peter*' – deeply moves me. I wondered if Peter had made it home. I asked myself what the middle-aged German made of all this . . . how and if he ever recalled that episode. I wonder if he was grateful, or if he had felt any affection towards the young men who had set them free. Often, embroiled in the videotaped story, I feel very close to Peter, and I partake in the closeness Granddad felt towards the German. I guess the point of storytelling is precisely this: to reach out from the past to touch our lives, to let us share an emotion, a closeness, and even affection for people we have never known and will never meet.

The Germans were not always keen on the kill either. Wehrmacht man Diekmann was captured on surveillance tape admitting that 'I can't simply shoot a man for nothing' (Neitzel and Welzer 2013: 94). Maybe so. Yet the title of this section brings me back to another, later interview carried out by my colleague Brescacin with Granddad Domenico. The topic of conversation had been the use of torture during the war. Granddad was adamant that under no circumstances should a being, animal or human, be made to die under torture by a human being. It was bestial, inadmissible. 'We [the partisans] eschewed torture absolutely', Domenico asserted. 'We decided early on: a captive was either saved, or dead' (Domenico Favero quoted in Conte and Strazzer 2003).

The panoply of sensory experience of war and conflict deserves thorough attention. Embodied knowledge of self, of other and of the world is not fixed, but rather fluid and reliant on a myriad factors apt to change at a moment's notice – that is why the fighters' perceptions could shift so rapidly, and their opinions diverge so dramatically. As a last remark, it must be noted that the notion of the body in conflict as body in pain has been implicit throughout this discussion, lurking at the margins of the stories and experiences therein, but not deliberately: the pain of the body, Scarry has noted, constitutes 'a reversion to a state anterior to language, to the sounds and cries a human being makes before language is learned' (Scarry 1985: 25). It is capable of upending, destroying and forever altering one's world. Perhaps the will or shunning of bodily violence depended on the implicit awareness of pain's impact on person and world: irreversible, destabilising, and ultimately hopeless.

3.7 Reconnaissance in no man's memory: the grim legend of Buss de la Lum

Alongside places of commemoration, some locales are not places of celebration, but rather infamous, contested and notorious: these, as we will see, are places of memory but not, for reasons we will argue below, places *in* memory. These locales loom large in the public eye and consistently generate newspaper columns, yet none of the partisans and resistance activists we have interviewed or whose memoirs we have engaged with mention it as meaningful – or even present – in their memory or experience of the war. Places like this demand a 'particular kind of attention to make sense of it, one that attempted not to defuse sensations of ambiguity and aversion, but to work with them' (DeSilvey 2006: 320). Illustrating these issues are the manifold meanings and attitudes converging around the anti-memorial site and alleged 'mass grave' of Buss de la Lum [Hole of Light] in the Cansiglio Forest at the foot of the Dolomites in northern Veneto. Here, official versions of events conflict with the recollections of late and surviving partisans. I seek to situate the liminality of this place in terms of its cultural significance and the implications of the abject nature of the dead bodies it concealed on wider understandings of death in conflict in a quintessentially Catholic country.

The Buss de la Lum is located on the Cansiglio plateau, one of 200 sinkholes in the karst rock, with a depth of 186 metres. According to right wing narratives, Buss de la Lum was a place of mass carnage perpetrated by the partisans against soldiers of the RSI and their civilian collaborators and spies. The legend of the place of mass massacre was born out of a contamination following events that happened in the wider area of the Friuli-Venezia Giulia and former Yugoslavia (*foibe* or mass graves). The presence of sinkholes in the karst uplands of Veneto are troubling for many because of the alleged killings of Italians at the foibe (Pirjevec 2009). The foibe were vertical caves on other karst uplands to the east of Trieste around the northern end of the Istrian peninsula that were used to dispatch ethnic Italians and enemies of the Communist partisans (Oliva 2002: 2; Pupo 2005: 5). The region had been awarded to Italy at the 1919 Versailles Peace conferences, but where ethnically Slavic communities had settled (Ginsborg 1990: xviii). The Slavic locals bitterly resented plans to Italianize the region in the interwar years (Cooke 2009). Once the Yugoslav-Italian border was re-drawn in 1945, it curled around Trieste but returned the bulk of Istria to Tito's Yugoslavia (Battaglia 1953: 50; Valdevit 1997). In vengeance and a form of what we today call ethnic cleansing, former Yugoslav partisans, nationalists and others evicted ethnic Italians from their homes across Istria. On the way, they massacred several Italians and threw their bodies into the sinkholes (Pupo 2005). Some estimate that over 4,000 Italian soldiers were thrown into foibe (Baldoli 2009: 299). In the Italian imaginary, the victims were thrown to their deaths in these sinkholes, and debate still rages about the *infoibati* (see comprehensive monographs above, sadly not available in English). Speleological expeditions carried out in the 1950s by the University of Trieste support the case against a mass grave. From the forensic evidence at Buss De La Lum, we can rule out a mass execution site in the style of the Yugoslavian *foibe* due to the following factors:

- Size of the phenomenon: fifteen to twenty individuals versus the alleged 'thousands'.

- Mode of execution. Prisoners were tried and executed in the surrounding woodlands. Only afterwards were their corpses concealed down the sinkhole. Fascist propaganda promotes the view that the bodies belong to individuals thrown in while still alive. There is no evidence, however, of a 'throwing plank' from which to push or throw live prisoners into the cavity, unlike in the actual Yugoslavian foibe.

One victim supposedly fell to his death. This was a spy who was fleeing from the partisans and fell to his death down the sinkhole. This story does not appear

Figure 3.2 The Buss de la Lum and the Silentes Loquimur memorial.

Photo: Sarah De Nardi

anywhere apart from in the memoir of former partisan Tito Antonio Spagnol, published after the war (Spagnol 2005); no other account corroborates it. Since the 1980s, nationalist and Neofascist groups have appropriated the site and gather yearly to mourn the unsung heroes and martyrs of Italian Fascism. The followers of the *Silentes Loquimur* ('we speak silently') Right-Wing group erected a cross and a gravestone to the alleged thousands of massacred Fascists at this site. The large black cross still creates tensions, attracts morbid media curiosity and, despite the forensic data collected by the speleological investigations, feeds the myth of a place of infamy and bloodbath in the collective imaginary. However, the partisans remain stubbornly silent with regards this site. The few veterans who openly acknowledge this place (Nino De Marchi, Domenico Favero, Giuseppe Giust) claim that the site was exclusively used to conceal the bodies of executed Fascists and spies; it was an attempt, Nino has claimed, to avoid repercussions and retributions against partisans' families in the surrounding areas. Moreover, an Allied Mission was stationed nearby at Hotel San Marco on Pian Cansiglio, and this particular partisan 'initiative' would have left them unimpressed, if not angry; and the partisans knew well that any conflicts with the Allies could have resulted in ceased or diminished supplies drops (Brescacin, pers. comm.). The fact remains, however, that the veterans I have interviewed were based in the area near Buss de la Lum and could not have ignored its existence during the war – not even those who deny awareness of its existence.

From the myriad headlines and articles in regional and national dailies (Figure 3.3), it is apparent that a tangible – albeit complex and confused – mythology surrounded this place from day one. This mythology ranges from eerie folk stories about mysterious lights (will-o'-the-wisp) and ghostly sightings of 'old relatives' of the dead, to uncorroborated declarations by local so-called 'ex-partisans' who admitted to, or claim to have assisted in, the hurling of living victims down the sinkhole. Even the existence of hard forensic evidence from the speleological expeditions seems unable to dispel the myth. In many of the articles I gathered on the tragedy, there is an emphasis on the perspective of the populations inhabiting the villages near Pian del Cansiglio. These groups have consistently come forward to speak to the press, volunteering hostile anti-partisan stories and harbouring a grudge dating back to the days of the resistance – when many were reluctant to give up goods and food items to the guerrilla fighters, even in exchange for coupons, and resentment still runs deep.

Doing an ethnography of absence at this site faces a cognate issue: the removal of memories of this place in and among the partisan community. Like characters in a murder mystery, we can physically place many of the resistance activists at the site of Buss de la Lum at some point or other, although they all hide behind the alibi of forgetfulness or ignorance. None of the partisans and their associates express a willingness to engage with this place. Some particularly self-reflexive resistance supporters advocate more transparency and urge for more understanding on the

Figure 3.3 'No trace of "*infoibati*" inside Buss de la Lum': a 1966 headline.
© Il Messaggero

part of the modern generations of the pressures and duress they were subjected to during the end of the war, yet they resist and oppose the remembrance of such a key site. In denying Buss de la Lum, what other choreographies of memory are opened up? The counter-memory of the site also entails the silencing of Fascist voices and the negation of Fascist victimhood in the context of an unpalatable civil war. What is the status of the victims recovered/concealed at Buss de la Lum?

Alongside resentful memories among the Cansiglio populace, doubt also lingers among the researchers and scholars engaging with the 'official' history and the mainstream production of knowledge concerning the tragic sinkhole, and it has to do with the actual undisputed guilt of those who were executed by the resistance (Brescacin 2013). Oftentimes partisans adopted a 'better safe than sorry' policy when faced with the task of dispatching casualties; this arbitrariness lies at the crux of the ugliness, feeding the bitterness surrounding the episodes at Bus de la Lum. The shameful materiality of the locale makes it a non-place: a hidden, illicit spatial hub not unlike the torture and detention sites of the Argentinean dictatorship (Salerno and Zarankin 2014). The late Giuseppe Giust admitted in an interview that it was a mistake to conceal the bodies out of fear of punishment, but assures us that no carnage took place. Another denied their presence at the site, when contemporaneous accounts place them at one of the executions as the perpetrator. Foot (2009) also observes that as part of resistance actions, bodies were frequently hidden; subsequently, a pact of silence accompanied that concealment. This behaviour sought to deny any form of burial or of remembrance to the families of Fascists and neo-Fascists – it constituted a 'double death' that entailed 'complete oblivion, even of the body' (Dondi in Foot 2009: 173). To achieve this end, resistance fighters often concealed bodies rather than allowing relatives to mourn the dead. The consequences for the perpetrators were also unhappy: they felt guilt and remorse, and this served to fuel their silences still more. In particular, this strategy took hold after the war in the midst of the reprisals from Liberation Day in April 1945 until the Amnesty of 1947: the wild days when partisans and locals (in)famously settled old scores with Fascists, collaborators or opponents: remember Baldini?

To this day, the absent bodies of Buss de la Lum haunt the site and the local imagination(s). The grim sinkhole defines the local community's identity, their resentment congealed around this site. These 'silencings, violent endings, devastating . . . losses and erasures' (Tolia-Kelly in press) would haunt and resonate for decades to come. In these parts, the resistance fighters have never been 'the good guys'. A reflection on the status of the bodies once contained in Buss de la Lum, their abject state and their ghostly haunting of the site and of the local imaginary leads us to the theme I explore in the following chapter – storytelling as a powerful act of affective materiality.

Note

1 Interview by Claudio Pavan with A. Busatto on 21 January 2014. Interview and Italian transcript online at https://www.youtube.com/watch?v=wxNjnG2jV1g

4 The haunting materiality of storytelling

> 'I still think you are stirring up trouble. What if someone who doesn't like your findings comes looking for you?' Warmly inflected in the dialect of the Treviso piedmont, this utterance comes almost unexpected on a sunny March afternoon. My Grandmother looks worried, the hand holding a cigarette shaking slightly. 'One thing', she continues, 'is to listen to the old codgers' stories out of respect, and another thing is to publish those stories that others will learn about'. I shake my head. 'What if some bad Fascist comes and makes trouble? I know who they are, you know. They are still around. But then they will try to sling mud on your Grandad's memory because that lot, not all were as nice as him, you know. They say the partisans did terrible things up there at the Buss de la Lum'. At the end of this monologue, as I light my own cigarette, she smiles. 'He would have been proud of you, you know'. I smile back, and we remain silent for a while.

4.1 Storying affects: wartime rumour as inter-corporeal practice

On 12 September 1943, when they got news that Mussolini was 'alive and free' because the Germans freed him, Turin born and bred teenager Zelmira cried with joy (Marazio 2004: 31–35). In the local shops, people whispered, 'They freed him? Is that true?'

'No, it's all propaganda. He's been dead a while!'

'He's gone to dust'.

But then a few days later, Zelmira heard his voice once more, weaker and less self-assured – but still the same beloved voice. Later that same week, Zelmira and a girlfriend watched the footage of Mussolini's liberation from the Gran Sasso prison at the Fascist cinema, but low grunts echoed in the audience and someone suddenly shouted, 'It's a lie! Mussolini is dead. He's been in the ground for a long time!' That is the second time we encounter that rumour in Zelmira's tale. She commented that the confusion around *Il Duce* embodied Italians' contradictory feelings towards him and the country's divided loyalties.

Keeping up the morale was important even among the Allies: much could depend on whether the troops felt strong or alienated, 'together' or disconnected. This seemed to matter especially to non-white American soldiers. The following is an exchange between Black African American 'Buffalo Division' veteran Lorenzo Bell and Myers Brown.

Myers Brown: You had mentioned to us in a previous conversation about how your unit managed to get back Columbus' ashes or something like that, can you tell us that story?

Lorenzo Bell: Yeah, up in Genoa, I guess it was during his birthday, some of the Italians had taken Columbus' ashes and hid them in the mountains. So we had a big ceremony and we restored the ashes. The 92nd division, they had a black choir with probably from the 1940s and 50s and probably into the 60's was called Wings over Jordan, a singing group. [. . .] And they came over and helped us in the celebration, and that was quite a feat for us. That brought back a lot of good feelings among everyone. I may also mention that in order to keep the morale up, we had shows that come over. There was a show called *Shuffle Along With Sicily*. OK, then we had sport events. We had football, spaghetti bowl between the Japanese soldiers and the 92nd division troops, in the 92nd division.

I highlighted in Chapter 1 the extent to which historical factuality is never conclusive or coherent, so that the events of the Italian war and resistance are tricky to assess and analyse even with hindsight. By telling stories and writing history, we give 'shape' to 'what remains chaotic, obscure and mute' (Ricoeur 1991: 115). In this chapter, I consider storytelling as a kind of shaping, a form of material culture which, albeit largely intangible, is still evocative and has great presence. Storytelling possesses a grammar of materiality and affectivity second to none. Here I extend the idea that the contradictions and ambiguities in the stories point less towards the 'obscurity of the event than the darkness of subjectivity: not what the partisans did, but what they *felt*' (Portelli 1997: 135, my emphasis). In an essay on the hermeneutics of imagination, Stark (1997: 124) observes that the 'narrative self relies on the imagination to synthesize the horizons of the past, present and future'. For Ricoeur, she continues, selfhood is a 'cloth woven of stories told' (Stark 1997: 124). I like the materiality invoked by the cloth metaphor, woven with a myriad stories affecting everyone who touches it. Imagination, after all, is part of the make-believe worlds we enact and inhabit (see also Navaro-Yashin 2012) and ultimately shapes the way we experience things.

The stories we tell and the memories we recount reflect what we have chosen to say about self and other (Fentress and Wickham 1992: 24). 'What are the stories we like to hear? [...] they are often the ones that confirm us in comfortable ways of thinking' (Turkle 2007: 323). We want to belong – we want to be told, and shown, that we belong, that we are not out of place. Ahmed pins it down handsomely:

> [w]e become alienated – out of line with an affective community – when we do not experience pleasure from proximity to objects that are already attributed as being good. The gap between the affective value of an object and how we experience an object can involve a range of affects, which are directed by the modes of explanation we offer to fill this gap.
> (Ahmed 2010: 37)

Stories localise and shape, empower and condemn, aggrandize and create an 'other' writ large. In this case, due to my autobiographical involvement in this historical event, 'my fictions blend with theirs' (Hoskins 1998: 4). For Bachelard, imagination perpetually links the human subject which imagines and the image itself. Imagination is thus recognised to be conscious of something other than itself which motivates, induces and transforms it: otherness is relational and interactive (Kearney 1998: 97). This chapter contains a section about rumour and gossip as particular forms of affective identity-makers and constructs in this relationality. L. White has stated that 'whether a rumour or gossip is true or false isn't what is important about it. What is important about rumours is that they come and go with great intensity' (White 2000: 13). Neitzel and Welzer take this point further in stating that flights of imagination, albeit difficult to identify empirically, are a part of the world in which we feel we exist (Neitzel and Welzer 2013: 156). What might (or not) have occurred, pondered Ricoeur (1991: 354) 'fuses the potentialities of the "real" past and "irreal" [sic] possibilities ...'.

How do we encounter such possibilities? How do they materialise in storytelling, then? The first point of contact with the materiality of remembered (and re-enacted) history, which is also living history the moment it is told or recreated, unravels through the affectivity and tactility of the oral history encounter. I like de Certeau's (1984) notion, further elaborated by Ingold (2000), of storytelling as a kind of *mapping practice*, whereby a narrator is essentially mapping out her or his story. In the following chapters, I explore this notion further and argue that rather than framing a story as a journey in a narrative manner, storytelling is an embodied practice which affords a performative understanding of journeys and stories lived and experienced. As such, the nature of the mapping practice(s) of the storyteller comes across as essentially sensory and performative. The idea that when a storyteller talks about their experience and engages others with their memories, this act can be considered an embodied mapping practice, has consequences for our material and social understanding of past events.

So, for example, the storytelling practices of Second World War veterans – whether in the form of interviews, diaries, mementoes or narrative memoirs – far from just expressing reminiscence, can become enactments of life itself as it unfolds in the present. These differently embodied and mattered memories express the making, experiencing and sharing of worlds, conjoined in the present moment of the telling (see also Pink 2009). Telling about experience turns material culture into a conversation and a story too (see Cameron 2012 for how 'storying' works in cultural geography, for instance), whenever elements such as gestures, recording devices and mementoes assist the storyteller in their mapping practice. In this active process, a storyteller invites others into a world they perceive as very close and immanent, regardless of chronological remoteness or geographical distance; '[e]thnographic texts are perpetually cursed with a loss of embodied meanings, but also potentially blessed by pluralistic desires and impulses' (de Certeau 1988: 227) – this, it may be argued, is a way in which affects enable the production of war narratives. In what follows, I situate myself and my autobiographical involvement and then better contextualise the historical context of the case study.

My main purpose here is to show how fundamental storytelling is to conflict, a concrete practice through which affects – call them the 'what ifs' or possibilities of open-ended and multivocal history – come to life. In a self-penned 1964 introduction to his iconic resistance novella *Il Sentiero dei Nidi di Ragno* (*The Path of the Spider Nests*), the former Italian resistance fighter, novelist and playwright Italo Calvino struggles to get to the point; by his own admission, he finds himself having to start over and over again. In one of his attempted incipits, he starts his mnemonic narrative by recollecting the unstoppable flow of stories about the war and resistance in Italy. Stories about what happened during the war, he complains in jest, have become so many that they risk spiralling out of control. In a 'multi-coloured universe of stories' (Calvino 1964: ii), people were 'brimming over' with tales – so much so that they 'stole one another's words from each other's mouth' (Calvino 1964: i). I love the 'brimming over' with stories hinting to the embodied, fleshy essence of stories, waiting to burst out of the storyteller's body and be shared with others at a moment's notice. At first this inference made me ask which, and how many, of all these runaway stories of all available wartime stories, versions and angles, have been committed to paper. I wondered what had become of all such stories entangled in memory, past and present, and to what extent they had become the subject of scholarly inquiry.[1] I felt like asking a slightly different question: what about the unquantifiable materiality of storytelling, the *Qualia* (Chumley and Harkness

2013; Lemon 2013) – that is, experiences of sensuous qualities and feelings such as anxiety, proximity and otherness – arising when atmospheres, hearsay and places prevail over the centrality of facts or the agency of persons and groups? What about the weight of stories, or the stories of things that cannot be seen or even interrogated?

> 'Violence is the driving force of history', according to popular wisdom. Whether true or false, this conclusion often leads us to study armed forms of opposition at the expense of civilian forms. Indeed, historians may be spontaneously drawn by what was 'spectacular', what was seen, what made noise – in short, by what left an impression.
>
> (Semelin 1993: 24)

> I put down each day's events as they occurred, . . . and . . . I did report stories and rumours that reached us, since they were part of the queer mental colouring of our daily life. . . .
>
> (Origo 2000: 11)

> Conversations [like these] are often like games of Chinese Whispers. Researchers in the fields of narrative and memory research have determined that stories necessarily change every time they are retold. Details are constantly invented, characters substituted, and settings changed according to the needs and wants of the storyteller.
>
> (Neitzel and Welzer 2013: 110)

Thus, stories shape and do not just reflect events. Stories can also highlight the concerns that are most important to storytellers and their audiences (Fentress and Wickham 1992), 'as well as what knowledge both groups possess and what historical facts and myths are familiar to them' (Neitzel and Welzer 2013: 111). In this sense, storytelling is a fundamental aspect of identity construction and enactment. In the final chapter of this book, I make a case for listening to each other's stories sympathetically in a way that can bridge even the harshest divide, but here I concentrate on the materiality of storytelling as a practice that gives meaning and orientates our lives and experiences. I conclude by telling three stories: two have to do with the realm of hearsay and gossip, whereas the other conveys the emotional distress that storytelling can engender if we get too close to the teller. In rehearsing these stories, I foreground the interactional nature of their context and content. The rephrasing and rewording of the stories' affective elements is my own and serves to prove that a story never truly ends with its telling, but rather stays with listeners and participants for a very long time.

4.2 The ontogenetic nature of storytelling: the snowball effect

The nature of memory work is interactive and ontogenetic – always unfolding and expanding, and perennially evolving; thus, emotions and affects like hate, love, pride and shame play a central role in what is transmitted as cultural memory from one generation to the next (Assmann and Czaplicka 1995; Hirsch 1996; Olick 2008). Engaging with emotions does not only affect the storytellers we work with. As we now openly acknowledge that we 'write ourselves' into research reflexively and inter-subjectively (Burkitt 2012), we accept that to become part of the story can be troubling (Mullings1999; Evans 2012). Joint storytelling is a profoundly moving process (Hardy 2012; Bondi 2014), and this is more the case when the subject matter of research overlaps with a researcher's own family or affective legacy. The 'narrative hospitality' advocated by Ricoeur (1996) lends an interesting lens to the interpretation of storytelling as an intersubjective process affecting all who partake in it. His notion of hospitality entails the 'making room' for one another's 'narrational identities' and the effort to allow these various narratives to be fluid and plural (Ricoeur 1996) and has been taken up by scholars interested in multivocality as a practice and a solidarity (see Jackson 1996, 2002). The notion of storytelling as a mapping or 'wayfinding' practice encountered in the work of de Certeau (1984) and Ingold (2000) is relevant here. For de Certeau (1984: 174), 'readers are travellers; they move across lands belonging to someone else, like nomads poaching their way across fields they did not write'.

By thinking of storytelling in this way, we engage with a person or group talking and narrating their tale while essentially mapping out their story for others – travellers or participants. As such, the mapping practices of a storyteller are essentially sensory and performative in nature (see also Tolia-Kelly 2004). If talking about one's experience and engaging others with one's own memories can be considered an embodied mapping practice, this has important implications for cultural understanding of past events. Far from being just an expression of reminiscence, the storytelling practices of Second World War veterans can become an enactment of life itself as it unfolds in the present, and can express the making, experiencing and sharing of worlds, conjoined in the present moment of the telling (Ott 2005; Andrews et al. 2006; Pink 2009). It opens up the affects channelled by material culture too, whenever other elements such as recording devices and mementoes assist the storyteller in their mapping practice. This is an active, not passive process in which the storyteller encroached others in a world they feel very close and immanent, regardless of the chronological distance in terms of calendrical time. As Cobb observes, 'Stories matter. They have gravitas; they are grave. They have weight. They are concrete. They materialize policies, institutions, relationships, and identities that circulate locally and globally, anywhere and everywhere' (Cobb 2013: 3). 'Stories that individuals tell about Self and Other, in everyday conversations, structure the nature of interpersonal interactions . . . as well as intrapsychic dynamics' (Cobb

2013: 7). In conflict resolution studies, a paradigm for understanding otherness and alterity in action has been offered by Coleman et al. (2007): the enmity system, defined as "the network divided into "us" and "them" ' (Cobb 2013: 7). While stories give shape to the dynamics of the enmity system, they do much more by shaping reality (Fentress and Wickham 1992). In a way, stories constitute the essence of a poetics of conflict experience.

Consider this: if a person witnessing events first-hand thought it significant to record rumours and hearsay regardless of whether these 'events' or narratives would come true or not, then they mattered; they must become part of the story we tell. Therefore, a strong case exists for an attention to affectual life and materiality of historical events and phenomena – to Qualia as material culture, however indeterminate. The cultural historical burden of war veterans and witnesses, as it is understood today, owes much to the ebb and flow of stories, intertwined, overbearing, and contradicting each other, as Calvino says. What Calvino did not explicitly ask is: how do we make sense of all these stories? What do stories do to the people who tell them and to the people to whom they are told? How does the temporality of stories act to bridge past and present? It is worth remembering the extent to which some commentators struggle with the subjectivity of witness accounts (Morgan 2009). These, they would argue, represent one-sided arguments; accounts are often not corroborated by checkable facts. And yet, 'to be effective', as Beaumont has noted, 'public memory must resonate with private, or individual memories of war, in a way that is complex and inherently difficult to document' (Beaumont 1995 cited in Scates et al. 2014: 207).

Precisely this putative difficulty of documenting memories is the fabric of affectual processes. It might be helpful instead to understand storytelling as yet another element in a dense and nuanced web of experience – an intra-action (Barad 2008). Intra-action analyses the ways through which matter comes to matter, whatever its nature, and is a useful framework for the discussion of affectual practices below. Unlike interaction, which presupposes external agents interacting as discrete yet tangential entities, intra-action has an intrinsic interconnectedness beyond the point of contact or overlap. Understanding affects as a framework to untangle intersecting memories, stories, doubts, false impressions and prejudice, I re-position the ephemeral yet pervasive energies in some of the places, objects and events of the Italian resistance as valid, usable research material – and by so doing seek to map out a material culture and working poetics of conflict experience. Re-inserting the imaginative and sensory into the resistance, civil war and occupation acknowledges the place of intangible elements – such as doubt, rumour and intimations – in the affectual life and materiality of historical experience. For Bates, 'what the stories mean cannot be separated from how they mean, so I consider their poetics along with their politics' (Bates 1996: 6). In order to appreciate how stories, rumours and hearsay may be understood to be central to the poetics of conflict experience in Second World War Italy, we should first understand the workings of affectual histories. 'Rumours are an emotional form of communication, spreading a feeling of something *monstrous* or *uncanny*. As such, they express an element that rarely occurs in the soldiers' conversations: feelings' (Neitzel and Welzer 2013: 158, my emphasis).

Rumours make up a significant part of how we communicate in everyday life. I have already mentioned the overarching problem with thick, performative, affectual narratives that are transmitted orally (like storytelling): we do not always know what we should do with them. The transcription of orality into written form can 'flatten out' the materiality and affectual 'matter' of speech. Writing things down also conceals the performative aspect of any interview, thus privileging what is said over how it is said, 'bleeding meaning from text' (Scates et al. 2014: 210). It is important to acknowledge that oral history interviews and memoirs, as any other archive source, require our belief as one version of events is preferred to others (see also Hoskins 1998: 4–6). Best practice still dictates that it is the researcher's responsibility to ensure that the narratives they collect have a grounding in reality. Might we instead, as L. White mused, attempt to attribute a materiality and historicity to stories that do not have a grounding in objective reality, but that the storytellers believed to be real – invisible or intangible things that *matter* to them?

Putative versions of events are also important to our understanding of wartime cultures. For instance, a propaganda-fuelled, idyllic and heroic vision of the war in Italy was often far from the truth. Sonia Residori (pers. comm. 20 February 2010) has argued that, during the war in Italy, a mythology had developed around the use of drugs in the resistance movement. She has suggested that real or imagined events and facts often got mixed up around the topic of drugs, whereby documented occurrences and substances existed alongside urban legends. By way of example, she discussed a palliative myth rife among people in Bassano del Grappa in northeast Italy: it was widely believed that injections of tranquillizers or barbiturates were administered to those condemned to death before hanging. This way, Residori suggested, local people made up a putative reality in which the patriotic partisans, who were often young lads, did not suffer as much as could be feared.

Elsewhere, Cappelletto (2003) has expertly reconstructed a narrative around a village tale of sorrow and loss following a Nazi massacre in Italy. The memories of the event, still jealously guarded, had become a myth through an almost ritual performance in which everyone played a part. The liturgization of roles in the tragic events that unravelled in the town assigned a part to everyone (the Nazis, the partisans, the villagers), and the main narrative formed around this solidified belief system. Although these memories were not negotiable, they were born out of myriad discordant versions of events – for those who blamed the partisans had different views from those who blamed the Nazi outsiders (Cappelletto 2003: 247). Claudio Pavone explained the grey area of partisan truces with the enemy as the consequence of 'tiredness, disillusionment, naivety, fear, [and] difficulty in relationships with the local populations due to the fear of reprisals' (Pavone 1991: 274). The lines between friend and foe were often extremely fluid and blurred. Elsewhere (De Nardi 2015a), I have asked to what extent actors in the Second World War in Italy really knew who their enemy was, and how the extreme ambiguity embedded in processes of othering and alienation impacted on the committing of violent acts and the spectacle of violence against others. Echoing Reddy (2001), it can be argued that there can be no emotional regimes without the experience of an other. Storytelling is therefore the privileged channel for the transmission of the affects and materiality of historical experience.

4.3 Action! The historical workings of affect

'How do roller coasters of contempt, patriotism, hate and euphoria power public scenes?' (Wetherell 2013: 2). The focus on affects is shifting attention away from discourse in an attempt to reinstate 'the energetic, the physical, and the sensual' (Wetherell 2013: 9) back into social studies and historical scholarship (but see de Certeau 1984 for a powerful pioneering work to that effect). To borrow from Curti (2008: 108), memories are 'performed and felt between, in and through bodies and thus always work through entangled forces of emotion, affect and memory'. Drawing from a rich and eclectic phenomenological tradition, we have acquired a critical awareness of the ways in which identity, emotion and embodiment interact to create meaningful social words of feelings; among others, Ingold (2000) has suggested that living in the world entails all sorts of barely quantifiable elements that make us feel 'at home' or otherwise.

History's purpose is primarily to interrogate facts, rather than second-guessing memories and perception. Some work on identity-making through emotional and perceptual stances has focused on the political working of local memory (Cappelletto 2003, 2005; Focardi 2005; Muzaini and Yeoh 2005; Ott 2005; Tolia-Kelly 2006) or on the formation of social mythologies (Fentress and Wickham 1992; Portelli 1997) rather than openly interrogating the emotional and perceptual grounding of historical experience. Seremetakis, for example, asked how we 'feel' historical experience through an interaction of memory, displaced and alternative pasts, which she refers to as 'experiential fragments'. These fragments, she argued, shape historicity – a process always constituted by 'act(s) of imagination' (Seremetakis 1994: 29).

There is a lively and informed debate that acknowledges wartime and post-conflict affects as all-encompassing energies implicated in the production of worlds (e.g. Nordstrom (1997), Dougherty Delano (2000), Saunders (2000), Cappelletto (2003), Jones (2005), Muzaini and Yeoh (2005), Curti (2008), Kivimäki and Tepora (2009), and Moshenska (2010)). These experiential places might be reified and embodied as places, objects and human bodies. If emotion is 'an action in a world made by others' (Beatty 2014: 557), then affect is an intra-action in a complex perceptual world animated by stories: Nordstrom's 'being-in-a-world-of-war' (1997: 180). In a war context, individuals and places of fighting develop an interconnectedness borne out of the materiality of emotions, identities and actions. These actions, in turn, inform identities, agencies, emotions and reactions in all actors enmeshed in a wartime intra-action (Nordstrom 1997), collapsing the separation of mind-body-intention. As Reddy points out, disagreement between feelings and thought processes is 'just the kind of clash of practices that can generate personal, social, and historical change' (Reddy quoted in Scheer 2012: 208). This line of thinking might illuminate the phenomena of resistance, occupation and collaboration unfolding in Europe during the Second World War.

To build on these notions is to contextualise historical experience and social action through the prism of affect and its materialities. The theoretical mileage afforded by an approach foregrounding the materiality of individual and collective imaginaries is potentially limitless; such an approach can fruitfully explore apparently other and apparently illogical perceptions and utterances people use to express the experience of the war and resistance. These 'Qualia' (Chumley and Harkness 2013; Lemon 2013) could then be re-valued – and approached – as significant data in a holistic understanding of the war and resistance.

Elsewhere (De Nardi 2015b), I considered that the interview process, or rather, intra-action (after Barad 2008) generates a deep mutual understanding, a rapport as it were, made up of, but not limited to, the emotional involvement of all parties present in the subject matter of the interview (Thompson 2000; Andrews et al. 2006; Pink 2009). Here I probe further into the energy and immanence created every time two or more individuals gather to share memories and impressions of the past. Even when an interview goes badly, or when no significant or relevant information is collected, something extraordinary happens. The encounter touches both (or all) of their lives, engendering an energy and a deep-flowing connection between human and non-human elements in the interview – such as objects, refreshments, family pets, the ringing of a telephone or doorbell, the batteries of a recording device going flat, the sudden or gradually increasing need to use the toilet, the scribbling of notes on paper, and so on.

Social scientists are interested in the relationship between performativity, embodiment, affect and materiality in the quotidian experience of individuals and groups (Ingold 2000; Hallam and Hockey 2001; Ahmed 2004a; Miller 2008; Butler 2009; Richards and Rudnickyi 2009; Saunders 2009; Lemon 2013). Investigators write affect into scholarship through an attention to emotion in thought and action (Beatty 2014). A crucial point of overlap in our research occurs at the junction between the representational and discursive, and notions of embodiment, irrationality and spatiality. So, for instance, Thrift (2000, 2004), Ahmed (e.g. 2004b), Tolia-Kelly (2004), Stewart (2007), Bondi et al. (2009), Wetherell (2013), and Cronin (2014), among others, argue that affect circulates through people, bodies, objects and places in creating atmospheres and energies. As such, affect seems to be intrinsically embedded in historical experience and in storytelling: it can inhabit discourse and stand out in the most mundane events (Whatmore 2006). In a similar vein, Bondi (2005a, 2014) unpacks the workings of not-quite-fathomable affectual energies penetrating and haunting oral history interviews: again, a practice not alien to discourse, be it personal, social or political. Brennan (2004) and Richards and Rudnyckyj focus on the profoundly 'transactional and intersubjective' character of affect in order to distance research from an 'intransitive interiorization' **or** inward-looking disconnect from the outside world which characterises terms such as emotion, sentiment or feeling (Richards and Rudnyckyj 2009: 73).

Foregrounding the affectual nature of historical 'moments', then, might be a powerful way to allow storytelling to stand the test of time. Focusing on the co-produced materialities of emotion and affect allows the cross-generational sharing, comprehension and appropriation of war stories, making a difference for the social greater good (Coombes 2013). Affects animate intersubjective relationships, and their materiality connects human and non-human agents together in meaningful ways (Tolia-Kelly 2004). These connections can then be transmitted, shared and re-negotiated on multiple levels and across generations (Bondi 2014). Stories usually told in a sitting room to great-grandchildren might then become amplified in meaning and resonance, providing approachable ways of learning about war and conflict for the wider community (see Pink 2009). As well as appreciating the many benefits of storytelling as an educational tool, I argue that the act of telling, of sharing a story, inexorably involves those who listen. It is the circulation of affects within and through the storytelling practice and its materialities that draw us in: the cups of coffee, embraces, banter, photographs and medals.

As well as powering storytelling and remembrance, affects are also a motor of political change and social action. The ideas that affect and emotion are expressed through political activism and social movements (e.g. Thrift 2004; Ahmed 2004b; Tolia-Kelly 2006; Askins 2009), that they emerge in economic transformations (Richard and Rudnyckyj 2009) or that emotion is a practice (Lutz 1996) are well known. The notion that large groups of people galvanise each other into a frenzy of social and political action is now similarly well established. Adorno et al. (1950) and Canetti (1960) outlined the psychological mechanisms by which crowds tend to polarise around a strong leader, and inferred that such is the root of Fascist movements. Decades later, affect is still mobilising the way we relate to such a galvanization. By thinking of the impetus, or drive, to mobilise people and places in more-than-representational terms, we realise that an affect exceeding the sum of individual responses powers scenes of political and social momentum.

Those working in the disciplines of anthropology, cultural and political geography, and the sociology and history of conflict are concerned about what makes the social and collective workings of historicity 'tick'; they look for what can be afforded by novel engagements with the interconnectedness of bodies and things (see, for instance, Muzaini and Yeoh 2005; Trentmann 2009; Beatty 2014). If, then, one is to consider storytelling as a way to gain knowledge about war and its many actors, we may find that an affect-driven ethnographic perspective is a powerful way to frame and interpret the associations between witness accounts, places, atmospheres and objects: a geography of 'being-in-a-world-of-war' and its pervasive, haunting materialities (Nordstrom 1997: 180). Emotion and/or affect have informed, to some degree, the rich interdisciplinary studies briefly sketched above.

None of these approaches, however, seem to encompass the evolution, from its origins through to its anti-climactic epilogue, of a momentous event in the European war such as the Italian resistance movement. Yes, Adorno and Canetti's 'crowds' were wired onto a predominant focus of attention, whether galvanised into political activism or sedated into docile subservience to a great leader; but things happened differently during the evolution of the resistance movement in Italy. The country had already had a charismatic figurehead (of sorts) in Mussolini, but dissidents and disaffected liberals were keen to break free from a dictatorship which, besides its alliance with the toxic German Reich, had dragged the country to a war that alienated most Italians (Lepre 1995; Pezzino 2005; Morgan 2009). Something else was needed, and a grapevine of rebellion started maturing around the discontent prevailing in wider society (Morgan 2003; Behan 2009). It may also be that the Italian galvanization towards resistance was not entirely due to psychological conditioning, as in the case of Adorno's crowds, but was rather animated by psychosomatic and emotional dynamics. Perhaps as the counter-regime stirrings rippled and spread, they behaved like so many interconnected and rhizomatic tendrils of feelings – or affects, as we have come to recognise them of late. As social beings, 'we are relational as well as rational . . . : as we relate, so we create' (Gamble 2015: 154).

Living through occupation and resistance entailed a poetics of watching, waiting and making do with day-by-day temporalities in which not much might happen. And when something did, one might not know *what* was happening right under one's nose. Veteran partisan Renato Pizzol recounted his experience on the day when the Allied forces rescued and liberated the part of the Veneto where he found himself in a way that I find deeply moving. He told me the following:

> I hear running along the trail just under my stakeout point, a rock over a precipice, and I hear voices and footsteps running, 4–5 partisans were running around. Then I hear voices coming from the other direction, from the village. Some spoke aloud, saying strange things. We partisans, we never spoke aloud, and this ruckus made me suspicious and agitated. It was an order to descend to the valley, it was Liberation! Then I head for the village, but many are ahead of me already. They say, we go down, but we did not use the word liberation, then, because it was a rhetorical word. Nothing, just go down, give up everything, I take my backpack, and I go down.
>
> (Interview 24 September 2011)

The immediacy and confused enthusiasm of the occasion, which no one yet dares label 'Liberation', is a typical affective event. The hushed enthusiasm grows into a shout, then another, and then everyone is summoned to the village. The energy of the event is contagious, even if people do not yet know what to call it. This is affect in practice (see Ahmed 2004a). The range of the affectual expression can span 'big moments' as well as 'more banal and everyday experiences, some of which may well be fleeting, equivocal and muddled' (Wetherell 2013: 43). As suggested above, affectual events can range from small, opaque events happening in the intimacy of the home to the portentous, euphoric moment of realisation that the war is over. During the Second World War in Italy, such events included resisting, whether actively or passively, but also permeated to varying degrees the social and cultural lives of those who chose not to support the armed resistance. Affects encompass the feeling of being taken by surprise as well as a shared emotion and atmosphere. Emotional communities who sided either with or against the guerrilla fighters or partisans performed specific affectual practices.

The hubbub and confusion following rumours of the Armistice had affected the whole of the country. In Emanuele Artom's diary, we read the following:

> September 8, 1943. Here comes Ugo [the Priest] who, as he walks up the stairs, says: 'They say they have signed the armistice.' Then we run to the town centre. There's great animation; everyone says the War is over, but no one has heard the radio. Instead C. comes out of his house and says he just heard on the Belgian radio that Eisenhower has accepted Italy's unconditional surrender and that he invites Italians to do their bit in driving out the Germans. But was Germany not going to surrender in a matter of days, then?
> (Artom and Schwarz 2008: 54)

Rumours of Italy's capitulation were rife, and people galvanised each other through the thought of the end of the war, despite the fact that no one had actually heard the announcement on the radio. Another partisan I interviewed, Giuseppe, recalled an affectual event which reflects the eerie materiality and open-endedness of resistance lives and events better than any theoretical intermission.

Q: Who warned you of danger?
G: Anyone and everyone. I like to think of a ritual we had, in my village, which I later tried to translate into a poem, but without success. Try to imagine a whole village with all windows shuttered. Silence. It always worked this way. You arrived in the village, and you could hear a pin drop, a total silence enveloped the whole pace, it's like an empty stage – but it is far from empty! Hear this: you arrive there, all houses hermetically shut off, and you are crossing an empty piazza, like a desert. But behind every shuttered window, a whole village waits, breathless. Or maybe you are breathless? At any rate there is always someone

there listening behind the shutters, so then they can intervene [mimics whisper behind a window]: 'Pssst! Hey you! Be careful!' After that, the scene became a desert once more. As if that whisper had never been. If no balcony shutters opened to a 1 centimeter gap, if we didn't hear any voice, any whisper, then it meant that you were safe- there weren't any Fascist or German roundups nearby. They always knew, up there.

Traditional historiography has sometimes felt uncomfortable dealing with this extent of explicitly subjective detail, and some have been unable or reluctant to engage with a perceived lack of immediately comparable, quantitative data. The fact remains that atmospheres, fleeting moments and enduring impressions constitute a large percentage of remembrance and memory work with veterans, reified in their evocations and stories (see Pavone 1991; Portelli 1997; Cappelletto 2003). How do we comprehend these utterances and re-present them in their intensely dramatic and visceral nature? Some accounts, such as Giuseppe's tale, rather than simply telling a story, almost cause the listener to literally hold their breath, like they themselves had done while passing through that village. The potency of such an affectual event is given by the open-endedness of the ritual performed by the villagers: if, by any chance, someone had failed to open a shutter, the partisans would have thought themselves safe and walked into a trap. What if that had happened? How many war events have been similarly affected by chance, by fleeting affectual involvements, and by such interconnected energies? Thinking about it, I lose count. Too many to recall, to be sure.

Laura Rival, drawing on Tim Ingold, states that '[r]elations are conceptualized as trails of becoming along which life flows like a river, through which understanding grows, and down which enduring organisms enmesh their conjoined histories' (Rival 2001: 219). Affects do precisely this: they are neither created nor do they create. Rather, affects evoke and materialise things: affects can lead to safety or danger. Affects embody materialities, flowing from photograph to shaking hand to welling eyes to rapt audience (as in my stunned participation in Giuseppe's story). Affects move and shake human and non-human lives in the time span of a few seconds or a few months. The importance of 'potential' energies animating storytelling should make a convincing case for a renewed attention to apparently incoherent, non-discursive historical memories, in order to prevent their disappearance from our final texts. Affects, then, go beyond an exclusive focus on human emotions. Like storytelling, affects do not just concern individuals and groups – they encompass the materiality of experience, and 'Qualia-like' elements such as places, atmospheres and possibilities. Storytelling as an affectual practice encompasses possible scenarios that might or might not come to be (Portelli 1997; White 2000). Affects and materiality also weave into non-human agents as a pervasive yet hard to pin down energy: self, identity, world, culture and being are inseparable. Building on our understanding of how affects work, I propose that affects liberate the circulation of sentiment, materiality and feeling to elements other than human beings, thus encompassing 'life's rich tapestry' in a more holistic and inclusive way.

4.4 Story one: constructing an American OSS agent as the Other

Here I engage with a particular kind of story; it goes against the grain of mainstream narratives, sowing doubt and scratching the established surface to reveal a veneer of destabilisation in the predominantly benign, unproblematic representations of US Allied officers in Italy during the war. This story unravels around the central figure of a man; it surprises many, because this man should, by all rights, be seen and perceived (and remembered) as one of the good guys. He is an American, who is constructed in social memory as an Other. Let us contextualise this strange tale: in the midst of the unimaginable duress and rawness of war and foreign military occupation, imaginations ran wild for many. Confusing propaganda and hearsay created a skewed materiality and perception of the world in which one lived – the 'queer mental colouring' mentioned by Englishwoman Iris Origo. However, it was not just the Italians who coloured their affectual geographies with imaginaries of reality and intimations: even within the structure of Allied Military Missions in Italy, rumours and myths were rife. Let us take as an example the case of the Taccoma Mission in the Belluno Dolimites range of northeast Veneto, led by the American intelligence agent Major Howard Chappell (OSS). While searching for partisan interviews in the archives of a local historical society, I came across recordings of interviews with former members of the Allied Mission and Italian patriots who had been associated with them. Amidst much technical intelligence jargon and military talk, I found recurring mentions of an alleged Italian conspiracy against Chappell. There are divergent versions: according to a predominant narrative, the *staffetta* (messenger girl) Maria, well acquainted with the local topography, warned Chappell of the existence of a plot to eliminate him. In another version, Charles Ciccone (another American OSS agent) insists that Maria came to him to inform him of the plot, and then asked him to tell Chappell. Remarkably, no one else in the Partisan Brigade or in the Operations Group in which Chappell and Ciccone operated had ever heard of such a plot or even of rumours. 'There were a lot of fantastic stories flying around' according to Belluno resistance specialist Vendramini, the interviewer of OSS veteran Al Materazzi (ISBREC Accession no. SO/56/1993). In the course of the historian's interviews with Materazzi, the American respondent claimed that Maria was very close to Chappell – perhaps even his lover – so that Ciccone's version seems illogical. If the two were so close, why would Maria go to Ciccone first and not directly to Chappell himself?

> There were several spies up there, you know? Rumours were going around thick and fast: being up in the mountains you didn't know what was happening

in the plains. You didn't have first-hand news, do you follow me? Instead you got hearsay, you were isolated. And you heard all kinds of stories. Some staffetta called *Maria*, don't know who she was, came up to me and warned me about a plot by the Italians to assassinate Chappell, but I couldn't believe that. He [Chappell] did not believe it either then, and I do not believe it to this day. No way.

(Interview by Vendramini with Tea Palman and Charles Ciccone, Belluno 3 March 1995)

On the other hand, the plot thickens. The stories around Chappell constitute a fascinating road map of the attitudes and nature of a man. John Ross had called him 'a deeply unpleasant chap' on another occasion (JR interview 1 March 2009). In the course of their interview, historian Vendramini and Materazzi conjectured about his likely sadistic streak (JR interview 1 March 2009). Materazzi narrated an anecdote that acts as a story within a story, positioning his former OSS colleague as an ambiguous figure possessed with a macabre imagination. The story went like this: once at a war reunion dinner in Italy, Chappell had publicly boasted about slitting the throats of two captured Austrian prisoners with the same knife he had used to carve a roast later that day. Materazzi and the other interview participants readily discredited the gruesome claim: a partisan present at the time recalled that on that day, Chappell had shot the two Austrians, but then he, the partisan, had had – extremely reluctantly – to slit their throats to ensure they were quite dead. In contrast to the partisan's bleak confession of a violent act he loathed perpetrating, Chappell the OSS agent had made an empty boast taking responsibility for that act of bloody violence. Why take ownership of something he did not do? For Materazzi, Chappell told his story with great gusto in a (fairly) inopportune situation, and fellow diners within earshot were flabbergasted by his callousness; some were put off their dinner. The element of the story the diners found most disturbing was the storyteller's linking of the act of slaughter of human beings with the act of carving meat for consumption.

Although merely a story without foundation, this utterance may reveal something of the man's nature and his instincts, dreams and reflections. Chappell chose to divulge a version of events that is more-than-representational and more-than-historical: it was the version that that storyteller chose to share. Such utterances disclose the workings of affect as they provide 'glimpses of stray facts, unformulated emotions – the feelings behind the "emotional background" ' (Beatty 2014: 550). Because no one can understand these feelings, a man who should have been a hero and a role model for Italian partisans and other OSS agents remains shrouded in mystery and baffles the memory of those who met him. The materiality of the act of killing goes a long way to shape the identity of this man and how he enacted this wartime persona after the end of the conflict.

The haunting materiality of storytelling 109

4.5 Story two: the Golden Column of Menarè

The materiality of stories is closely interwoven with the materiality of immaterial things – such as objects and places that have disappeared or become part of a nostalgia or fantasy world (see also Buchli 2015). Recent research on the presence of absence and the agency of absent things posits that 'absence . . . may have just as much effect as material presence . . . We thus take absence to be as much of an occurrence in real life as presence' (Bille et al. 2010: 10). Here is how.

In 2010, persistent gossip and hearsay prompted Pier Paolo Brescacin to investigate a curious phenomenon relating to the resistance and liberation of the Menarè neighbourhood in Vittorio Veneto. The historian had grown up hearing rumours about an event that allegedly changed the face and fabric of a community literally overnight. According to hearsay, several civilians and some members of the armed resistance formations had suddenly – and inexplicably – acquired great wealth at the end of the war in September 1945. How? The rumours had echoed through the decades because what had happened had been extraordinary: in the frantic days between the end of April 1945 and mid-May 1945, the time when Italians were waiting for the Allies to tell them what to do next (Brescacin 2010: 20), the Allies had bombed a column of retreating Germans carrying gold, and stolen Italian currency and Reichsmarks. In the course of the bombardments, several lorries carrying safes, crates of currency and jewellery ransacked by the Nazis from Jewish Italians and families hiding rebels had been blown up. Quietly, the populace had waited for the cover of darkness to get their hands on the loot (Brescacin 2010: 15). Apparently a few individuals living in the Menarè area had looted the retreating German vehicles, and so Brescacin, a member of the same community, embarked on an auto-ethnographic endeavour to establish whether there was a historical basis to the gossip – and discovered that there was. The precise events had subsequently been hushed up due to the illegal nature of the deed, but their memory lingered on in the form of rumour and gossip. The deed was to enter the local mythology (Brescacin 2010: 3).

The enduring significance of the Golden Column for Menarè bears witness to the imagined strength and intensity of that assemblage. Although no one knows what or how much exactly was taken from the bombed column, the population of the local area has mythologized the events and the objects that made some people rich overnight. Those who were the alleged thieves or opportunistic misappropriators of the precious metals and currency were even affectionately called 'Conti Colonna', an Italian wordplay on Conte, Count and Colonna, Column – the Column Counts. The fascinating fact of the matter is that although suspicions fell on certain people and their families due to their suddenly improved material status, some of the so called Counts were very discreet and invested their illicitly acquired goods and currency wisely and gradually, so that there was no apparent immediate change in their circumstance and lifestyle. More intriguing still is that despite the singling out of the category or 'outgroup' (see Chapter 2) of 'Conti Colonna', the names of those who fell into that category or outgroup are not known.

When Brescacin held a conference to launch his book on the subject in 2011, the assembly hall was packed to the rafters with curious audiences avidly waiting for what they thought would be the climax of the evening: the full names of those who had illicitly appropriated goods and currency from the German lorries – the list of 'Counts'. When the audience realised that the names were not forthcoming, some were so disappointed that they protested, and some even left the lecture uttering insults under their breath towards the scholar. So, not only has this category of people been created and negotiated without any knowledge of the identity of those who were supposed to be in it, but the fact that a category of people to blame/ admire existed was sufficient for the greater community to feel good about their own lesser (but honestly gained) means and fortunes.

In February 2013, I interviewed six individuals who had been Brescacin's witnesses, and they seemed reluctant to come up with names of people they suspected of being the perpetrators, whereas they had furnished him with a substantial list. These six people, aged between 80 and 88, told me fairly consistent stories of the bombing, the smoke coming out of the lorries, and their surprise at finding them pillaged in the morning, but they abstained from sharing their suspicions with me. Actually, that is not right: they claimed they *knew* exactly who had participated in the looting of the Golden Column but withheld the names, claiming that it was best to let sleeping dogs lie. I took the reluctance to share their suspicions with me as a sign that although I was (roughly speaking) a native of those parts, I had since left the community and severed my roots with the place. I could not be trusted with the suspicions lest I inform the 'suspects', leading to legal action against the respondents. I was no longer part of the local affective fabric of the place – how could I understand how it felt to live with this open secret in the midst of an ageing community of memory? It might also be that the very nature of the deeds and its repercussions were, and still are, perceived as a strictly local affair – not to be shared with the wider public. I can understand this reticence and it does not trouble me, because at the end of the day I was not interested in the names: I was interested in the significance of the looting of the German lorries and its place in wider narratives of the war.

What fascinates me is the idea that an assemblage of objects that no one, not even those who stole the items, had actually seen in its entirety, could become lodged so pervasively in the local imagination. Judging by the unprecedented turnout at Brescacin's book launch, this long-gone, invisible assemblage still haunts local lore (but see Renshaw 2011). Those objects had been only fleetingly present in material form in the public arena, while they were still inside safes and crates in the lorries. And even then they had still been, in a way, the (looted) property of the retreating Germans. Was the local population's obsession with these spirited away goods purely a matter of greed and envy?

4.6 Story three: expected and unexpected emotions

This story engages a very different affective register to the previous ones. In telling this story, I am the most exposed: it is a story within which I am intimately implicated, and it brings out the lights and darkness of the resistance and civil war event with great, ruthless clarity. It is a story which offers an alternative and non-canonical explanation of wartime events, in a way which has made other scholars uncomfortable. I approached this ethnographic encounter differently, aware of the multivocality and open-endedness of memory. Further, I was aware that 'rather than dismiss informants' accounts as imaginative "interpretations" – elaborate metaphorical accounts of a "reality" that is already given – anthropologists might instead seize on these engagements as opportunities from which novel theoretical understandings can emerge' (Henare et al. 2007: 1), I sought to let these new understandings emerge and inform my knowledge of the events, not to purge from the research process, however painful that would prove. And painful it was.

The story goes like this. A., an ex-Partisan and once my grandfather's best friend, invited me to his home to share his resistance experience. Before my visit, I learnt that towards the end of the war, the Communist Partisan formation in which A. had a leading role executed 124 Fascist soldiers in RSI uniform and threw their bodies in a river (Maistrello 2001; Brescacin, pers. comm.). These were unarmed young lads who had literally just been dispatched to the frontline in the last frantic days of what the Fascist leadership knew was an already lost war; it is likely that most, if not all, of these lads were yet to fire a single shot (Brescacin 2013: 124). After the war, the Communist brigade's officers in charge went on trial for war crimes for the killings. The acts of the trial, which I will not name in order to protect A.'s identity and those of the victims, state that

> there had been no chance of a proper defence for the culprits [the men in uniform], as they were accused of nothing in particular [besides being potentially Fascist]. Their death sentences were not publically announced but simply carried out. The life and death of each officer had depended on the wildest chance and arbitrariness.

The perpetrators were amnestied in the late 1950s as the deed was ascribed to the 'sensitive' context of the anti-Fascist war.

In speaking of the various places and environmental contexts he had known, navigated in and inhabited during the resistance, A. carefully avoided any mention of the fatal riverside killing ground; this, despite the fact that the avowedly geographical stance of my questions should have encouraged him to talk about his experience at this location – the main geographical feature of the territory patrolled by his formation. But our shared autobiographical affects enabled me to 'read the silences'

(Rosenwein 2010: 19), and to sense that the moment was not right. During our second encounter, I tentatively asked him about the shooting, careful not to imply that he had a greater extent of complicity than any other brigade member. He firmly denied his presence at the river on that day, adding that the Fascists were armed – despite what he called 'revisionist' claims to the contrary. In his version of events, A. contradicted a reliable archival source that placed him at the execution site – and the implicit assumption that the executions would not have happened without his authorization made the inconsistency all the more chilling.

In front of me was an elderly gentleman living alone: he had lost his wife to cancer when they were both in their late thirties and never remarried. A.'s life seemed to me to be defined by his resistance persona and by his close friendship with other veteran partisans. He certainly sought to project himself as a caring, benevolent figure with me – a surrogate granddad, now that my own had passed on. His silences and omissions, however, had troubled me and troubled him also, so much so that he had to cut short our first encounter. Much as I tried not to picture A. on a riverbank ordering the taking of young lives, during our meetings, violent images superimposed themselves on my conscious thought processes, intermingled with unconscious feelings of sympathy and family loyalty that rejected that same imagery. As an affective process, our second encounter entailed a set of 'background feelings which are . . . long-lasting, moving in and out of focus' (Wetherell 2011 3: 12). After all, would my grandfather have been this man's close friend if A. was bad? More to the point, was I supposed to forget my grandfather's and A.'s ordeal and challenge the greatness of the feat of their peers? Many would judge any such 'objective' interpretation of historical events as a betrayal (see also Pickering and Keightley 2012: 121).

I found it distressing to either confront or forget A.'s experience: my affective autobiography as a member of the partisan community was keen to engage with A.'s resistance story, accepting its contradictions unquestioningly – something about blood being thicker than water? Yes, indeed: as Domenico's grandchild, I found myself truly cherishing the cosiness of A.'s lounge, as I drank coffee and I smiled at his funny anecdotes about my mother and aunt as young girls. As an anthropologist, I had to contextualise and cross-check A.'s facts, thus challenging and contradicting the old-timer where it hurt the most. I knew I would have to return home and report that contemporary written and oral sources placed Respondent X at the site of a mass murder, although he denied resolutely that he ever went near it. I had witnessed the 'denial of the origin, the unfolding of a dead past' (de Certeau 1988: 47). Affects can be 'funny, perturbing, or traumatic' (Stewart 2007: 2). My encounter with A. was all of those things, but mainly perturbing. I am not ashamed to admit that I had a little cry about it; I cried because I felt sorry for this elderly man, for myself and for my grandparents. How to turn this story into scholarship? Should I?

4.7 Conclusion

In this chapter we have seen how the embodiment of stories, 'mythical' objects and rumours constitutes an invisible materiality of the conflict. Stories do much more than just structuring and verbalising content – they move, 'emerge, and affect us in the very act of their telling' (Cameron 2012: 588). Stories perturb, other, and divide. The ethnographic encounter with veterans and their families engenders much more than data or evidence for a story already established. Fieldwork with veterans and their 'things' represents a 'collapse of the experience/analysis divide, such that the experience of things in the field is already an encounter ... with meanings' (Henare et al. 2007: 4). The alterity and closeness experienced through the ethnographic encounter with veterans and their memories makes up a compelling, powerful mixture of affective and sensory thickness that threatens to attack logical thought and defies traditional modes of scholarship and academic writing. I chose to embrace its confounding otherness all the same: how else to disclose, and become part of, the world of that redolent, non-absent past?

There is more. When an Other is constructed and positioned as 'alien' in stories, they become 'disorientated and unmappable' and 'difficult to locate, situate, personify and identify' (Weber quoted in Ahmed 2004b: 135). And yet, ethnographic encounters, storied and affected, still somehow feel part of us: as if we belong with them, and as if they have been with us for a long time. Could it be that they feel familiar because they are? Even the most personal stories represent fragments of mutually interwoven narratives reaching out for others' stories – those of family members, forebears, friends, enemies and strangers. This may be what Ricoeur (1996) meant when he posited that the game of telling is part of the reality told (1996: 294). One does not have to be related or connected with veterans to share in their stories. By teaching schoolchildren the tales of the civil war and its experience in English secondary, I have not only become a part of the storytelling process and woven new threads into the rich and troubling tapestry of the conflict – I have implicated my British-born students as actors and participants in the story, by writing about it and discussing it in class, many miles from the places where the dramatic events of the resistance and occupation unravelled. Their heated discussion about the ethics of the civil war, their gaping mouths at hearing the most audacious partisan actions or the sombre silences with which they came to terms with civilian massacres –they all became part of the story. It is out of my hands now, and has reached a whole different and fascinating new realm of telling, performance and feeling.

I drew on a psychoanalytical approach that explores the non-verbal elements of interviews (see Bondi 2014) during my interviews with A., and much more went on than was verbalised or committed to tape. One way of understanding the 'largely non-verbal, out-of-awareness, process of building trust or rapport is in terms of the "transmission" and "reception" of unconscious "messages"' (Bondi 2014: 48).

More-than-verbal affective messages had gone back and forth between myself and A. during our meetings; a mutual trust and rapport had formed the base of our shared autobiographical emotion in a way that had little to do with strict historical accuracy. A. verbally communicated less than what we both knew to be a much more troubling experience. Violence and death had hovered in the room with us but never materialised: we were both haunted by the presence of a memory that lingered uncomfortably 'at the margins of speech' (Seremetakis 1994: 3).

The verbal and more-than-verbal elements of interviews must be understood as an emotional kind of force or energy we co-produce with the storytellers and their worlds. Do we reach out to the other's world even when it is full of pain? Can we bond over an untrue story, and use the information we glean for academic purposes? Using Heidegger's notion of historicity as full of possibility means that yes, we can and should encompass alternate versions of the past into our overall narrative. The phenomenological mission of historiography is to 'disclose the silent power of the possible' (Heidegger 1953: 360), that is, to bring to the fore possible versions of events *other than* the one that allegedly occurred and for which documentary evidence exists.

In order to overcome an ontological shyness to incorporate the ephemeral and the ambiguous, a solution might be to stop thinking of stories as data and start thinking of them as bridges to the other's world. Stories told are not finite exchanges to be archives, but rather the start of a conversation affecting the hearts and lives of many. This is what Ricoeur (1991) meant when he suggested that we reach out to others' stories using our imagination and sympathy and, most importantly, we do so via our own stories. Stories and events made up or real, visible or invisible (like the looting of the 'Golden Column'), constitute so many meaningful and entangled affective processes shaping and intervening on the perception of the war. The second story recounts the affective workings of a community divided and haunted by riches but united in the curiosity to find out who had taken advantage of the looted material. The materiality of that absent present is significant for any reconstruction of wartime morale, perceptions and affects.

Those who looted the column are technically criminals whilst being constructed as community heroes at the same time – they have become accidental icons. The looters' illicitly acquired riches shifted and shaped their subsequent identities in ways that would not have been possible if the bombed lorry column had not been there. These people embody the contradictions of war and conflict: they inhabit the tension between culpability and victimhood, between moral and immoral. The impact of an illicit assemblage on the notions of citizenship and war victimhood created in them a marginalised yet celebrated identity separated from that of the majority of the population. In a similar fashion, the Communist veteran partisan who was complicit in a brutal act of violence against unarmed men in RSI uniform has set himself up with a dual identity of moral ambiguity: 'guilty' for scholars and the law, and innocent for the community of his peers and loved ones.

In Chapter 3 we saw how, through the examples of two 'marginalised' modes of embodiment, being female and being Jewish, impacted on the subjective experience of being part of the resistance movement. In Chapter 3 we analysed the significance, perceptual position and ontological nature of the bodies of Fascists and spies executed and disposed of in the sinkhole of Buss de la Lum by the resistance, asking whether their being 'abject dead' defines them as material culture, as non-subjects in light of their liminality. Following this reifying thread of materiality and identity, I next turn my attention to the most tangible form of material culture by arguing for embodied and affective engagements with war-related objects and mementoes as part of the present/absent entanglement of the materiality of memory.

Note

1 For a critique of Holocaust storytelling, see H. White (1992) and van Alphen (1997: 95).

5 Competing materialities

Presence and absence in the material world of the war

> [Anna takes out some photographs. She stands next to me, delicately emanating the fragrance of Parma violet, a delightfully timeless scent which always reminds me of my late Nonna Dina.] 'These lads here, they are the partisans of the Mazzini Brigade', she says. 'This is Partisan Possamai – we called her Irma'. [She takes a picture out of the lot and gently strokes it. It shows a smiling young woman in a sunny garden, which makes Anna's next words sound chillingly at odds.] 'She was captured and tortured in the Castle of Conegliano. The Germans did it. She was so badly tortured that she was unable to have children . . . afterwards. The castle was a base of the SS, they had occupied it and there were interrogations chambers in the tower'.

> There are moments when we are struck by a feeling of strangeness . . . Perhaps we sense the inadequacy of human knowledge in the fact of the brute that-ness of the natural world; . . . perhaps the familiarity drains away from ordinary objects, leaving only *mute intruders*.
>
> (Withy 2009: 1)

5.1 The material turn in the social sciences: things 'matter'

At the time of writing, I questioned the appropriateness of an academic publication to weave the story of a strange, unsettling experience for Italy and Europe as a whole. In conducting this past-present ethnography, what have I accomplished? A way to (momentarily) avoid being plagued by this kind of uncomfortable question is to turn, as many have done, to things themselves – to the elements of our ecological selves. This book began as a result of my encounters with things that belong to nature, discourse and society – in other words, I have sought to trace a poetics of conflict experience through narrated things, remembered things, loved things and mourned things. Withy's quote (above) reveals the ultimate uncanniness of the

Figure 5.1 The infamous castle of Conegliano.
Photo: Sarah De Nardi

worlds we inhabit: the people and things in them have the power to confound and to become intruders. Things populate our mutual sphere of experience whether we like them (or understand them) or not. In reviewing the memories and impressions that shape this current work, it seems to me as if 'things', material and immaterial, do have a way to influence and filter out the realities we live and remember.

In this chapter, I devote my attention to things, visible and invisible, to do with the memory of the conflict. They are what Olsen (2003: 87) calls 'the physical and "thingly" component of our past and present'. Our things and other people's things (in the broadest sense of the term) play a fundamental role in the way we orientate ourselves in relation to the past and to our present – objects and things being not finite entities but portals that propel us forward as well as back into the past, through interaction, dialogue, evocation and affects. And interaction is key, as no memory lives in a vacuum.

War mementoes and relics may symbolise the grief, loss and mourning associated with memory, events and places (Saunders 2000: 45), yet they also increasingly tell us about people's everyday experience of war as they are contextualised within wartime cultures (Moshenska 2010) and affectual performances and processes (De Nardi 2014). Methodologically, a historical attention and an a-where-ness (Osborne 2001) to affect and emotions lets us consider 'the specific situatedness of . . . doings. It means trying to get a look at bodies and artifacts of the past' (Scheer 2012: 217).

The 'material turn' in anthropology and related disciplines over the past twenty years has explored the embeddedness of material objects in human social life and the values that objects (and the materials they are made of) acquire through craft, interaction and exchange (Neisser 1993; Hoskins 1998; Ingold 2007; Miller 2008; Saunders 2009). The idea of pregnant and porous multi-agent materialities and embodiments has been with us for a while; in Levinas' words,

> to be alive means to be currently involved in a complex network of mystic 'participations' in common with the other members, living or dead, of his [sic] social group, with the animal and vegetable groups born of the same soil, with the earth itself.
>
> (Levinas 1998: 49)

This is an idea espoused by Tim Ingold as well, who asserts, 'to describe the properties of materials is to tell the stories of what happens to them as they flow, mix and mutate' (Ingold 2007: 14).

Phenomenological and post-phenomenological thinking, then, reminds us how ineluctably interconnected with our material worlds we are. Materiality, as a manifestation of agency, becomes a collaborative process embodying the human and more-than-human elements of our world. As advocated by 'artefact-centric' anthropologies of recent years, the fact that a thing is understood to embody or contain different worlds and different natures (e.g. Henare et al. 2007) suggests that we have to think imaginatively about what things 'do' and not just what they mean. 'How things were' is not a tenable proposition for thinking about any historical period, but even less so when thinking about war and conflict, and the identities formed and enacted in such a context. We might recall Heidegger's position on the becomingness and possibilities afforded by historicity – the material condition of our being-in-history. Therefore, we might want to open up possibilities and understandings of the war using materialities and the multiple voices incarnated in things – the material world – to seek a connection with that non-absent past and its reverberations in the present.

An emotional and affective engagement permeates our orientation in the world as much as the physical handling of objects in the everyday. 'We are moved by things. And in being moved, we make things' (Ahmed 2010: 33). Things take centre stage in any serious discussion of socialisation, in the wake of Latour's (1993) conceptual bridge between human and non-human actors. When purporting to understand reality in its various elements, he asked, '[i]s it our fault if the networks are simultaneously real, like nature, narrated, like discourse, and collective, like society?' (Latour 1993: 6). He went on to complain that traditional practitioners underrate the possibility of an anthropology of the modern world. The reason for this paradox, he posits, is that unlike the traditional subjects of ethnographic study, Westerners have become too disconnected – not seamless enough to be able to weave harmonious webs of nature, culture and narrative.

In the recent shift towards new materialism (e.g. Braidotti 2006; Barad 2008; Ahmed 2010; Coole and Frost 2010; Dolphijn and van der Tuin 2012), the dualities of body/thought and self-world are being rewritten through the lens of the posthuman (Connolly 2013). This is a drive towards a reinstatement of the material and the sensory in the ways in which we humans perceive, organise, plan and desire to live our lives: for Classen and Howes (2006: 202), we use touch as a 'medium for annihilating time and space and establishing an imaginative intimacy' with the past possessors and users of objects. I wish to extend this notion to stories, equally as important to someone's materiality and identity as objects.

Over and above its new-materialist concerns, the affective turn in the social sciences has problematized the embodiment and materiality of the researcher in fieldwork, positioning constructions of the self at the forefront of scholarly practice and inferring that, as with all social action, fieldwork is embodied (Tolia-Kelly 2006; Pink 2009; Wetherell 2013). As a result, we are now well aware that emotion, memory and cognition are interwoven and mutually constitutive (Burkitt 2012). Memory, too, is a 'thing' with properties. How do we remember through 'things', and why does it *matter* so much (Hoskins 1998; Kavanagh 2000)? For Deleuze (1991), echoing Bergson, memory is just one of many possible entities, such as imagined events (see Chapter 4) that become co-present in the now and may be able to engender political awareness and action. Thus, for Trentmann,

> The focus is not just on what things mean but on how things are *done*. Practices have a dynamic force of their own, creating sensations, competencies, and plans of doing more or doing things differently. They are entangled in a creative interplay with materiality.
>
> (Trentmann 2009: 297)

Trentmann makes reference to theories in psychology investigating implicit memory (or procedural memory) and its role in socialisation (see Proctor and Dutta 1995; Groeger 1997). Things can disturb us if we are unable to understand them or cannot relate to them on a personal level. When confronted with the baffling alterity of things that we do not understand and find hard to 'translate', we might be lacking the parameters or concepts to engage with them (Henare et al. 2007: 12). Without terms of reference, we are troubled by the alien artefact we observe in a documentary about extraterrestrials or the antique relic encountered on museum trips or archaeological excavations. For David Lowenthal (1985), the past is indeed a foreign country, whose artefacts may be thought of as strange souvenirs from an exotic (and sometimes all-out dystopian) elsewhereness. When confronting the otherness of others and their possessions, we might feel perplexed if we do not comprehend what they are about. In other words, these alien 'things' that have arrived from somewhere else bear the marks of this elsewhereness (Straw 1999). The creative force thriving in the interrelatedness and intercorporeality between things and dwelling practices is crucial to my discussion of conflict material culture. Saunders' work on trench art (2003, 2009) provides a useful sounding board for a discussion of Second World War materiality: he makes a compelling case for everyday objects as meaningful actors in shaping people's quotidian experience of the war and the subsequent 're-memory' of others (Tolia-Kelly 2004).

An attention to things can bring together thinking on fieldwork and research into the materiality of the everyday and the workings of memory and identity. In *Biographical Objects: How Objects Tell the Stories of People's Lives* (Hoskins 1998: 2), Hoskins confesses: 'What I discovered, much to my surprise, was that I could not collect the histories of objects and the life histories of the persons separately'. People and their objects, she argued, are ontologically intermingled – inseparable. They belong to what Neisser (1993: 387 ff.) has identified as the 'ecological self', the assemblage of embodied and socialising elements that sit on or around our bodies in the everyday.

Besides promoting a conceptualization of stories and places of conflict as part and parcel of a complex wartime materiality, I also consider here the physical remnants of the war – for instance, a melancholy poem/letter and photographs of desolate ruined villages in their emplaced essence as material culture, beyond their representational value: as co-constituting identity, emotion and memory with the storytellers. For Fahlander and Oestigaard,

> Materiality is modified by people, made into artefacts, reused and remade, and given new meanings in an endless chain of re-negotiations. The world we live in is material – the world is an artefact – we conceptualize it, modify it, construct new constructions – to live is to participate into an endless series of material modifications of worlds that are already made.
> (Fahlander and Oestigaard 2004: 37)

As with Hoskins, when I set out to do my ethnographic fieldwork, I had not anticipated that I would be worrying myself so much with *things* that I would encounter, evoke, conjure up and attempt to translate. In itself, the strenuous process of translating from the softly inflected local dialects into Italian first, and then into English, already highlighted and delineated the different materialities inbuilt in auto-ethnographic learning and research. The thick materiality of interviews has often proved overwhelming, and after every research encounter I felt exhausted – emotionally, intellectually and physically. The potency of interview mementoes, and the materiality of the intensely affective gestures of the ethnographic encounter with memory, can become almost disorientating (see De Nardi 2015b). During an interview, gestures and objects are like 'souvenirs from the traversed landscapes of the journey, signifiers of "other" narrations of the past not directly experienced but which incorporate narrations of other's oral histories' (Tolia-Kelly 2004: 1).

The poetics of conflict experience unravels in the field as well as in the museum, gallery space (see Saunders 2009), or the living room among the clutter of cups, saucers and recorder batteries. It is, it seems, all about the materiality of stories as they unravel.

In the previous chapters, I introduced the notion of competing materialities and hostile embodiments; in other words, I explored some of the ways in which conflicting material cultures and alien bodies contributed to the widespread sense of tension, precariousness and hostility experienced by all during the civil war and occupation years. But what about the intensely bodily and emotional objects that serve to evoke and narrate those harrowing experiences in the present? Who engages with these objects? Let us call them mementoes for now. Csikszentmihalyi (1993) argued that 'objects reveal the continuity of the self through time, by providing foci of involvement in the present, mementoes and souvenirs of the past, and signposts to the future' (quoted in Kavanagh 2000: 103). No, thinking back to the photographs depicting the last moments of Armando Baldini (Figures 1.1 and 1.2), we can say something more on their significance as meaningful things. Are they mementoes? And if so, whose? Whose future signposts are they?

Through these pages, we have accrued a sense of how materiality is central to our understanding and interpretation of the events and legacies of the Italian civil war; let us now for a moment reflect on how these affects and material presences are imbued in the artefacts of Baldini's execution. Although Edwards (2009: 24) observes that photographs are usually apprehended as a 'visual trace of the appearance of a past moment in its apparent entirety', this is clearly not the case here. The pre-execution photographs testify for and convey a fragmentary sense of possibilities, an incomplete register of pride or regret, of joy and sorrow felt and resonating in the photographer, his or her surroundings and the event they were about to witness. It is not the archival finiteness and indexical precision of the images but rather the fragmented, irretraceable incompleteness of the scene that haunts us. I wish to explore in more depth how photographs, as well as other 'memory objects', contribute to creating the sense of 'being there' that pulls us, fascinated and rapt, into the past and its maze of memories.

Here, and throughout this book, I position the materiality of 'things' and bodies of the Italian civil war and resistance through the lens of otherness, but also think of them as having an agency given by their material and sensory 'properties'. In line with recent thinking about an object-centred anthropology (e.g. Henare et al. 2007; Leach 2007; Miller 2008), this chapter explores the different embodiments and materialities of things by taking as a starting point the fact that otherness can be thought of as a property of things (and bodies). Understanding this alterity as a quintessential property of wartime objects is, I contend, essential to their understanding and their connection to the present and the future.

The material culture of the Italian civil war and occupation period is made up of the often weird and unsettling souvenirs of elsewhereness and the familiar things that constitute the everyday. Following on from the previous chapter, here I continue to interrogate the role of materiality of storytelling, but focus not on the stories being told and their manner of telling, but on the visible and invisible objects and things that embody or reify those stories in the present. Next I reflect on the materiality of the interview process, asking what objects contribute to the affects that circulate during the 'research' encounter. I then offer further considerations on the affective nature of wartime materialities, and then turn to frontline objects: *objets de guerre* encountered in the field, as it were. In the subsequent sections, I consider a varied assemblage of meaningful things that channel affects, and I explore the ephemeral material culture of sleep and sleep deprivation.

5.2 The materiality of the interview

An interview is an encounter with the materiality of another's life and experience. Redolent objects and interview-related material cultures profoundly affect the researcher; they ask to be remembered, to be spoken about, to be written about, perhaps, although the written word can never equal the intensity of the experience of engaging with such material. While Turkle (2005) and Barad (2008) make the point that we think through things, I would propose that we feel through things, too. This 'spotlight' on mementoes/objects as sites of feeling represents an interesting approach to the materiality of interviews: reflecting on the interconnectedness of experience and feeling leads us, for instance, to ask how the intercorporeality of interviewee, interviewer and object (scrapbook, medal, photograph, poem) shapes the interview experience and creates an event in the here-and-now, where memory comes alive through the encounter of/between persons, places and objects (see Edwards 2009; Hancock 2009 for mesmerising forays into the materiality of the photograph and everyday objects). Materiality offers a useful toehold into otherwise ineffable worlds of experience.

But how do uncanny, perplexing and discordant elements of memory emerge in materiality? Ernst Jentsch's (1906) use of the word materiality suggests that a lack of orientation is bound up with the impression of the uncanniness of a thing or incident. Does this kind of uncanniness reside in some thing's unsettling presence in someone's lifeworld or memory? Or does the uncanny colour a willing or unwilling absence from memory? Does the uncanny inherently inhabit the preservation, discard or loss of things? Is it possible that new categories might have to be created in order to explore the uncanny materiality of wartime objects? Here I discuss the affective properties of objects relating to the conflict and its experience. I then explore the different affects channelled by the presence and absence evoked in objects and texts. Beyond theorising about the experience of those I have come into personal contact with and narrating the things through which they felt and remembered about the war and their experience, I also have a duty of remembrance towards people and things – both artefacts of conflict. Not unlike elderly relations who entrust a precious memento or keepsake to a younger relation or friend, the older persons I came into contact with were entrusting their memories to *me*. We, together, have created a novel and dynamic materiality by means of our encounters and our mutual liking and respect.

This materiality has not always been a happy one. In Chapter 4 I performed an affective 'biopsy' of the uncomfortable ethnographic encounter with a veteran whose version of events did not correspond to historical evidence, and which brought to the surface all kinds of raw and grim feelings of guilt and responsibility. On the whole, however, there is a creative positive energy in narrating, retracing and mapping out a story, be it a tale of life, death or nostalgia – affect also lives and thrives in the phantomic and spectral (see Navaro-Yashin 2012).

As potent affective forces, presence and absence trigger memory, shape experience and map out the future. In delineating our identities, our life paths, where we come from and where we are going, present and absent 'things' in our world guide our understanding of what it is to be alive. The way 'things' affect us so powerfully and enduringly is given by the experiential approach that we have to objects, places and other human and non-human beings in our world – we engage with them through our bodies. 'A three-dimensional archive; a phenomenological journey through the spatial layerings of another's personal archaeology': thus, Hancock (2009: 114) evokes the experience of 'being' and engaging in the surroundings of Charleston, Virginia Woolf's house museum. The import of the emotional and affective registers of memory objects cannot be understated.

5.3 Wartime tangibilities: on emotional absence-presence

I argue here that an object or 'thing' is constituted as an emotional presence with its own properties, a distinct materiality, and agency, even if it is no longer with us, because it looms large in memory and perception, tangible or intangible as it may be. It is what Maddrell (2013) calls 'absence-presence', and it inhabits the realm of the make-believe, loss, mourning and trauma. We have no choice but to start thinking of wartime 'things' in conceptual terms that exceed and disrupt the binary presence-absence. Liviano Proia commented on the difficulty and duress of resistance lives, but also on the presence of hope – hope, he told me, was all that propelled them forward despite the many adversities.

> At the start of 1945 . . . you could start seeing a smile appear on the faces of those who until very recently had gritted their teeth, tightening their belts. . . .
> (Interview 6 August 2011)

The gritting of teeth and tightening of belts are elements of everyday-conflict lives, affecting the fighters, their enemies and the civilians at large. Are these 'things' (is hope?) not as much part of war material culture as grenades, shrapnel and medals?

In the Italian civil war of 1943–45, the sides in the conflict were deeply uneven. Their poetics was fundamentally, ontologically different. On the side of the Fascists and the Germans, we are dealing with traditional army strategies and fighting tactics. The resistance, on the other hand, fought an avowedly guerrilla war. The Germans and Fascists had formal headquarters, barracks and physical, emplaced strongholds; the resistance had none of those things – it was transient, placeless and invisible. They had to be, because buildings and base camps were potential death traps. Due to the very nature of the organisation and strategy of the resistance, material culture in the strict sense is scarce. The partisans had to leave no traces of their passage, lest the local population be punished or suspected of collusion with the 'rebels'.

The partisans had to learn to disguise their presence wherever they went. That is why when we think about the materiality of the resistance, we tend to engage with the absence of things, bodies and places, rather than a presence. Or it might be even more useful to think of the resistance's material culture as constituting an absence, a melancholy hiddenness, as in Domanska's (2006) idea of an 'absent present' materiality. The lack of shelters, everyday things like cooking implements, washbasins, bedding, and so on, sets the resistance apart from traditional war material culture. We have to turn to other tangible and intangible things to understand the everyday materiality of the people who lived through the events – to understand their quotidian lives.

On reflection, materiality is by far the most intuitive and self-explanatory avenue into another person's memory. Consider the closeness of heads leaning over a photo album; the sharing of old letters, yellowed and stained by age and loving fingers (see Edwards 2009). Mementoes of the past are everywhere around us in our material- and memory-saturated world. How many times have we daydreamed about a snapshot into the physical past, through a handshake, an embrace, or a piece of well-weathered clothing? Whether tangible or intangible, war and conflict leave traces on bodies and in memory. In her wartime diary, Sonia Ciapetti (2007: 16) comments on the duress of eating 'by candlelight' and we get a sense of an invasive ambience made of acrid smoke, which Sonia likens to a 'being' sticking to bodies and clothes in a messy, sticky smoke layer of soot. The homemade heaters, meanwhile, once or twice nearly killed Sonia's mother due to the carbon dioxide emissions in the poorly aired rooms. Is smoke a 'thing', part of the material world (Ingold 2007: 4; Saunders 2009; Buchli 2015)?

This is history inscribed on the body and affecting the body. It is through our bodies that we can gain entry into someone else's sensory past. We can feel a real closeness to someone, partaking in their recollections of being hungry, cold, injured, or pleasantly sated and warm after a long hike or dangerous action. A keen awareness of the innate tactility of memory has been with us for some time (Appadurai 1986; Domanska 2006 et al.), but never before have we become so conscious of the link between the body, memory and the objects and places that make memories and recollections meaningful to an individual or group. Do things create and partake in that closeness? Do things make a story 'come together', materialise in an affective event?

Ankersmit (1996, 2005) contends that an experience of the past, such as the feeling of 'being there', is fundamentally at odds with our cognitive discourse about the past. Thus, the more we write about history, the more context we create, the more we will have the feeling that the reality of the past itself is buried under a layer of discourse and contextualization (Ankersmit 1996). In other words, the more we know the past, the less we can experience or feel it. The boom in 'collective memory' has gradually disembodied remembrance by ascribing an official, quasi-strategic facade to processes of recollection and celebration. Even when scholars have turned their attention to negated or submerged memories, the memories of persecuted or marginalised social groups, a focus on the politics of memory contestation has sometimes brought about a disembodiment of such recollection. And yet the memory of losers, stigmatised persons, and 'outsider' memories are intensely, if not quintessentially, tactile and embodied by the very virtue that they have survived in oral form, never written down, never committed to officialdom. Or when they are written down, the ritual of remembrance can become very dangerous.

On many occasions throughout his wartime diary, Emanuele Artom commented on the danger of his keeping of a diary. He called this act 'potentially deadly' (Artom and Schwarz 2008: 61) and ultimately an irrational endeavour, yet also thought of the diary as a tangible form of his everyday life – a way of making peace with himself, preparing for the future and making sense of the world:

> This diary represents my only intellectual pursuit and I don't want to give it up; on the other hand, sometime in the future, I will take pleasure in reading these horrible soiled pages, these dirty, bent, stained pages penned with an old crooked pen.
> (Artom and Schwarz 2008: 113)

The diary serves as a bridge between the present and the future at a point where danger has ceased and hindsight colours the distressing past with a pleasant patina; sadly, we know now that Artom would never have the opportunity to reminisce on the stained and ripped pages of the diary after the war, because the materiality of the diary survived the fragile mortality of the storyteller.

Figure 5.2 Dead partisans Mario Cappelli, Luigi Nicolò and Adelio Pagliarani, 1945, Rimini.
Source: Wikicommons

5.4 Frontline materialities: evocative objects and booby traps

5.4.1 *The eagle and the death cult: Fascists and their materiality*

One episode in Zelmira Marazio's diary recorded the pomp and officialdom of the Fascist rituals. The description of one event conveys in vivid terms the flavour of Fascist materiality: the brass band playing military songs and the singing crowd; the large Tricolore flag hanging from the balcony of an official's palazzo; the multicoloured *gagliardetti* (insignia) of the various 'departments' glittering and waving in the slight breeze; the soldiers' proud tears (Marazio 2004: 68). An Italian flag proved potentially deadly for civilians in the Perarolo village in German-administered Alpenvorland. Caterina Marinello reported that:

> On St Catherine's Day [28 April] 1945 my husband Beppino and I realized that the retreating Germans had set fire to the hills where our house was. We had been away and were walking homebound when we saw the eerie light of the fire on the hills in the half light, we were afraid that the Germans would surround our house and harm us! We considered turning back and running but we were paralyzed. Afraid of capture, Beppino remembered a little silk Tricolore

handkerchief in his pocket. He put it in his mouth and tried to ingest it, but he had no saliva. He retched and coughed.

(Amantia and Svaluto Moreolo 2004: 168)

The apparently harmless object (the patriotic Italian flag handkerchief) becomes one with the panicking body in the act of self-preservation, but the body failed Beppino.

In his war diary, Florentine Fernando Togni (1988) recalled his deployment in the Fascist Barbarigo Battalion, which on 23 February 1944 was bound for Anzio – the frontline. He recalled how his comrades were suddenly silent, inward-looking, each seemingly 'lost in his own expectations'. They were twenty-year-old or even younger lads, motivated and sustained only by their Fascist faith. In order to boost morale, their superior had given the young recruits new insignia to pin to their lapels: two gladii enclosed in a laurel wreath. The pomp and regalia of old Rome was supposed to motivate them towards 'victory or death'.

In another episode, Zelmira recalled the final moments of a Fascist officer of the Alpine division on his deathbed in late 1944 (Marazio 2004: 112). A mutual friend put the dying man's alpine hat close to his face and the latter kissed its long black feather. This is another example of the redolent materiality of Fascism, and an everyday example of the Blackshirts' quasi-fetishist fascination with their symbols and regalia. Indeed, the *presence* of the uniform has been conceptualised as a mainstay of wartime materiality. Here is how former President of the Italian Republic Eugenio Scalfari remembers his relationship with the Fascist Party and its paraphernalia:

> I received a phone call. [. . .] It was a female voice asking for the Fascist Eugenio Scalfari. I qualified myself and said, this is him. 'You are to come to Palazzo Littorio tomorrow. At ten a.m.'. I was troubled by that call, by the harshness of the tone and the icy impersonality of that voice: 'The Fascist Eugenio Scalfari must show up tomorrow at ten at palazzo Littorio, in full uniform'. I adored my uniform. The following morning, I was especially fastidious in my dressing ritual. The outfit was extremely elegant. My jacket – it was called a Safari Jacket [*Sahariana*] at the time – the grey-green jodhpurs, the boots, the shoulder details, the same stars on the sleeves, the light blue neckerchief and, of course, the signature black shirt. . . .
>
> (Scalfari 2008)

What do the diary of a doomed young Jew and the shining uniform of a Fascist have in common, if not their persistent presence in memory and emotional embodiment? 'Things' populate our ethnographic descriptions, building a bridge between ourselves and the worlds inhabited and experienced by the people we work with. Even when consciously refusing to explain away 'things' from those other worlds using our own rubrics and our own distinctions (Leach 2007), we use them to scaffold our story nonetheless. Those worlds are present, they are right there in those 'things' we touch, draw, photograph, observe or imagine in our mind's eye if they have disappeared or have been lost. If we think of their affective potency as a presence, war mementoes inhabit a particular kind of presence: the longing for peace, the silent suffering of violence, the loss of loved ones and the spirit of political engagement – and, often, potent sentiments such as hatred and revenge. Whatever the affect inhabiting (or haunting?) an object, whenever it is used to engage others with a story, a memory, or simply a glance back to the past, reveals a great deal more than finite memories: the redolent thing becomes the start of a conversation. Whether a diary or a uniform, a thing-with-memory can reach out to us and bring us closer to its non-absent past (Classen and Howes 2006).

The object does not only play the role of active agent in an interview explicitly geared towards exploring someone's memories. Rather, the photograph, handkerchief, letter and button also become a part of an affective assemblage alongside the recording device, the cups of tea or coffee, the clearing of the throat, the hesitations and the silences. Objects achieve this interconnectedness and embody this presence by their physical presence with us in the room, or they might feel close-by even if they are not *physically* there. One does not even need to touch a memorable thing to feel a connection with it – the fact that its mute, yet eloquent presence shapes the encounter is enough. As a direct appendage of bodily affects and emotions, wartime mementoes embody the past in a way that goes beyond words and gestures. That is why it is so difficult to do these objects justice when committing to written words research which was the spoken word. 'Things' bridge the gap between individual memories and the affective worlds of today (Tolia-Kelly 2004; Turkle 2005).

How then to engage with mementoes – the redolent presence of things that serve as a channel to another world, simultaneously distant from yet close to our own? I suggest that things with pregnant pasts constitute sites of feeling, not just receptacles of recollection. By inhabiting a site of feeling with the person who remembers, we can get closer to their world. For the researcher, flicking through a diary or a collection of letters can be enough to feel a real closeness to the writer. Memories *matter* – in the sense that through the engagement with human and non-human bodies, they are matter. Material culture studies (e.g. Gibson 2004; Turkle 2007; Classen and Howes 2006; Miller 2008, 2009; Dudley 2009; Edwards 2009; Navaro-Yashin 2009, 2012; Saunders 2009; Moshenska 2010) have become increasingly preoccupied with the interpersonal dimension of artefacts as social and cultural catalysts, and with the role of objects and their sensoria in the making and unmaking of worlds, memories and meanings. For Saunders (2009: 38), in a world at war 'where speech failed, material culture could intervene'. I propose that we continue to give a voice to the shared materiality of things, and that we turn our lens on the ways in which redolent war-related objects and mementoes inhabit sensory worlds, and share and refract affective intensities in the here-and-now.

5.4.2 Frontline objects

In a recent news story, a team of historians published an account of recovered booby traps the Germans had planned to use during the war against the Allies (BBC News, 29 September 2015). In both World Wars, 'souveneering' was popular with militants on all sides (Winter 1979; Saunders 2009: 43). Yet soldiers at the frontline were also aware of the existence of booby traps. Private Whatmore recalled an episode in which he and a companion faced such a risk first-hand:

> [o]nce there was this German laid out in front of us, he had been dead about a week. My companion went through his pockets, although we had been warned against going through dead Germans' pockets in case there were booby-traps in them. Anyway this chap went through this dead chap's pockets and he came back with a gold pocket watch. He couldn't wind it up himself, He was all a tremble, whether it from fright or nerves I do not know, so I wound it up for him.
>
> (Whatmore, IWM Accession no. 2703)

Thus, the taking of a watch or any personal items from a dead enemy was a risky activity, given the danger of booby traps. The presence of souvenir-worthy objects could orientate the uncomfortable and perilous materiality of the frontline, leading some to take risks in order to 'own' a trophy. Still, the apparel and possessions of the dead Other were sometimes too tempting; sometimes carrying of weapons and articles of clothing belonging to the enemy had the same intoxicating effect.

The taking of and craving for souvenirs affected civilian life too. Florentine teenager Sonia Ciapetti's first encounter with a German soldier, who halted the car driven by her father on a suburban street, also centres on a valuable object as a putative catalyst of violence and danger (Ciapetti 2007). Sonia pre-emptively noted that she had always had an 'inexplicable' aversion to Germans even when they were still Italy's allies. She saw that this German soldier sported ten watches on his left arm from wrist to bicep. When he said something in German pointing to his watch-decorated arm, young Sonia immediately thought that he wanted to add their watches to the collection. Then she noticed that he was drunk, unsteady on his feet, and also that he looked very young, blond, tall and very thin. As soon as Sonia's father proved to him that neither of them had a watch, he let them pass. Later that drunk German would be killed and his death would spark a cruel reprisal against those who lived on that street: several houses would be blown up. But had it been worth it? Sonia asked in her diary.

During the war, things had the power to change perceptions and realign identities. Countless partisan memoirs evoke the ephemeral materiality of lives lived on the move, but civilians also recorded their impressions of the fleeting, yet powerful, materiality of the resistance. In her memoir, Magda Ceccarelli (2011: 267) recalled a meeting with a man who escorted her up into the Piedmontese Alps at Acqui to inspect the local partisan stronghold. Magda surveyed their lodgings, their equipment and their weapons. She thought the lads looked 'strong' and were well prepared to fight the Germans. Enrico Lowenthal's (2015) memoir is similarly punctuated with his enchantment with the shiny, luxurious war equipment sported by of the American GIs he came into contact with in November 1944. As part of the Allied mission in Piemonte, Enrico's formation was supported by a group of OSS agents (Lowenthal 2015: 98 ff.). Enrico expressed his delight with the equipment that the Italian partisans could suddenly make use of: brand new shiny backpacks (he called them 'gorgeous') and the fabulous K Rations, the meals in a paraffin-sealed tin complete with a cigarette, matches and a small roll of toilet tissue (Lowenthal 2015: 99). Enrico or 'Ico' wrote of these alien objects with an awestruck fascination mixed with delight. The American materiality was so far removed from the misery and dirt of the Italians' clandestine resistance lives that the partisans viewed such creature comforts as dazzling. In the days that followed, eighteen-year-old Enrico wore the new American uniform and equipment with infantile pride:

> After we had worn our new American uniforms with a machine gun on a shoulder strap, I started strutting about the village squares, proud as anything. I was such a kid. Maybe I overdid it with the showing off, because rumours of our collaboration with the Americans started circulating aplenty.
>
> (Lowenthal 2015: 101)

5.5 Absence as an affect: the shadow-play of memory

But what about the materiality of absence? Domanska (2006) has problematised the disembodied nature of much historiography by pointing to the intrinsically embodied and material nature of our knowledge about the past. So the question, both methodological and theoretical, becomes: how can we, as social scientists, trace absence? How do we follow and describe the movements, the attachments, the translations and representations through which absence becomes matter and through which absence comes to matter? The polysemic nature of the word 'trace' is appealing for our purpose here. For it denotes, first of all, an active and spatial act of drawing or mapping out something.

On Sunday, 31 October 1943, Corrado Di Pompeo's letter to his evacuee wife Antonietta reveals that he found comfort in familiar things, in the belongings of his loved ones, and in thoroughly cleaning their home (Di Pompeo 2009: 28), which he then reported in great detail to his wife. That was his way of coping with separation. Corrado called his home 'a sad little house' (Di Pompeo 2009: 29) because it had been emptied of the warmth and loving presence of his wife and children. Left behind working in a minor administrative role in Rome, the lonely man learnt to find some comfort in the materiality of the one-way letters to his wife, and in reading their past love letters and the family photographs. He admitted that never before then had he appreciated photos more. The materiality of nostalgia is writ large in Corrado's handling of his small sons' objects, too: he surrounds himself with blankets, wooden toys, and his wife's small pink bag (Di Pompeo 2009: 27). Corrado was completely and consciously politically unaware: he is only concerned with his family; on one occasion close to Christmas Day 1943, he complained about the enforced 7 pm curfew due to the fact that some Germans had been killed by 'god knows who' (Di Pompeo 2009: 71). In the crushing vice of his affective everyday void, Corrado found solace in the making of things – he discovered in carpentry an antidote to his anguish (Di Pompeo 2009: 35). He kept on making things to kill time, futile things, useful things – superfluous pieces of furniture and storage. In Margherita Ianelli's diary (n.d.), we find a poignant exemplar of the intensely present-absent materiality of the war in all its potent loss and grief. Margherita recalled how a battle between local partisans and German soldiers had broken out in her home – an event in a chain of violence that would result in one of the cruellest war crimes in the history of the whole Second World War: the Marzabotto civilian massacre. In the aftermath of a clash on 4 October 1944, two men lost their lives, although we are not told exactly who had died – possibly because the terrified twenty-two-year-old was not herself privy to that information. We then learn the following:

> Our first job was that of burying the dead. They [*we do not know who she refers to here*] looked in their pockets and found pictures of saints and family photos. My husband and my brother in law helped us bury the two men at the edge of a field. My mother in law would often visit that gravesite and pray. When asked why, she would answer that every dead person was the same, united in their eternal loneliness.
>
> (Margherita Ianelli n.d.)

The materiality of the dead men's possessions is the only clue to the identity of the deceased fighters: the possessions of images of the saints positions them as Catholic Italians. Without this moving detail, we might not know who Margherita and her family buried on that grim October morning. Her mother-in-law's silent prayer at the makeshift gravesite bore witness to the futility of death.

5.5.1 A paper cenotaph: Bruno's memento

I held in my hands two battered sheets of paper, bearing a thick typescript text slightly faded by the frequent handling of many hands. Bruno Canella, one of the partisans I interviewed, had introduced me to this most moving of artefacts. This was a letter/poem written by his then severely ill wife in remembrance of an episode of their resistance lives. As I held in my hands this redolent thing, I was

> **VECCHI INDIMENTICABILI RICORDI...**
>
> Tante tante cose sono cambiate da quei tempi al mio paese.
> Vi è passato il progresso, vi è giunto il benessere conquistato dal duro lavoro dei suoi abitanti e persino l'espressione dei volti e il modo di vestire sono cambiati. Tanti non ci sono più, tanti nati dopo sono ormai grandi, ormai uomini. Quando vi ritorno accarezzando a volte un bimbo, lo guardo e cerco di indovinare nei suoi lineamenti il viso del padre o della madre che furono della mia età.
> Molto è cambiato, ma la mia casa, la mia vecchia casa, così nota per me in ogni suo angolo, è ancora là anche se per me ora è inaccessibile. Ma non ci vuole sforzo per ricordare: è tutto ancora così vivo e presente tutto ciò che è passato per quella casa! Lo dicevamo tante volte allora: *"Se questa casa potesse un giorno parlare..."*
> Noi qualche volta abbiamo parlato per lei, abbiamo raccontato come sia sempre stata brava e pronta ad accogliere i nostri compagni e come sia stata fortunata a non essere incendiata dal fuoco dei tedeschi. E' ancora là la mia casa, ha cambiato solo il nome del padrone e il colore dell'intonaco.
>
> *******
>
> Quante ore, quante serate vi abbiamo passato in compagnia!
> Allora era la più bella casa del paese, dopo quella dei Pascoi che fu incendiata nel rastrellamento del settembre del '44. Attorno al fuoco del suo grande *larin*, che mio padre tanto amava perché gli dava la gioia di qualche spiedata, ci trovavamo abitualmente noi sorelle con Astorre, Rossi, Parco e mio marito, ma la casa ed il fuoco accoglievano chiunque avesse bisogno di ristoro o di nascondersi. Ne ha visto passare tanti, e tanti ne ha ospitati la mia vecchia casa! E i ricordi più vivi si riferiscono al duro inverno, forse per quel fuoco così luminoso e caldo davanti al quale i nostri uomini tentavano di asciugare e di riscaldare quei calzetti di lana così ruvidi, così grossi e così sempre bagnati. Rivedo Rossi lavorare abilmente con la pinza, che portava sempre in tasca, un pezzo di fil di ferro e farne un paio di mollette per voltare le castagne che arrostivano sulla brace. Risento i porcaeva di Parco, mentre Astorre ci ragguagliava sulla giornata. Nasceva fra di noi un chiacchierio concitato, mentre istintivamente tendevamo l'orecchio nel timore di sentire il rombo di qualche motore. Eppure in quell'ansia che non ci abbandonava mai, ogni tanto, echeggiavano le nostre risate: momenti in cui ci sembrava di dimenticare la dura tragedia che stavamo vivendo. Ricordo le colorite espressioni dei nostri amici:
> *"I ciaparia e faria un spolveras!" "Tasi che magari da qua a do tre di saron in simitero..."* e subito per scaramanzia: *"...a portarghe i fiori ai morti."*
> Quando fuori nevicava ci sentivamo più difesi e in quelle sere mio padre ci suonava con la fisarmonica qualche valzer e noi cantavamo qualche coretto in sordina, bevendo qualche cosa di caldo... quell'orribile caffè... benedetto a volte da un po' di graspa da troi. Fu proprio in una di quelle sere nevose che festeggiammo il

Figure 5.3 The poem, Page One.

not yet fully aware of its significance. The affective potency of the papers I was holding spoke of the emotional pull of absence alongside the heart-wrenching effect of a presence. After I returned the sheets to Bruno, he began to unravel the magic of the object by reading from it. As he was moved to bitter tears, I felt that the story emanating from the interaction of this elderly man and this object engulfed us all, in that room, at that time, and led us all to become participants in the story being told.

Briefly summarised, this text recounted an anecdote: an episode that, in its apparent simplicity, not only aptly illustrates the day-to-day 'feeling' of living underground resistance lives in the mountains, but also the emotional worlds the protagonists inhabited during and after the war. In this incident, a partisan friend of the couple, 'Barba' [Beard] had sought shelter at Bruno's fireside to dry off (it was snowing outside) and to partake in a homely meal of roasted chestnuts and grappa before returning to his partisan formation, temporarily stationed high up in the rugged, inhospitable Dolomiti alpine peaks. The text emphasised how this situation had occurred several times before, and yet this particular encounter was life-changing. Shortly after Bruno and his wife's friend Barba had left their home, a Nazi patrol arrested Barba on his way back to his hideout. That was the last time the pair ever saw him, their last encounter before his execution. 'I want to thank you, dear old house, for helping us give our friend the gift of a few last moments of warmth and serenity' Bruno read out, before his voice broke. Memory, nostalgia, anger and grief make Bruno's story 'matter', and in so doing they include his wife's story in its affective potency and agency. Bruno the patriot was grieving for his murdered friend, so movingly remembered in the poem written by his beloved wife; while Bruno the husband also grieved for his own wife, the author of the story, whose memory still haunts the pages he was reading and who was, at the time, still alive in the next room – 'a million miles away' (in Bruno's words) in Alzheimer's limbo.

Bruno was grieving for her too, as if she was already gone. In the crumpled pages of the poem he read out, or rather performed, memory and emotion escalated in an overlap of past, present and future. Bruno was shaken with the unfairness of it all – his murdered friend never got a chance to grow old and shall forever be remembered for his garish woolly jumpers and long, thick russet beard; yet the one who had been able to grow old, Bruno's wife, had become very sick.

Bruno's heartache may be seen to take on a double connotation: at the time of writing, Bruno's wife had sadly passed away, but at the time of the interview I sensed that he had long been mourning both his loss (her companionship) and her loss – her wit, talent, and above all, the negated possibility to reflect and metabolise her wartime experience like he did. Bruno had been mourning two persons through the performance of the poem: his friend (dead) and his wife (terminally ill). The poem, originally written in longhand, then typewritten, and finally printed out by a nephew using a computer, consisted at the time of Bruno's performance in those two well-thumbed, inkjet-printed sheets. The poem, or story, or memento, perhaps also through its sequential incarnations as longhand script to computer printout, had taken on the significance of both a site of memory and a site of feeling. It was, one may even argue, a site of mourning where a tension between presence and absence (see Kidron 2012: 14, 16) deprived him of the actual objects Bruno longed for – a paper cenotaph of sorts. Without this poem and its powerful links to place (the house, the fireside), love (his wife, their friend) and loss (death, illness) it embodied, which in turn opened up endless stories, possibilities and interpretative meanings, his encounter with me would not have been the same.

5.5.2 The night is a thing: the poetics of sleep and sleep deprivation

There is, I believe, an ephemeral materiality of night, sleep and sleep deprivation during the conflict. This issue provides an example of how the peculiar nature of nighttime and darkness, and the traces or absences left by sleep and lack of sleep, can inform the everyday sensory experience of the war. As a fundamental part of the veterans' remembrance, the irregularity or lack of sleep looms large in the experiential landscapes of the resistance in particular. Partisan commanders were aware of the need to routinely police and discipline the body of the fighter in several ways to ensure the safety of an armed formation. The nighttime geographies of the civil war are made of silences and concealment, but not always. 'The night is a thing, an entity, when you are a partisan' Cesare Marzona mused during our interview. As a 'thing', the night entails its own materiality, its sensorium, and its code of conduct. Was the night an ally of the clandestine resistance? Most storytellers I have engaged with seemed to agree. For all their better logistical organisation and greater numbers, the Fascists and Germans still got anxious when darkness fell. Lorenzo Altoè recalled:

> Once, the Fascists and Germans were in this remote mountain area, isolated, and they were terrified of us partisans; they always had their lights on after dark, flashlights and so on. Once the Allies misread those lights for our drop site signals and dropped a whole load of supplies right in the lap of the enemy.
> (Interview 18 December 2011)

Falling asleep during a night watch roster was unthinkable for partisans. Someone should always be alert to approaching danger. 'A partisan on guard duty that fell asleep would have been shot' (De Nardi 1976: 42, quoted in Behan 2009: 64). 'On the other hand, if someone who had been viewed with suspicion suddenly left the camp overnight, it was almost inevitably taken as a sign that an enemy attack was imminent' (Behan 2009: 65)'. The cover of darkness was perceived, therefore, as both a shelter and a danger; reduced visibility was a blessing or a curse. Another fighter, Aldo, explained to me why falling asleep at your lookout post was a bad idea:

> During the autumn-winter of 1944 we had with us a Neapolitan lad; one night they assigned him to night watch between two and four am outside our hiding

spot (a hut). So he asks me: 'Listen Aldo, I'm scared. Come keep me company'. I agree and join him at 2 am. In the meantime, that night, our Brigade Commander and a few others were due back from an expedition. I join my friend under a thorn bush and we speak, softly. He is white as a sheet with fear, so we chat quietly, you know, I want to comfort him. Then we hear a shot. Oh god! The Commander had returned and seeing as we had not noticed their arrival, he fired a shot on purpose to scare us. I am not armed, for I had only joined the watch guy to keep him company. We would have been unprepared for an attack, unfortunately, as we had been engrossed in our talk ... We were punished harshly.

(Interview 30 August 2010)

This lad, a southerner, felt out of place in the cold woodlands of northeast Italy. His alienation became pronounced at night, when he probably felt more alone than ever. In order to exorcise the potentially fatal outcome of sleeping on night watch duty or not enduring marches that lasted all night, in some divisions the Allies offered to share their supply of amphetamines with the partisans. Use of amphetamines by the US Air Force during the Second World War is well documented; in the Vicenza region, US pilots allegedly shared their supplies with partisan chiefs. One veteran partisan in the Vicenza area (Attilio Crestani, interview August 2003; Residori, pers. comm. 20 February 2010) admitted candidly that the *little pills* prescribed by the Allies made night marches and actions on no sleep at all much easier to endure. He did not know and did not ask what was in those pills, he said during his interview with Sonia Residori – all he knew is that they sure helped. Artom also commented on the usefulness of *Simpamina*, an over-the-counter Dextroamphetamine compound that made dangerous action and prolonged lack of sleep easier to bear, although it made them irritable and 'wired' (Artom and Schwarz 2008: 118). One can only imagine what the sensorium of a young person not accustomed to the use of amphetaminic stimulants must have been like, taking into account the concomitant side effects of paranoia and restlessness characteristic of such drugs – adding a further layer of anxiety onto the already hefty burden of worries and concerns that guerrilla fighters had to engage with on a daily basis. This kind of intangible materiality informs wartime memory as poignantly as objects that we can see or touch; as such, this ephemerality deserves to be incorporated in our storytelling and publications.

5.5.3 'I shouldn't have asked them for it'. Wilma's guilty prize

Wilma De Paris had been a young woman during the war; she was born in 1921 in Trichiana, a village in the Belluno Dolomites. The whole province of Belluno had been annexed to the Reich as operation zone Alpenvorland, and Germans loomed large everywhere in Wilma's tightly knit mountain community. She decided to be part of the resistance movement, and we have seen in Chapter 3 how frustrated she was by her inability to join the men up in the woods due to the fragility of her female body. She had taken to sleeping rough, without mattress or pillows on the barren floor, to feel closer to these brave men through pain and discomfort of the body. Nonetheless, Wilma turned out to be the most helpful and bravest staffetta in the area despite her impossibilty to take up arms. In her autobiographical account of the war (De Paris 2005), she wrote candidly about her experience in German-occupied Trichiana. Yet at Liberation, which in the Alpenvorland region took place later than in most of Italy (3 May 1945), Wilma did something she later came to regret. In the honest, heartfelt pages of her memoir, we learn that on Piazza dei Martiri (formerly Piazza Campitello; see Figure 6.1) a crowd was forming, awaiting the official Allied speeches, and gloating over the parade of the German military prisoners who had not managed to flee north and were detained in town. The Germans, Wilma wrote, had an edelweiss on their hat as part of their insignia. Wilma and fellow partisan Tëa Palman approached one of the prisoners in the column, and she asked for his edelweiss.

> I asked him to give me his edelweiss as a gift. Before I knew it, the whole column had taken off their edelweiss and held them in their hands, ready to give them up. 'I only need the one' I said. At that moment, with bitter sadness, I understood what a humiliating gesture the giving away of the edelweiss would be, for them. I should have never asked them for it.
>
> (De Paris 2005: 98)

After the war, it is possible that Wilma kept that edelweiss. The centrality of the humble alpine flower in her memories of the war cannot be underestimated; whether Wilma kept that edelweiss as a memento or not, this is a poignant example of how a thing lingers in memory as much more than an aide-memoire. A thing becomes imbued with powerful emotional investment and shapes self-perception after the events have passed. In an informal (sadly not recorded) interview in later life (Amantia pers. comm. 2015), Wilma is understood to have commented on the edelweiss, saying that she still felt guilty for humiliating those lads. This led me and Amantia to speculate that Wilma assumed that her request to have the German prisoner's edelweiss, in her newly found position of superiority as Italian partisan, had hurt and mortified the prisoners. In her imagination, Wilma had probably associated her spontaneous gesture with the wider pain and humiliation that the German prisoners experienced in the wake of their defeat. This sad little story, one of a myriad tales from the war, may seem insignificant. Yet this tale of regret encapsulates the poignancy of absence and is but one of the many little nooks and crannies of history left unexplored by mainstream scholarship: never underestimate the power of the imagination, of the 'what ifs' in making and understanding our world.

5.6 Reflections

I have sought, somewhat hesitantly, to give 'body' and essence to the intensely affective nature of wartime mementoes in this chapter. Photographs, wounds, poems, mementoes and even imaginary assemblages (remember the looted German column of Menarè?) loom large in the memory of the war, intensely interwoven with people, places, bodies and feelings. To call war material culture 'objects', separated from the recounting subject, seems untenable: I would argue instead that the veteran's world of feeling is channelled through the body's interaction with these storytelling mementoes, which in turn become not only sites of memory but also sites of feeling. In my encounter with veterans, their families and friends, things have been active agents of remembrance and engagement. From the photocopy to the offering of food and drink, objects and things have been an active presence in the interview room. I believe it is because I let them 'speak' in tandem with their owners and facilitators, entangled in their lives through their material presence. Whether dwelling in the past or in the present, 'things' have told many a meaningful story in the course of my research. To explain away or marginalise objects as tangential to the stories being told would occlude the unique sensory sharing experience of the ethnographic encounter. We might instead engage with things as well as with persons with a humility that can render them approachable as means of discovering more, and more in depth, about past events and their *present* affects.

As can be expected, during the course of wartime research, interviews and encounters engage with objects and things that incarnate an absence as well as a presence. Some mementoes issue forth from violent acts – a watch stolen from a corpse, or the scarf taken from a loved one's bloody corpse as a keepsake. Anna's photograph of her friend, identified as 'Partisan Irma' (quote at the beginning of this chapter) testifies to the power of photographs to evoke the sense of loss, presence and intense love by an elderly woman for her unfortunate friend. In Elizabeth Edwards' words, 'photographs are spoken about and spoken to – the emotional impact articulated through forms of vocalization' (Edwards 2009: 25). This is indeed the case in Anna's story, whose deep affection for her friend emerges through her delicate stroking of Irma's face in the photograph; the smiling young woman in the photograph jumps out to us as a fragmented episode in Irma's life, an incomplete strand of her life story, one obscured by a dark fate.

The photograph reminds Anna, and us, of a moment of bliss before the unfortunate was tortured and rendered infertile through enemy brutality for her underground resistance activity. In this sense, as Kidron (2012: 4) observes, 'objects that silently encapsulate and perform pasts that have culminated in death or near-death experiences are especially affecting and haunting'. Such objects speak of the encounter with death directly, without intermediaries: they are the relic of a life brutally and unnaturally terminated. They become corollaries of murder, associated with sad or ugly thoughts; and yet, when someone cherishes and stores them, they can take on a more benign, warmer quality of nostalgia. Apart from those objects explicitly guarded and engaged with as war trophies (the reward for the kill), even those objects appropriated in death can become the portal to a new life, an engagement with others, and they can tell a story of presences, of absences, and of immense, heart-breaking love.

6 Landscapes of fighting, feeling and hoping

Place as material culture

> In every town and piazza in northern and central Italy, you will find a reminder of the resistance: tales of the torment and the ecstasy of the rebellion against Fascism and German occupation. Far less numerous are the reminders of the civil war and military occupation inscribed in the vernacular. As I crossed Piazza dei Martiri in the northern town of Belluno, I superimposed the grisly pictures I had seen that very morning in the local Resistance Studies institute's archives onto the serene sunlit scene around me. In the pictures, dated 1944, the lifeless bodies of six partisans hanged from lampposts at the corners of the square overlooking the busy café and office building at the south end of what was then called Piazza Campitello. Up here, the Fascists had no jurisdiction; this town was part of the administrative area called Alpenvorland, annexed to the Reich. The Germans hanged many local patriots up here. I wondered what the square looked like in the aftermath of the bleak events – in between the murder of brave Italians and the renaming of the square at the end of the war. A phantomic space full of ghosts, to be sure. I shivered, then turned off the main square and, its melancholy affects still trailing behind me, headed towards the train station and home.

6.1 Hostile landscapes and the vernacular of terror

Q: *How did you feel revisiting the places of your resistance after all this time?*
GG: My heart was saddened at the thought of all those brave lads who were no longer with us. I saw these places and remembered how I had lived there. I recalled what it felt like actually living there on a daily basis, you know? All manner of things came back to my memory, flooding in. I remembered the family who gave us shelter, the friendly locals. . . . With hindsight it's easy to make sense of events.

140 *Landscapes of fighting, feeling, hoping*

Figure 6.1 Piazza Campitello/Piazza Martiri, Belluno.
ISBREC Institute, Belluno. Reproduced with permission

Q: How do you mean?
GG: The Buss de la Lum ... it's a myth. I know very little of it. I never saw it before the war, I only visited it afterwards. A priest there was saying that partisans were bloodthirsty bandits who filled the Buss de la Lum with Fascists and Germans. I followed the Trieste researchers' examinations. They found five corpses, not 500. The corpses were taken to a nearby town, Caneva. I have seen the documents. Buss de la Lum was a Fascist cover up. Of those bodies, one was a partisan.

[Brescacin: *There were more than five bodies . . . let's say twenty.*]

GG. Well, then. To answer your previous questions, when they take schoolchildren to the places of the resistance, I think the kids try to *live the stories that happened there*. Although that is sometimes difficult, you see, 'cause at school they are spoon-fed nasty anti-partisan propaganda on a daily basis.

(Interview 10 March 2011)

This exchange, in the context of an interview with veteran partisan Giuseppe Giust, is an example of the atomized and often contradictory remembrance of the war. Our conversation stimulated the veteran to reflect on several issues that this book explores: the sense of loss of comrades and things once loved, the everyday dimension of partisan lives, hospitality, the refusal to 'go there', the denial of negative places, and younger generations' desire to make sense of the ugliness and mess of the war by trying to relive those stories imaginatively.

In everyday experience, embodiment, action, and landscape are intimately interconnected, so that material culture cannot exist without bodies just as storytelling cannot come to life without its constellation of places and actions. The separation of themes and concepts into the different chapters of this volume has been an artifice necessary to break down the complex poetics of conflict experience into coherent chunks. Life is not like that. So in a sense, the arguments presented in this chapter also belong to and feed back into the overarching themes of previous chapters. Here I argue that to be 'at war' means to engage in a 'fundamentally bodily making and unmaking of the world' (McSorley 2014: 121). The notion of intra-action (Barad 2003, 2007) draws in the role and agency of more-than-human agents in the creation of meaningful worlds of interaction and significance – 'practical entrapments' (Hodder 2012: 163). How did the actors in the civil war and the Germans relate to their surroundings – their *Umwelt?* The key questions are thus – how did various actors experience their entrapment in space and place? What opportunities did places afford? What traces (if any) did they leave of their world-making or unmaking? (Ingold 1993, 2000; Tilley 2004; Bondi 2005b; Legg 2005; Andrews et al. 2006; Hill 2013). In order to tackle these questions, I reinstate the spatial into war and resistance master narratives that often, by privileging the political and tactical aspects of the war, come across as bloodless and curiously abstracted (Neri Sernieri 1995; Gentile 2012). Instead, mapping out spatial perceptions of places and landscapes of the civil war foregrounds their messiness. I maintain also a recurring focus on the everyday embodied knowledges and impressions that the protagonists of the war carried of self and other as the war drew to a close in early 1945. Here I use the strategies with which civilians, fighters, Germans and Fascists made and unmade places as spatial metaphors for the unravelling of their stories. In memory, a strong sense of place (pride and patriotism) is often accompanied by an equally poignant sense of being lost or disorientated in accounts of partisan life and German and Fascist memoirs and interviews. Being grounded and being lost are part of the same spatial and perceptual story.

A sense of loss and disorientation in the memory of the conflict went hand in hand with disidentification, that is, the removal of a person or persons from the naturalness of place (De Nardi 2015a). The Italian language has a wonderful adjective to indicate the confused emotional and mental state of one feeling out of place and disorientated: *spaesato*. Literally, this translates as 'without a village' (from *paese*). It is a term employed often by my respondents when they seek to describe their experience during the war. Some used the term quite literally: nine veterans had *seen* their villages go up in flames following German and Fascist reprisals. *Spaesato* echoes Heidegger's use of 'unheimlich', not as just feeling strange but literally 'not-being-at-home' (*Heim*) in a world where one is otherwise already immersed (1998: 258).

To begin, I return to a fundamental theme introduced in Chapter 1: the altered, unsettling new spatial understandings and transformed practices which inhabiting the post-Armistice world involved. The Armistice of 8 September 1943, I have argued throughout, does not only mark a temporal watershed in the lives and experiences of everyone who happened to be on Italian soil – but the day Italy switched sides also acts as a boundary between perceptual and emotional worlds. Here, I emphasise the embodied, immanent spatial experience of resistance fighters and their allies – be they men or women, armed or unarmed, and their enemies (the Italian Fascists in the first place through recollections, storytelling, memoirs and sketches). Learning place anew after 8 September 1943 entailed the adjustment of bodily knowledges and social modes of interaction (see also Neisser 1993: 394). Nothing would ever be, feel or look the same. We might think of the changing situation of Italians, Germans and the Anglo-Americans in the aftermath of the Armistice as a novel cultural-geographical configuration – a new spatial awareness, and an unexpected and unpredictable Being-In-The-World.

The experience of Norman Stone is telling (1996). In recounting the shelling suffered by his unit (attached to the 2nd and 5th Leicestershire Regiments) during the Salerno landing taking place between 4 and 5 am on 9 September 1943, Stone reported:

> It was dark, nobody knew what was happening, people were shouting out 'where's your company, where's this, where's the other?' and eventually we did get sorted out and took up an emergency position outside the town. . . . As I said the nearest approach I can say . . . is like a crowd of people on Filbert Street turns out, adding darkness to it as well.
>
> (Interview, Leicester Oral History Archive)

Unable to draw on any similar experiences, Stone aligned the memory of the scary events of that night by positioning it within the familiar geography of his everyday life: Filbert Street in Leicester was once the site of the Leicester Football Club stadium. The veteran attempts to make sense of the world, to organise the uncanny geographies of fear in reassuring terms – the rowdy crowds on match day. There are so many stories like Norman Stone's, and they are all emplaced in real or make-believe places.

Resisting and fighting were intrinsically geographical practices that left behind a distinct material culture and a unique way of organising place in memory. In veterans' recollection, things and places are turned on and off, hidden or foregrounded to express one's passionate recollections or to fence off the obstinate refusal to admit one's guilt. In engaging with places of conflict and resistance, in a sense we do not just learn about places and things that happened and left a trace, however. We also get to understand life through its ruination; we come to comprehend the world through its coming apart (see DeSilvey 2006). These are the affective geographies we have to work with, or, to stay with Heidegger, the spatial 'moods' operating in the conscious and subconscious experience of those who remember. The dark forests of wartime memory are riddled with booby traps, ruins – and booby traps in ruins; they are traversed by paths that can lead one to frightening places (see the haunting case study at the end of Chapter 3, or A.'s removal of his past self from the site of a massacre in Chapter 4). The past's otherness – or its strange, misaligned likeness, as in our case – can be moving and unsettling.

If wartime memories are a forest, I have made my way through it thanks to the insights and emotions of the veterans; I followed the clues left by those who wrote about their own journeys after the war, and the more painful footsteps of the unfortunate ones who mapped out with mortal wounds on their bodies their one-off, one-way journey. Predictably, being guided by veterans meant that I have often ended up nowhere. I do not use the metaphor of the forest simply for effect: woodlands feature insistently in the memories of the civil war. The forest, I was told a number of times, was 'very good for hiding bodies'. Dead or alive? I asked. Both, one answered. *Our living bodies, and, of course, dead bodies.* To 'orientate' and map out the ways in which veterans navigate the treacherous forests of war, I draw on their personal travelogues through two mutually informing themes: the making of places and the unmaking of places. 'Unmaking' practices include the deliberate destruction and obliteration by an enemy faction, the site of massacres, and the deliberate tactical concealment of the places the resistance fighters passed through and dwelt in. Unmaking also refers to the conscious and subconscious refusal of acknowledging a place.

6.2 The making of places: opportunity and consolation

Temporality, indissolubly tied to place, was suspended in a configuration of embodiments and perceptions unique to the experience of war and conflict. Time was, for some fighters, an entirely relative concept; despoiled of quotidian rituals and knowledges, days and nights became an unstable roller-coaster ride of surreptitious escapes, enforced silences and uneasy and exhausting mobility. Time left its mark on the fighting body: wounds and hunger, bruises and fleas, sleep deprivation and exhaustion were part of everyday life, and marked days and weeks in the partisans' non-linear microcosm of attacking, moving and hiding; attacking, moving and hiding, and so forth. So for 'Ico' Lowenthal (2013: 124):

> In the bizarre life we led there was a partial disconnect from any sense of time. When I read again my notes and the very concise diary I kept back then I realize that the entries are not dated. To be honest we were only vaguely aware of the date on any given day. We lived day by day and we eventually only learnt that it was Christmas or Easter from the civilian population's celebrations.

A relative and fluid temporality was a fundamental aspect of the transient and precarious existence of the armed resistance groups. It makes sense, after all: when you have no knowledge of where you will spend the next night, the day of the week becomes irrelevant.

Fear and displacement are qualities of the everyday materiality of many partisans' memories; the sense of being a little lost or risking to make a 'wrong turn' especially haunted the first few weeks and months in the resistance. These feelings shaped how equipment and weapons were used: more cautiously at first, more spontaneously as violence took its toll on the fighters' habitus. With time and through communal effort, partisans started getting used to the mountains and to their newly dangerous and transitory lifestyle. While the fighters explored these landscapes and worked out the best ways to adapt them to their need to hide, rest, move and plan, they also effectively learnt anew about the natural world, and renegotiated their relations with these environments accordingly.

From woodland to ravine, from cave to mountain peak, partisans had to comprehend what they were dealing with (De Nardi 2011; see Favero 2003: 72 ff.). To 'comprehend' means to encompass, to become one with, hence the 'com' (Latin *cum*) prefix. The resistance had to quickly work out the best strategy of spatial interaction. Their initial struggle to know places must have been similar to the early stages of learning a foreign language: the struggle to understand and decipher signs and sounds, the difficulties in making oneself understood, and the effort of generating a sense of increasing comfort – trying to feel at ease. Some veterans, on the other hand, claimed that this process was not particularly taxing.

Others adapted very quickly to new surroundings and learnt to get by. For example, Giuseppe Giust (who originated from a mountain region) enjoyed nature and 'being in those places. I adapted to the landscape very easily – I think it's ... that we were so young'. By contrast, Giorgio Vicchi talked of a longer, more involved negotiation of being and environment:

> We [Partisans from Bologna] knew nothing. We learnt by making mistakes, constantly, to learn, to find out about things. [. . .] A march that would have taken ... a shepherd ... one hour, took us seven or eight. We took the wrong turns, went down the wrong path. Once you made a mistake, you never repeated it ..., because you created landmarks ... you learnt as you went

along. Place names helped a lot, they were essential. [Laughs] If you read my war diary, you will find that I wrote the place names all wrong – they were dialect names, so you can imagine! [. . .] You see, I had never actually read or seen these place names, for to write them down . . . God forbid! So I had created my own geography, with my own place names, and I went by that.

(Interview 20 December 2010)

Interestingly, Giorgio uses concepts like 'learning' and 'geographies' to articulate how he incrementally engaged with these environments. Other protagonists tried to express the gradual ways that they came to know, address and move though environments (through the environment's affordances, perhaps; see Ingold 2000; also see Pink 2009). Giuseppe Taffarel talked of developing a 'sixth sense' as a partisan while moving across landscapes:

Then you all stop, and I proceed almost creeping forward like a cat, nice and quiet. I stop by a bush from which something that looks like a rifle neck protrudes. So I walk around and I throw a rock at the bush. Nothing moved, but that would've been the case if someone was hiding in it . . . it turned out to be a large branch. But that's what I mean by having your six senses in constant alert. You did develop a sixth sense for danger, you know.

(Interview 4 August 2011)

For Taffarel, natural elements that may once have been perceived as mundane and everyday were now appraised for their potential to hide enemies. In other instances, landscapes that mountain-dwelling partisans used to associate with familial events or their work in the high pastures suddenly took on a new, sinister veneer of uncertainty and danger. Similarly, Italian resisters' sensations of fear and uncertainty were highest in places of apparent safety, such as an inn, haystack or barn. The enemy routinely reconnoitred these places, on the lookout for weary partisans taking a stealthy nap. Here, partisans were most vulnerable to betrayal. Giorgio recalled how they knew when danger was coming: 'We knew the countryside very well, every hedge and fence. And if we heard the sound of a car, well, back then in those remote country lanes the only cars belonged to Germans. So you ducked away!' (Interview 5 December 2011).

Buildings of any kind, even barns and foresters' huts in remote locations, were at best passing places – transient locales to be occupied for a few hours or nights at most, or used for hurried brigade meetings. Offering hospitality to partisans, meanwhile, could lead to the death of civilians. Lorenzo Altoè told me:

There was a peasant house we walked in to ask for a glass of water; meanwhile the German trucks that intercepted us before arrived at the farmhouse, and the lady, desperate and terrified, let us out of the scullery; if we had been found there the bastards would burn their house down . . . so I run [sic] out the window. Afterwards I learned that the Germans had exacted revenge for the two comrades we had shot earlier and they ... killed the two farmers who had taken us in, poor things. Horrific.

(Interview 18 December 2011)

For several reasons, buildings were no places to linger; they did not afford rest or safety for their owners or their illicit guests. Partisan 'Lupo' Zanolin's memoir evoked the sixth sense and sensory sharpness needed to survive in the everyday:

> A house across the square from the church had been turned into a prison. The Germans slept in a room by the cells and a sentinel went back and forth under the portico. He went fifty metres until a barrier and then turned back. The Germans wore shoes with studded soles that made a loud noise. You would hear the sound of their footsteps loud and clear. So we waited to hear his footsteps moving away from us.
> (Zanolin and Brescacin 2013: 31)

Let us for a moment imagine the reverberating sound of German footsteps moving away: the tangible multisensoriality of storytelling reveals to what extent the soundscape of guerrilla and resistance was a fundamental aspect of the fight (see also Classen 1993). The places of clandestine resistance were marked by furtive silence, as Renato explained in his interview:

> Then I hear voices coming from the other direction, from the village. Some spoke aloud, saying strange things. We partisans, we never spoke aloud, and this ruckus made me suspicious and agitated.
> (Interview 24 September 2011)

In this case, the loud voices announced the long hoped-for outcome of the war: the Allies had arrived in Montaner on 24 April 1945.

The spatial habitus of the resistance, the Fascists and Germans exceeded a purely tactical dimension. Contemporary accounts remember how the partisans literally '*merged with the land* where they were born, and for which they are fighting, while the Fascists are regularly described as outsiders in league with the foreign invaders, even though they, too, may have been local natives' (Portelli 1997: 132). The mobile, untraceable and elusive presence/absence of the resistance fighters unnerved the Germans. Hence, in Field Marshal Kesselring's memoir, we read that the Wehrmacht found the enemy's tactics disorientating:

> In small groups or singly they ran amok without restraint, doing their nefarious work everywhere, in the mountains, in the Po valley, in woods and on roads, under cover of darkness or fog – but never openly.
> (Kesselring 1954: 271)

In one of the most infamous battles of the European front, Monte Cassino (17 January – 18 May 1944), numberless Germans and Allied soldiers lost their lives in a carnage of tactical failures and sheer horror. For Germans and most Allied soldiers, the frontline at Cassino was something they had heard about from comrades but not experienced until they were deployed there. In his interview, German paratrooper Robert Frettlohr described his 'blind' voyage to the frontline: when his division was moved to Cassino at the start of February 1944, German paratrooper Frettlohr admits he did not know where Cassino was or anything about the place; he did, however, have a notion that the valley of Monte Cassino might be a gateway to Rome, presumably located on the 'other side' of Italy (that is, on the Tyrrhenian coast). They got there, and what they found was worse than anything they could have imagined.

In a letter home dated 12 March 1944, German soldier Helmut K. recalled his adventures in a foreign Italian landscape:

> I found myself on a reconnaissance mission, a solitary wander hour after hour. I hunted for Partisans, and came to know the land and its stormy beauties. I got to know the people, with their good and bad sides. I sat by an Italian fireplace with the family of a lawyer with fugitives, and we talked about family, kids, gardens and houses, and about music and culture, and I found friends in this cultured family – my Italian is coming along nicely.
>
> (Tagebuchsarchiv Accession no. 3261, 1 p. 42)

In carving out a semblance of domesticity, Helmut tried to make himself at home, to feel like he belonged by that bourgeois Italian fireside. His interaction with the locals became an opportunity to create a little serene space within a hostile nation peopled with stealthy assassins.

When anti-Fascists and Italian soldiers dodging the Nazi draft dashed to 'the hills' upon the Nazi occupation after Armistice Day, many of these individuals arrived in upland spaces they had seldom, if ever, encountered before. They were also thrown together with people of differing motivations, politics and backgrounds. For many, this was a disconcerting experience laced with feelings of dislocation, alienation and fear. Place-making would be not only desirable but a tactic necessary to survival. Out of loneliness and fear, one created one's own little space. Displaced fighters, fleeing prisoners of war and Allied stragglers experienced disorientation and placelessness, eloquently and movingly explored and recounted in various resistance narratives and war memoirs. In the semi-autobiographical novel *Annarosa Non Muore* (*Annarosa Won't Die*), for example, Giovanni Melanco (2002) tells of an encounter between his character, Alfredo, who is familiar with the local mountains, and Leo, a partisan from

Bologna in the Po valley; the latter reveals his profound unease in the unfamiliar surroundings:

> You have to help me – I feel lost without you. . . Where I come from, mountains don't exist, and all these highs and lows, valleys and hills and mountains disorient me, dizzy me, and I don't know which way to go.
>
> (Melanco 2002: 85)

By contrast, Alfredo responded thus:

> I feel at home! We roam the mountains I know well. We make for *my* mountains over there now. The thought makes me feel free, happy . . . On top of a hill, we stop in the shadow of a thick hedge. Leo, left behind, calls out to me (. . .) 'I can't take any more uphill climbing, I am going to cough up a lung . . . you know I don't understand these mountains of yours. Take me to the plains and I will be your guide.
>
> (Melanco 2002: 86–87, my emphasis)

Of course, the retreat to the mountains constituted an extremely complex experience, as the above quotes suggest. Mountainous contexts inevitably affected how the resistance operated and orientated and guided partisan life in the everyday. The relative freedom from Nazi-Fascist control in uplands allowed different forms of social organisation, rules and relations, but the business of guaranteeing shelter, food and safety – place-making – was more time-consuming (Behan 2009). Also, for some partisans, time in the mountains could be transient: Ginsborg (1990) notes how during the harsh winter of 1944–45, when the Allies had controversially advised the partisans to 'stand down' for a few months and their enemies launched manhunts through the forests, most partisans retreated from the mountain to the better conditions of the foothills and plains anyway. Nevertheless, the hills became the symbolic site where the resistance was focused – and this symbolism endured through the post-war years.

Conversely, some Germans found the landscapes of northern Italy sufficiently familiar and similar to their own homeland that they felt at ease, so to speak, and appreciated natural beauty spots. On 29 September 1943, Otto A. wrote positively about the area in which he found himself with his formation – the northern village of Santa Lucia.

> Here the landscape and countryside are manicured and rather beautiful. The fields are tidy, the orchards plentiful and rich, and the farmhouses and country houses are pretty; in fact *they would not be out of place in Germany*. The women

and girls all wear make-up but look clean and nice. I have already seen many beautiful ladies here. The men around here scrub up well too. Children are clean and well behaved – I have also seen several pretty kids.

(Tagebuchsarchiv Accession no. 802/II, my emphasis)

The emphasis in the above excerpt is mine: I wanted to highlight how even some Italian places and things – characterised by pretty, tidy houses – could recall home. After all, successful place-making practices live and thrive in the realm of make-believe, affording the opportunity to carve out one's own place in uncertain times (Ingold 2000; Navaro-Yashin 2012).

6.3 The unmaking of places

In February 1945, a few months after joining the German Wehrmacht as an Italian volunteer (for undisclosed reasons) at the age of twenty, Fulvio Aliboni decided to desert. He left behind a written account of his extraordinary and rocambolesque escape (n.d.). After sneaking away from his camp in the middle of the night, Fulvio spent two days hiding, waiting to make his next move. After twenty hours without drinking, he became very thirsty. Under cover of darkness, he carried on for one more day, passing through villages and towns. Incredibly, his escape was facilitated by the fact that he was still wearing a German uniform. Among the pages of his memoir, we find a poignant reminder of the extraordinary and alienating materiality of ruination when Fulvio described the destruction of a house where he had previously found shelter. In mourning the building where he had found brief respite, the fugitive wrote of the surrounding countryside as a bleak theatre of destruction. The idea of the *uncanny* also populates the pages of Fulvio's memoir: all the villages he passed were deserted, dead still in the summer heat, and he felt as if he was encountering 'fairy-tale hamlets'. That is a fugitive's perspective: we can almost *feel* the anguish of a runaway person in those pages, almost delirious after days without water and human company; the chronicle of Fulvio's personal odyssey is thick with excruciatingly alienating and terrifying detail.

Indeed, when we consider the unmaking and unravelling of certainties, becoming alienated and estranged in one's own native place must be one of the most unsettling experiences. The uncanniness of feeling out of place emerges from most veterans' memories. Echoing Freud and Jentsch, Moshenska has aptly commented that the uncanny is 'the unusual interplay of the familiar/safe and the unfamiliar/frightening that it embodies. For Freud a common manifestation of the uncanny is the disconcerting effect of familiar things encountered in alien forms or contexts' (2012: 1198). For van Alphen (1997: 201), the uncanny is circumscribed to enclosed spaces and bound up with confinement, silence and loneliness. In this context, I argue instead that movement and transience were the triggers of a sense of upended or warped reality: the suddenly constant enforced movement between, to and from places in itself felt *wrong*. Corresponding to a disrupted and unknown spatial organisation and (mis)orientation was, by and large, a skewed temporality and relative timelessness. The fighters' days were marked by attacks, and the dates that loomed large for partisans who were in contact with the Allies were those of the launches of equipment, food and ammunition: beyond creature comforts, the essentials of survival.

But let us return to the beginning: 8 September 1943. Armistice Day for the Italians. Capitulation day for the Allies. Day of Wrath for the Germans. After a life-changing event, like Italy's sudden change of sides in the conflict, 'a new experiential knowledge about the vulnerability of solid objects, like bodies . . . and buildings, . . . transformed their experience of seeing, feeling, and moving in the world' (Wool 2013: 421). A vernacular of terror crept over once familiar places, penetrating the local affective geographies and disrupting familiar (and familial) practices from within. The themes of placelessness and dystopia following foreign military occupation has been a constant feature of this book because, arguably, it has always constituted a potent leitmotif of memory. The sense of losing one's home while staying put haunts many – we can begin to glimpse the feeling of not-quite-loss by thinking of Merleau-Ponty's metaphor of the phantom limb sending confusing signals to an amputee's brain . . . the eerie itch which reminds one that things are not quite as they ought to be (see the next chapter).

The fear and threats occurring on a daily basis transformed the partisans and activists' geographical *habitus* and the networks of places and affiliations that they had enacted before the war. The conflict dismantled their place in the local affective topographies. The old politics of belonging or exclusion no longer held true; their task-scapes (after Ingold 2000) were riddled with booby traps. But what was the alternative? Interestingly, a bourgeois perspective on the emplacement of the war would have differed greatly from that of farmhands, mountain dwellers and working-class urban individuals. Hence, educated middle-class Emanuele Artom's resistance experience took a different form to that of rural partisans such as Aldo, Renato and others. Refined city dweller Artom wrote in an entry dated Friday, 10 December 1943:

> Today I brought him [a friend] to my house. As he entered the first room on the ground floor, where, if truth be told, I never live, he said: 'I would love to have a camera because some time in the future, if we are still alive, we will have a laugh looking at the rat-infested dumps where we've ended up' and, seeing that I tried to defend my lodgings, he continued 'if they'd told you that you would have to live here two years ago, you would've died of fright'.
>
> (Artom and Schwarz 2008: 100)

It was unusual enough for a partisan to live in a house, but the particularity of local circumstances dictated that the partisan was to occupy a derelict house for a few weeks, and thus inspired amused pity in his equally bourgeois associate. In this instance, the light-heartedness of the episode is darkened by the fact that Emanuele would not live to look back on his experience or indeed make light of it. Afterwards, the dismal ruination of a building he briefly inhabited would surely seem heavenly in comparison to the Fascist and Nazi interrogation rooms where the youth would suffer unspeakable tortures (Artom and Schwarz 2008: 5). Did Emanuele remember or long for those decaying walls while in captivity? Are the wounds on Emanuele's body not his own intimate geography of war – his broken body on the gallows the final stop in his short journey?

6.3.1   Home, falling apart

When war and conflict unmake place, home can become a hornet's nest, and the safety one felt before becomes irrelevant – at risk, or, in the worst-case scenario, gone for good. Nedda Zanfranceschi, the teenage partisan we first met in Chapter 3, commented on the destruction of her hometown:

> After the bombardments the people of Treviso lived in terror. Even the school was in ruins, you know, and the station . . . the whole city centre, up in smoke. Everyone down in the shelters! Something like the Twin Towers. But so pointless. How cruel the English were- how ferocious, bombing us like that. Why, asked everyone? Couldn't they leave the partisans to blow up trains and factories?
>
> (Interview 13 October 2010)

Nedda orientated her tale around the familiar earthworks of her young everyday geography: the school, the station. After decades, she still blames 'the English' for the sudden loss of her world. At the same time, places of traditional safety and comfort became threatening and dangerous given these changing contexts. Lavinia F. told me how her home and village, previously places of refuge, became perilous sites where partisans were particularly vulnerable:

> How did I feel? In constant danger, hunted, stalked, that's how. I felt threatened by [collaborating] Italians as well as the Germans [. . .] I felt uneasy anywhere near or in the village . . . it was full of enemies. I felt unsafe in my own home because I feared being followed. Spied upon, on my way down from the woods . . . After the missions I kept looking over my shoulder, always, always.
>
> (Interview 4 December 2010)

Figure 6.2 The remains of a church where the SS slaughtered the civilians of Marzabotto, south of Florence, between 5 and 9 October 1944.

Source: Wikicommons

The home could become the setting of something much worse: violence could encroach into the domestic space and disrupt the familiar geography of the domestic sphere. Margherita Ianelli, twenty-two years old in 1944, lived in the tiny mountain hamlet of Marzabotto in the Monte Sole hills south of Florence – the location of one of the most infamous German civilian atrocities in Italy (Cooke 2000; Baldissara and Pezzino 2009). Here, the SS-Panzer-Aufklärungsabteilung 16 led by Walter Reder slaughtered some 770 civilians (forty-five were toddlers under two years of age) and terrorised the few survivors who escaped. Margherita recalled that on the night of 4 October 1944, an unexpected gunfight broke out between the Germans and the local partisans – despite the fact that she, like others, had been convinced that the partisans 'were no longer there'.

> After five terrifying days cooped up in a cellar shelter, the soldiers allowed us to go back home. What we found at home did nothing to relieve our fear. On my bed we found a soldier, he'd been dead for days; outside my room there was another soldier, asking everyone who went in or out for water; in the kitchen, pools of congealed blood and broken glass. We had no idea what had happened but of course, with what came later [*the massacre*], we forgot about small things like these.
> (Ianelli n.d.)

In recounting their journey through the forest of remembrance, several veterans vividly relived the physical discomfort felt in certain locations. I could tell, from the way they suddenly became animated, sitting up, gesticulating, that they were trying to recreate that other frightening world in the comfortable room we sat in. Giorgio Vicchi and Renato Pizzol told me how the clandestine nature of the resistance entailed fear of displacement and a sense of the world starting to fall apart around you; and I think that that fear equally affected local individuals newly anxious in familiar landscapes, and people from further afield finding those environments intimidating.

As the rank and file of the resistance grew, anti-Fascists from mountain communities witnessed the arrival of newcomers at the same time as they too had to decide whether and how to resist. For a partisan from the Cansiglio region, the reconfigurations embedded in the resistance markedly changed his local landscapes:

> I knew the Cansiglio forest very well . . . [and] the topography of the forest is second nature. We [Partisans] had a kind of hut in Cadolten, and we moved through the *casere*, night after night, from one *casera* to the next, always moving . . . I had spent my childhood and adolescence in the forest. Very different business, doing the Partisan thing there! [. . .] I mean I couldn't feel at ease anymore.
> (Interview 15 January 2011)

The war had perverted Aldo's established dwelling practices; the Armistice upended his world, and now he had to go about *his* landscapes performing disturbing and unsettling tasks. Another site of intense alienation looming large in the new vernacular of terror was prison. There is no room in this chapter to devote sufficient attention to the geography of incarceration for military and political crimes linked to the resistance, but here I encompass prison in the remit of liminal spaces in which some bodies belong. More to the point, the war and occupation opened up the negative space of the prison to those who would otherwise never set foot in one – be it as prisoners or visitors. Fifteen-year old Nedda Zanfranceschi felt utterly out of place in the Fascist prison cell she ended up in due to her activity as a messenger and aide to the resistance.

> I was put in prison a second time in December 1944 – this time for a month, for suspected resistance activities. I shared a cell with two prostitutes and some thieves. It was, simply put, a nightmare. I slept on a rag on the floor, and I was so scared of the bombardments. The thieves luckily were local women, good women, and they recognised me for what I was – a terrified little girl. They made sure that the syphilis-infested prostitutes did not get too close to me. *I was clearly out of place in that prison cell!* Most days the prison master came in and shouted, Good grief, girly – remind me again what are you doing here?
> (Interview 14 October 2010, my emphasis)

My emphasis in the passage above indicates the incongruous, dystopian experience of an innocent girl trapped in the corrupt adult space of the prison with tainted individuals (prostitutes) and criminals. There were, then, some places where female bodies belonged, and places where, by society's conventions at the time, they did not. Not only were women who participated in the armed resistance perceived as out of place, vixens and amoral; there were places in the everyday vernacular of the war where they would not be seen as 'fitting in'. In her memoir, Wilma De Paris (2003: 81) recalled such a situation, when she found herself alone in Belluno before a mission on a dark, gloomy morning in the middle of winter:

> I knew that grappa warms you up and thought about going into a café. I had never been in a café or a bar before, not even to order a coffee, because I was shy and ashamed of being seen. What could I do? But I braced myself, went into this bar and ordered a shot of grappa. The barman looked me up and down, but he served me without saying a word. I sipped the harsh spirit slowly.

The café bar, a traditionally male space in Mediterranean cultures, would be patronised by married women and couples but lone girls were observed, at best, with condescending curiosity – even in the relatively more emancipated north of Italy. Wilma's reluctance to enter a café to procure a glass of Dutch courage was met with pre-empted curiosity and judgement by local men as she sipped the strong spirit.

Later in the war, when the Germans retreated from Florence and started pushing northwards towards the Gothic Line (the frontline), they left devastation in their wake. The German retreat first towards Fiesole and then onto the Gothic Line is remembered by Sonia Ciapetti (2007) as an awesome and terrifying spectacle. A diary entry describes in vivid terms the chaotic and sensorially saturated materiality of a retreat unfolding as a motley, makeshift assemblage of donkeys, carts, horses, lorries, cars, bicycles, cannons, motorbikes and any manner of moving vehicle. The events unravelled to the sound of barked orders and desperate yells to men and beasts. The chaos, seemingly endless, lasted the whole night. Sonia then commented on the destruction left in the wake of the German retreat: the explosions destroying the city's noble, ancient streets and the old fragile bridges on the Arno. She personally surveyed the damage:

> I went to explore the devastation, and by walking on the piles of debris I felt like I was perpetrating one more act of violence against the remains of stone and wood, the materials so lovingly and laboriously carved and sculpted by our forebears.
>
> (Ciapetti 2007: 64)

6.3.2 The unlikely comfort of the uplands

If persecuted in their villages and towns, the partisans had the option to retreat to the relative safety of the hills. Dissidents and activists would often leave their homes in order to ensure the safety of their families and loved ones. Once away from the perils of one's treacherous neighbourhoods, however, the lives of activists were exacerbated by the transient, nomadic lifestyle in the mountains. Veterans tell remarkable tales of endless movement and of the efforts to erase traces of their presence to protect the civilians who helped them.

> Sudden interruption – Enemy Cossack Troops are reported to be in San Francesco which is kms away, and held by Garibaldini. We have packed up radio and all kit and are ready, if necessary, to flit. The old woman in whose house I have a room is nearly in tears and thinks it will be burned to the ground. But we will leave no trace of our lodgement. I don't particularly like the idea of running tonight, it's started to rain again, and the radio makes it no joke.
>
> (Tolson 2007: 110)

The experience of leaving home to embrace partisan life could be harsh. Some could not quite cope with it. Giuseppe Giust recounted:

> I felt a little anxious, but not as much as one of my friends. We climbed this hill and he realised he was so far from his family and familiar surroundings on this strange hilltop, he started crying saying that he missed his family, and his dad was sick and needed him. We told him that if he felt that way he shouldn't stay and he should not be ashamed to go back home. Which he did. I don't want to say his name now 'cause he was taunted, after the war, well, some [partisans?] called him a coward.
>
> (Interview 20 December 2010)

Movements and transfers mainly took place at night and, predictably, several veterans recounted their difficulties in adapting to this practice. Most young Italians joining the resistance had until then experienced and lived in comfortable (if humble) family homes or shared student lodgings in university cities. Most were unaccustomed to travelling across wild mountainscapes, to daily marches and to sleeping rough (and briefly) where and when they could. By contrast, Allied SOE officer John Ross reported that in his recollection, many British field agents were less troubled by their sleeping conditions: unlike many of the partisans, the Brits were acquainted with army life and before that, he added, with tough conditions at boarding schools. Those factors made the British more adaptable to a punitive life in the field (interview 3 December 2010), whereas many Italians were upset by an endless mobility that made 'home' seem ever more intangible and further away. Some likened moving around so frequently to the life of vagrants. Lowenthal (2015: 124) wrote that:

> Our vagrant life, consisted of sleeping in the woods, cooking our food in abandoned huts, and all the while we were covered in lice and fleas. We washed when we could, in a stream, and almost always without soap. If we got ill or injured it was pretty nigh impossible to have access to medical aid or supplies.

The themes of alienation and loneliness in the mobile life of the guerrilla fighter surfaced repeatedly through many of the partisans' interviews and memoirs. Aldo De Bin remembered how:

> At night we marched for kilometres on end. During the day we could rest a little. Mostly in casere, if the owners were on our side willing to run the risk and shelter us . . . Even so, we were still anxious, on edge. [. . .] There was so much loneliness, especially at night. You thought of your previous life, how lovely and peaceful and calm and happy it was, you know, being at home.
> (Interview 4 August 2010)

Beside and beyond the heroic 'myth of the resistance', therefore, we find another set of memories that outline a more mundane daily grind that could be fearful and uncomfortable, and left partisans struggling, exhausted and physically debilitated. Giorgio Vicchi wrote of the alienation inherent in constant movement, as well as the physical strains:

> a long and strenuous march . . . after 13 hours en route, a blizzard catches us out . . . we carry on regardless in an exhausting march lasting all night. . . . The shattering march had some really difficult moments. The woods, and the snow, in places one and a half metres tall, have hindered recognition of the right path.
> (Vicchi 1984: 495)

6.4 Searching for invisibility: stealth and secrecy in everyday materialities

Resistance life was precarious. The core idea of guerrilla warfare is that mobility and invisibility are key. To the sedentary and visible presence of Germans and Fascists corresponded the mobile elusiveness of the resistance. The fighters must leave no traces leading to their occupation of a cave, a barn or a cellar – the lives of selfless villagers or farmers depended on their discretion. The partisans, therefore, had to train themselves to pass through spaces and places undetected. This strategy meant leaving the landscape undisturbed, and cleaning up after themselves as thoroughly as possible – unmaking their transient worlds on the go.

The nomadic dimension of resisting, although often mentioned in diaries, memoirs and oral history interviews, has been largely excluded from substantial historical studies of the phenomenon – as if the precarious existence of groups of men and women did not play a hugely important role in their identities, in the way they lived and identified themselves in relation to others. The unmaking of places entailed the obliteration of material culture: in tracing their own invisibility, the fighters had to erase the material traces they left behind – from food remains and used bandages to paraphernalia and excreta. It was essential that the Fascists and Germans did not suspect that they had dwelled in any one place, lest they start mapping out likely places of shelter and makeshift HQs that would likely be used by a partisan group on other occasions.

For the Germans, the stealth and cunning of the resistance were a source of constant anxiety. Sources report that the unnerving work of the partisans immobilised operations, sometimes for days on end, especially when resistance groups managed to blow up bridges and thereby impeded the movement of heavy artillery tanks and lorries. Here the material culture of Fascists and Germans differed the most from that of the resistance: whereas the former two embodied traditional warfare and deployed bulky, highly visible and structured logistics, weaponry and modes of transportation, the partisans made use of makeshift shelters and meeting places and carried light weapons, using donkeys (whenever possible) as a mode of transportation, but mostly walking to get from one place to the next (see also Ingold 1993).

Unlike their Fascist and certainly their German counterparts, who dwelled or settled into modern dwellings in urban and suburban areas, in houses and apartments confiscated from Jews or expropriated from local families (but also often shared with the property's original occupants), the underground fighters adopted an almost pastoral and decidedly anachronistic way of life. Members of the resistance had to relinquish the modern comforts of a sedentary life rhythm for a highly mobile lifestyle dictated by contingency. They had to adopt an antediluvian, archaic lifestyle – with no telephones, almost no electricity, only candle light and paraffin lamps to read and play cards by, huddling by the odd fireplace to keep warm and dry their rain- or snow-sodden clothing and boots. When overnighting in the open air, the making of bonfires would lead to detection and certain capture, so long nights were spent shivering in makeshift sleeping bags.

By contrast, most Italian Fascists carried on living in the same exact material surroundings as before, except perhaps when they were transferred from a big city to the countryside or from the south to the north. In that case, a brusque shift in everyday materiality and environmental surroundings also dictated the need for a certain degree of adaptation for the Italian Fascists, who often lamented the primitive way of life of the mountain folks. As a rule, despite the comfort of often elegant lodgings in historic palazzos and villas, the Germans struggled to adapt to the Italian surroundings due to a series of crucial temporal and cultural factors.

Before 8 September 1943, Germans and Italians had, to an extent, shared in the common materiality of a war against the Allies, both troubled by aerial bombings by the RAF and US Air Force – both targets, and both running scared. After the Armistice, Germans in Italy became enemies almost overnight and had to learn how to protect themselves from a hostile populace (except in certain German-speaking pockets of the far northeast) and from the cunning aggression of the newly formed resistance bands.

Some fighters and most messengers inhabited competing and parallel places and social roles. Those who were able to pose as Fascist soldiers by day and partisans by night, like Lorenzo Altoè, tell extraordinary tales of literally inhabiting two worlds. He went back and forth between a Fascist division and a resistance band, providing invaluable intelligence to the partisans. He admitted to feeling amused when his commander in chief warned him to watch out for partisan activity in certain spots and to 'keep his eyes open' (interview 18 December 2011).

The ability to 'split oneself in two' was not only a life saver: others morphed into different personas intermittently and even in between partisan roles according to circumstances. Enrico 'Ico' Lowenthal, the young Jewish partisan whose false identification papers pronounced him a year younger than his actual age and of Italian stock, was able to rejoin his family living incognito in a tiny mountain hamlet after months spent in a leadership role in a resistance band. At home, he shed his uniform and regained his identity as Enrico Lamberti, seventeen-year-old high school student. 'After a change of clothes I morphed again into little Enrico Lamberti' (Lowenthal 2015: 104). 'Ico' was then able to hide in plain sight in the hamlet for a few days, even participating in communal events and rubbing shoulders with the high honchos of the Fascist rank and file. On one occasion, the elite marine squad Decima Mas' orchestrator Prince Junio Valerio Borghese looked on approvingly as Ico, along with the village teenagers, shovelled snow and ice from the streets (Lowenthal 2015: 105).

The unmaking of places could also take place under more sinister circumstances. The Germans tended to burn to the ground any edifice and village where the resistance had been active, or supported in any way by local inhabitants. Back then, destruction and dereliction served as stark reminders to the populace that disobedience brought about annihilation. The destruction the Germans left in their wake bore witness to a melancholy absent presence, that of once-lived-in landscapes of resistance, voices and laughter and talks still resonating in hollowed-out barns and shuttered windows. When we engage with the remnants of the war, we encounter 'unsettling ghosts of place' (Bell 1997: 827), caught up in burnt-out parlours and incinerated churches in an 'endlessly present past' (de Certeau 1988: 37). Conflict memory is enmeshed in everyday 'practices of incorporation' and 'practices of inscription' (Hills 2013: 381). These entanglements link our present-day places and contexts to our pasts and to those of the ancestors.

6.5 The marginality of bodies, the liminality of the river

The river Sile played a macabre role in the history of the civil war in the locality of Roncade (Treviso). In 1944 and 1945, the river became a tableau of death and reprisal to showcase the violent killing of Fascists and partisans, indiscriminately set to float downstream in allegorical intimations of death and ruination. The local priest, Monsignor Citton, is one of the sources recounting the macabre role played by the river in the local geographical imagination.

> The ambushes began – during the day unknown, distressed-looking faces were seen around town. But at night, there were ambushes in the outskirts, especially at crossroads. Usually the partisans came from Monastier or the Sile lowlands. The Sile became a flowing cemetery for thousands of victims tied to rafts, tortured and naked, nailed to planks, decapitated. The riverside communities, those living on the river banks, they pushed the victims to the centre of the current so that they could be washed away to the sea. The river was a catwalk . . . for the macabre parade of murder victims of both political colours, as a warning to villagers along the Sile bank. If at first the bodies had been thrown into the Sile out of practical reasons, the next use of the river was to violate and mock the bodies: the trend took off and horrible, disgusting death allegories appeared on the water.
>
> (Citton n.d.: 5)

According to local witnesses U.P and S.P. (2012: unpublished interview with Gianni Favero), the admonitory display exceeded its purpose to dissuade locals to get involved in partisan fighting or reprisals against the resistance; instead, the almost mediaeval spectacle of death went beyond the representational in the channelling of something abject, primaeval and powerful: the quasi-biblical destruction of life and mercy in the areas affected by the corpse 'parades'. The *memento mori* would shake up local imaginations, especially when the victims became indistinguishable, frozen in a macabre parody of everyday acts such as playing cards or driving a vehicle. The enactment of death by the fighting contingencies served to remind the locals that they could be next. Citton continued,

> More and more corpses kept flowing by, in full view of the settlements along the banks, as mementoes for the peasants who were horrified and fascinated at first, but then got almost used to it towards the end. One day, six corpses of Fascists in uniform flowed by: their bodies fastened to the inn table where the partisans had caught them by surprise as they were playing cards; the partisan had then attached the cards to their dead fingers with barbed wire. Another time my brother saw three corpses, arranged like a horrible convoy, hands and feet fastened to the body in front of them, all with wooden planks under their

bellies to make sure they floated; and horrible placards, bearing slogans such as 'slow – bends ahead'. I think they were Fascists, but it could have been Partisans. Dead men of both sides became a common sight on our river.

(Citton n.d.: 5)

A witness recalled that 'I think they were Fascists, but they could have been partisans': the identity of the corpses had ceased to matter. The strategy of corpse disposal in the river had more serious consequences than traumatising the population: river contamination (Citton n.d.: 11) deprived the local inhabitants and their livestock of drinking water. In the intensity of the retelling, the conjured up tableaux do not imply distance: they feel very much present. The bodies of victims slowly polluted the waters as they unravelled the seams of the local dwelling perspective, corrupting the natural order of things. Yet, the witness also added, after a while even the villagers living right along the river banks 'got used' to the horrible spectacle. These stories are not descriptions, but rather relived sensory events, either of places and actions directly experienced by witnesses or paraphrased by local oral historian and journalist Favero. 'The threshold of discomfort and aversion . . . can also be a threshold to other ways of knowing' (DeSilvey 2006: 321). The materiality of the town and river in Roncade had been disrupted by the introduction of an otherworldly, abject element that destabilised and corrupted.

For better and for worse, the emplaced postmemory of the war events is still with us, seared in the act of remembering. There is no room here to unfold the complex affective afterlives of war zones and sites of fighting for veterans in the nuanced thoroughness they deserve. Yet I choose to take an optimistic stance towards their memories: even if towns like Roncade are unable to erase the horrors which once polluted its river, I like to think, as Giuseppe Giust suggested, that when young people visit the places and memorials of the conflict, they try to comprehend that ugly chapter in their country's history by trying to relive the partisans' experiences. Perhaps, as they walk about or take photographs, some of them ask themselves what they would have done if they had been in that situation: would they have joined the resistance?

6.6 Going back

One thing is certain: these places are not to be forgotten, despite some veterans' attempts to purge them from their memories. I conclude this chapter with a story from Robert Frettlohr's experience. The German, who had arrived in Monte Cassino for the first time on the way to a field hospital in February 1944, had been a prisoner of war in Britain and then settled in northwest England after his liberation. Frettlorh told interviewers from the Imperial War Museum about the time he eventually returned to Monte Cassino for a reunion some forty years after his experience there. The site's *presence* moved him to tears because it looked new and

Figure 6.3 Destroyed German vehicles in Monte Cassino, May 1944.

Source: Wikicommons

unfamiliar to him – the reason being that the reunion marked the second time he had seen the town of Cassino itself during the day. In the long months of the war, Frettlohr had only ever encountered the town and its environs at night. His unit used to hide in a rock shelter in daylight hours ('an artificial shelter, as the whole hill was of granite and you couldn't dig a hole in it'). The most moving thing for Frettlohr, apart from a view of the beautiful little town in broad daylight, was visiting the cemeteries of Monte Cassino: the site where German, French, Commonwealth and Italian soldiers rest together. 'Thousands of crosses under the sun. We were all young lads really. That's what hurts'. His soft crying was discreetly recorded by the tape, the cathartic unspooling of a decade-long affective build-up – leaving me wanting to comfort the man, but unable to from my position at a desk in the museum's research room in the year 2014.

In the preceding chapters, I have explored various material and embodied practices of life during the civil war and occupation, tracing the precarious geographies of emotional, sensory experiences and engagements. By telling Frettlohr' s story, I have demonstrated how emotionally close we can get to the worlds inhabited by veterans through the connective tissue of remembrance, affect and material culture. Like Frettlohr's nocturnal existence at Cassino, a mantle of invisibility (intentional and not) has been cast on dystopian memories of the war, but conflict affects endure. I have reviewed some of the ways in which the various actors in the civil war positioned themselves and others in space and place, paying attention to mechanisms of imagination, opportunity, disorientation and displacement.

Through an emphasis on the materiality of places for charting presences and absences, I have made a case for attending to the geography of conflict and its hidden, visible, official and non-official places of fighting and resistance in an interdisciplinary manner: in this case, a cultural-geographical perspective augments existing military historiographies in producing a more grounded, complex sense of what happened in these landscapes, and to whom. Memory is populated with smooth places of pleasant recollections as well as regions of silence redolent of other places, other bodies and other things lost in time. As a rule, identities and materialities had coincided with established affective geographies before Armistice Day, 8 September 1943, and then became disrupted, atomized and confusing afterwards. The day of Italian capitulation to the Anglo-Americans, I have argued, acted as a spatial as well as a temporal marker of change. The rents in the social and emotional fabric that followed this fracture would have lasting, indelible consequences for everyone.

7 The conclusion of a journey through regions of silence

> This is history. History which is determined by posterity, by those who are absent, with a judgement that can no longer change anything – the judgment by those who are not born of those who are dead.
>
> (Levinas, *Entre Nous*, 1998: 25)

By way of foreword

The title of this chapter takes its cue from Merleau-Ponty's (1996) description of the uncanny feeling of a phantom limb – the longing for something that is no longer there, even though we feel it still ought to be there. Here I use the term 'region of silence' to denote the underlying sense of loss experienced during the war, but also the lack of something, the absences *felt* in the course of the conflict. Echoing de Certeau, we might say that the writing of this book has been an attempt, on my part, to appease 'the dead who still haunt the present' (de Certeau 1988: 2); it does not, however, seek to offer them 'scriptural tombs' (de Certeau 1988); rather, it seeks to connect their past lives with our own. Without losing sight of the historical specificity of the Italian story within these pages, I have also sought to contextualise it (and myself, and my familial materiality) in a much wider-ranging web of resonance beyond the years of the civil war. I, too, have a place to tell some of this story, but the difficulty was knowing where to begin. The 'story' is bigger than I am, after all. So in the end, I focused my storytelling 'gaze' on a game-changing event: the Armistice of 8 September 1943, the date in which Italy switched sides. Using this event as a pivotal point to understand wartime experience, I set out to investigate the materiality of practices and processes that had previously been analysed as a political-military phenomenon. The precipitates of that momentous day reach into the present and future in a myriad of complex ways that there was no room to adequately unpick in this book.

7.1 Compassionate scholarship: using affect and postmemory towards a recognition of the uncanniness of civil war

In order to bring forth an explicitly experiential perspective of the Second World War in Italy, I have collected, conjoined, untangled, questioned and brought together a myriad of stories and attempted to understand them as ethnographic events in the present – as hauntings, filling the archive, interview room and the page with redolent materialities. War stories do not allow us to 'get over' them. Most of us seem to have, at least, a half-baked opinion about that war, but this level of becoming intimate with that history rarely percolates into academic books and journals. Stories of the Second World War matter: that is why we continue to care about the war today; we feel it is close to us still.

In writing about the poetics of conflict experience, I have been working closely with the Italian case study while occasionally stopping to consider the implication of the Italian events on the wider historical and anthropological epistemology of storytelling. It has often occurred to me that the questions I posed in the introduction to this volume and which inform its underlying line of inquiry seem eerily, if unsurprisingly, topical at the time of writing. I started wondering about things like: what is the social, cultural and emotional impact of foreign bodies moving through and across one's home turf? How does the idea of foreignness affect perceptions of persons and places? How do people cope with the regions of silence clustering and congealing around each other's strangeness and mutually constituted non-belonging? De Certeau has postulated that intelligibility can be established through a relation with the Other. But how? For Jentsch (1906: 4) 'the traditional, the usual and the hereditary is dear and familiar to most people, and . . . they incorporate the new and the unusual with mistrust, unease and even hostility'. All of those questions are of vital and urgent relevance to the reality of mass displacement and emigration brought about by the ongoing Middle Eastern crisis as I write. As we still worry about others' motives and compatibilities, it would seem that human nature and our ways of engaging with the worlds of others have not changed much since the Second World War.

We might say that the unnatural presences and longed-for absences in the material culture and memory of the war constitute regions of silence. The events following Italy's capitulation caused many to adopt the strange, unnatural role of runaway, clandestine fighter, spy or displaced person. In shifting to a transient and precarious existence, individuals would no doubt have noticed troubling little differences and absences in everyday life, trivial things that nonetheless made them feel out of place. In that sense, this book has covered vast swathes of such regions of silence. The epigram at the start of the chapter, moreover, reflects another phenomenologist's view of history as ineluctable and melancholy *post hoc*: a history populated with dead people and absences; a postmemory of trauma and hopelessness. But in this final chapter, I make the case that, on occasion, silences (and silencings) can be broken, and absences become present through our empathetic engagement. Let us start with the sources: Artom (2014: 112) summarised the atmosphere of the wider war, in its places and landscapes, thus:

> The frontline is here: on every turn of every road you might run into Fascists; at the back, there are the meadows, the woods, the trails where we try to hide. Partisans fall, the Fascists fall, every day the newspapers announce new massacres and the war proceeds over time slow and heavy as a huge monstrous snail, which leaves behind a large trail of blood.

His region of silence was the war as a whole – a landscape marred by the red trail of blood left by the giant snail of war, which would cut his life short in a horrific manner. The silent frontline passed through every road, slithering around every corner. Here a silence becomes embroiled in vanishing perceptions and eroding human compassion. It is a silence in which all of us, readers, protagonists and writer, have partaken, by letting ourselves be 'sucked in', thrown and troubled by the events narrated through the pages of this book. And yet I have tried, to the best of my ability, to let these pages be non-silent. In the following section, I use Primo Levi's resistance experience as a way into the ambiguity of civil war; here, a heady mixture of historical fact and rumour takes us into unchartered waters and unexpected places in memory.

7.1.1 An intermission: Levi, the partisan

The concept of the uncanny, which I have explored previously, can be exemplified by a story about Primo Levi: in this case, the uncanny arises when we are unexpectedly confronted with an element in our understanding of him which does not correspond to our concept of Primo Levi-ness. It is not widely known that Levi had been a resistance fighter before being deported to the Auschwitz death camp. His short spell with the Piemontese and Valdese resistance in Alpine northwest Italy (September to December 1943) had all but slipped through the cracks of historical memory until Sergio Luzzatto embarked on a mission to reconstruct Levi's contribution to the armed struggle against the Germans and the Fascists in his home region. Luzzatto's reason for investigating Levi the partisan has all to do with a fascination with the uncanny (as well as a desire for sensationalism, some have argued): his book revolves around an ambiguous line in Levi's chilling masterpiece, *The Periodic Table* (*Il Sistema Periodico*, 1975), in which the author compiles a series of vignettes about 'life' in the death camp. Among the stories narrated in the book is an autobiographical fragment in which Levi confessed to harbouring a '*segreto brutto*': an ugly secret.

In *The Periodic Table*, Levi hinted at an event that had occurred three days before his capture, when he still belonged to a partisan formation. Roughly translated in my own words from Italian (I do not presume to convey anything close to the haunting beauty of Levi's style), his confession went like this (1975: 136):

> We had been coerced by our conscience to carry out an execution, and went through with it, but we came out of it ruined men, annihilated, ardently yearning for the end. We wished to end it all. Yet at the same time we desperately needed to see each other, to talk to each other, to help each other exorcize the haunting of that recent memory. Now we were finished, lost, and we knew it. We were trapped, each of us in his own trap, and there was no way out but down.[1]

These powerful words led Luzzatto to investigate the events preceding Levi's capture in order to find out whom Levi and his companions had executed, and why their enactment of violence made them yearn for their own death.

After painstaking archival searches, Luzzatto allegedly uncovered the truth, eloquently and elegantly unravelled in his controversial best-seller *Partigia* (2014): Levi and his partisan comrades had shot two young friends and protégés who, presumably, had not deserved to die for their deeds. Luzzatto postulates that the two lads had been stealing from the local peasants – perhaps because they were starving. A source not included in Luzzatto's book, Pastor Adolphe Barmaverain's diary, casts a more sinister shadow on the two dead partisans. The two boys, the diary claimed, had bullied an elderly Jewish lady and eventually driven her to suicide. Does this change our perception of events? Whom do we believe? Whatever we believe, we shall never know. The likely desperate want and need motivating the lads' behaviour towards an innocent person, the still disputed guilt of the boys (only that source alleged that the two had perpetrated a horrific deed), and their young age (seventeen and eighteen) makes their execution by older comrades and mentors the stuff of tragedy. What do we make of these particular stories? Whom do they affect? More importantly, how do we position ourselves in relation to storyteller and the story's characters? What do we *now* think of Primo Levi, which we did not feel before? If anything, Levi's story demonstrates how absolutely nothing – no event, person or action during the war – can be understood as a clear-cut representation. His experience illuminates a more fruitful way of thinking about the horrors of war and conflict, which I discuss below.

7.2 Making place for a future

Why bother writing this book? Whose ugly secrets would I uncover, and with what authority was I to expose them? With hindsight, *I thought it was a story worth telling* in this fashion. As stated in the introduction, I was dissatisfied with the way that the Second World War is under-represented in critical anthropological literature, confined to the shelf of the military or political historian (but see Portelli 1997,

2003; Cappelletto 2005 for illuminating ethnographic perspectives on the war). In mainstream representations, war is often 'emptied of human content ... a rarefied choreography of *disembodied* events' (Scarry 1985: 70, my emphasis). And yet war is rather all about 'unmaking and remaking in which familiar or taken-for-granted objects of knowledge and structures of meaning are overwhelmed and transformed' (Brighton 2011: 102). In putting these words to paper, I feel that an engagement with the materiality of the Second World War could significantly widen the scope of what we can learn about resistance, displacement and occupation processes over and above the Italian case study.

What is missing from much contemporary historiography on the Second World War is an attention to the experiential side of the conflict: the imaginations, sensations, prejudices and hopes and dreams making up the everyday lives of those who lived through these momentous events. In sum, I wrote this book to lend an experiential perspective to a historical period and its many stories, because they mean a great deal to me: *pace* Levinas (1998), my writing has been an endeavour to restore the voices of the dead to the discourse of the living in a world populated by possibilities, absent presents and present absences that reflect how life *is*. An experiential approach to recent history fulfils three main purposes: it bridges the gap between past and present, involving younger generations in the understanding of what has come before; it opens up the plurality of historical interpretations to move away from elitist accounts and into the everyday memories and postmemory of the survivors and their descendants; and, as an experiential perspective, it is closer to the lived, everyday reality of the protagonists: it brings to the fore the shocking, mundane or heart-warming little facts and anecdotes of a war making and unmaking worlds in every town, village and city in most of Europe.

I use the concepts of the uncanny, postmemory and affect to pave the way to an inclusive, humane and compassionate way of thinking about the war, what people did (or did not do) and the places where big and small events unfolded. The uncanny, intended as the sense of something being out of place, unsettled and unsettling, works in synergy with affect, conceived as a way of 'perceiving' moods and atmospheres in the world, and with the workings of postmemory. Postmemory, as a mode of perceiving the past and relating to it in the flesh, body and soul, reacts to the stimuli of the uncanny as it is not a direct experience or memory, but rather a learnt, or sensed, sense of the other – of someone else's memory that becomes part of us. The workings of affect and the uncanny in memory and postmemory of the civil war have brought us here: to a final discussion of the overall experience of the conflict in its many facets.

History, wrote de Certeau, is 'probably our myth' (1988: 21). And yet the events of resistance and occupation are not a closed discourse from which we can distance ourselves. They still haunt the present. Throughout this book, I have attempted to show that the views and perceptions commonly held about the war might not be necessarily true to people's experience, intention and hopes. In Chapter 4, we saw how rumour and hearsay have coloured and populated our received wisdom of the war in the same way as facts and actual events. Take, for instance, the myth of 'the good German' in storytelling (Pavone 1991: 154; van Boeschoten 2005: 53), a trope found in wartime stories all over Europe. The trope, attributing humanity and kindness to one of the enemy outgroup (see Leyens et al. 2000), is prominent in some of my interviews, too, for example, with Lavinia, who lamented the mocking, often odious attitude of Fascists towards her but reported kindness on the part of German officers through offers of help to lift and carry heavy carts of food rations for her family. We ask ourselves why some, and not all, characters were invested with this innate quality of goodness. The myth of the good German echoes the Christian trope of the merciful Centurion from the apocryphal Gospels and finds place in Catholic resistance practices and understandings (Pavone 1991: 154); after all, 'the Germans repented, the Fascists did not' (Pavone 1991). In many of the interviews I carried out, the same conviction is true of the Fascists, upon whom the heaviest blame falls. But what if *anyone* wearing the RSI uniform (for whatever reason) was invested with the same evil characteristics as bona fide Fascists? In other words, did Baldini really deserve to die?

How we remember his death matters, too. Levinas postulated that we have a complex relationship with temporality and memory, whereby we experience 'a past which concerns me, which "has to do with" me, which is "my busyness" [sic] outside all reminiscence, all retention, all representation, all reference to a recalled present' (1998: 150) – a kind of transcendental postmemory. Through affective postmemory, we establish and enact a connection to history emotionally and affectively, by reaching out, or homing in on, the stories of those who lived (and died) through the events: we project something other (the past) as if it was our own.

Ricoeur's invitation to reach out to the stories of others via our own stories, empathy and imagination (1996) was my starting point; I have strived to be co-present with other voices, to fill the silences with possibilities that may facilitate the flow and passage of stories in ways that have hopefully involved, intrigued, and perhaps moved the reader. The stories related here constitute competing materialities, conflicting identities, dissonant emotions and paradoxical 'things' – part of a wider poetics of conflict experience. The writing of history, de Certeau suggested, is about representing something that is lacking . . . and to 'make a place for a future' (de Certeau 1988: 85). If something's lacking, and we need it, then we shall write about it. A book such as this may then endeavour to be a work of compassionate historiography, collaborative ethnography or the mapping of the emotional geographies of a network of people, things, places and events that changed Europe forever.

To tell the story of the Italian war, I started from the mainstream narratives of the war in Chapter 1. There, we traced how official conflict narratives are slotted into a comprehensive story which provides a 'comforting' sense of identity and belonging for the average citizen. Then, in Chapters 2 and 3 I moved on to consider how wartime affects inhabit and circulate in embodied identities. By tracing these identities, I then explored how people made sense of their world at war through storytelling; I have taken an active and sympathetic listening stance to the nuances of storytelling, like gossip, rumour and make-believe (Chapter 4). I then turned to the sites where stories live: things and places. But are things and places really separate? Arguably not. Chapter 5 devoted attention to materiality, the 'thingishness' of things (Straw 1999), to sites of memory and wartime mementoes, real or imagined. These meaningful 'things' and places have the potential to tell stories that align or depart from the mainstream narrative. Chapter 6 panned out to the wider landscapes and places where the events of the war unfolded: far from being a backdrop to the action, places have folded back into the story, hiding and revealing actions, imaginaries and everything in between. Places have patiently waited for their turn to take centre stage in the second-to-last chapter because I believe them to be the most powerful agents in this story. Places, in their being constituted with the sum total of the affects and materialities present in this book and much more besides, are silent (but eloquent) storytellers.

Memory is capable of transforming places, and transfiguring people and events, through the production of stories; memory and postmemory are relational – remembrance never occurs or develops in isolation, but along with relationships – 'memory is a sense of the other' (de Certeau 1984: 87). Just as postmemory is the sense of something other, something missing.

Scholars from as varied a disciplinary background as psychoanalysis and oral history have argued (Conway 1996; Thompson 2000; Cappelletto 2003) that 'the memory process depends on that of perception' (Thompson 2000: 129): that is, in order to metabolise a memory, one must first *understand* it. For instance, without a cultural framework in which to make sense of the momentous decision to oppose the Nazis and the puppet Fascist regime, those individuals who delivered messages, weapons, food and effectively provided intelligence to the armed partisan bands in the mountains or in the woods are not necessarily aware of the historical significance of their own actions. It would not be until later, when they started sharing their stories and memories, that activists and veterans began to metabolise and *make sense* of their experience.

The sharing of memories, Calvino's 'many stories', effectively created a conglomerate of cultural memory and local identities, as each town and village has their own different, unique story to tell about the war and occupation, and different degrees of complicity in collaboration or resistance. Thus, the temporality and representations and 'meaning' of wartime actions are closely linked to individuals' preempted intimations of the futures and their memories of the past (see also Pink 2009). In this sense, both memories and predictions of the future can be considered ways of imagining. Imagination is crucial in the making of everyday reality. For Pink (2009: 45), imagination is a 'more emplaced everyday practice carried out in relation to the multisensoriality of our actual social and material relations'.

7.3 Engaging with the poetics of conflict experience

Levinas posited that history is determined by posterity, 'by those who are absent, with a judgement that can no longer change anything' (1998: 25). What if that was not always the case? What if novel engagements could make a difference, and allow the dead to be relevant to our present and actively shape the future once more? This might be accomplished through a reflexive approach to posterity, a move towards minimising or at any rate not relying so much on hindsight. Hindsight bias allows people to

> position themselves on the side of foresight and knowledge, whereas in reality people who find themselves in the midst of a process or historical transformation never see where this process is headed. [. . .] People who share an illusion can never recognize it.
>
> (Neitzel and Welzer 2013: 35)

With hindsight, we can make many assumptions about the rights and wrongs of the civil war and German occupation, but we need to turn to the overarching atmospheres, materiality and actual interaction of embodied identities (the sources) if we are to engage in a meaningful and informed dialogue with that unpalatable past.

I also want to ask – how to conclude a story like this? Or rather, how to bring closure to the hauntings present within these pages? 'The end of the story is what equates the present with the past, the actual with the potential. The hero *is* what he *was*' (Ricoeur 1991: 114, emphasis in original). Have the present and the past come together, and do they resonate with the potential of things to come? Cobb (2014) has provided a definition of a conflict as a situation characterised by markers such as violence, exclusion and displacement. In an attempt to rationalise and finalise the loose ends and potentials brought up in the preceding chapters, I use the notions of violence and exclusion as rubrics of experience in this 'final' space of reflection. I use these ugly 'categories' of war to try to make sense of the troubled poetics of conflict experience. I suggest that we need to better understand our own mutual autobiographical materialities in order to learn how to respond humanely and (at least attempt to) accept and understand the materialities of others; this might then, arguably, be a first step in resolving the painful memories of decade-long conflicts.

7.3.1 The poetics of violence

The public display of the executed bodies of Benito Mussolini, his mistress Claretta Petacci and twelve Fascist bigwigs, hanging upside down from petrol station pumps on Piazzale Loreto on 28 April 1945 (Ginsborg 1990: 67–68), was an event of magnitude not unlike 8 September 1943. It was the end of days. In her memoir, Magda Ceccarelli (2011: 311) described her visit to Piazzale Loreto and the crowd's reaction to the corpses of Mussolini, Petacci and the Fascist leaders. Everyone agreed that Petacci was 'a looker'. In the next few days, Magda tells us, everyone was 'all smiles'. Strangers smiled to one another in the streets and on the trams (2011: 315).

Despite an enduring fascination with the events of the Second World War, and the importance of understanding the dynamics of violence in general, there is reluctance in the public sphere and in the educational sector to address the complexities of engaging with or representing the perpetrators. The story of an Italy united against the Nazis has been challenged time and again, but never in terms of its emotional and experiential dimension. What is more important is that diverging and unaligned stories have been silenced for the greater good, and for example, spats and disagreements between politically incompatible partisan formations have been whitewashed, in order to project a united front in the battle against 'evil' Nazism and Fascism. I have proposed instead that a root of the violence and a facet of its justification in the eye and heart of the perpetrator lie in the perceived difference, abjection and alterity of an enemy displaying competing materialities and incompatible embodiments; in turn, this misunderstanding and misalignment led to infrahumanisation, then and now.

> The other is the only being whose negation can be declared only as total: a murder. The other is the only being I can want to kill. The triumph of this power is its defeat as power. At the very moment when my power to kill is realized, the other has escaped.
>
> (Levinas 1998: 9)

Is killing another a letting go? Does infrahumanisation entail a little killing?

Yet it was not all doom and gloom. Human nature is wonderfully eclectic and surprisingly effective in preserving fairness and decency, even in the face of the most dismal danger and deprivation. A glimpse of 'humanity' exists in the midst of the grimmest wartime episodes. Amidst the betrayal and the fury, some felt that they had to preserve their values and moral compass intact. Some did not, and some others prefer not to talk about it.

In the chapters of this book, we have perceived, through intertwined stories of violence, mercy and reconciliation, that everyday life during the resistance and occupation spelt danger for almost everyone. Both sides in the conflict claim their people suffered the most losses. For years, resistance mythologies delineated a heroic endeavour where brave men (and sometimes women) gave their lives for the freedom of Italy, fighting against the un-Italian madness that the Fascists incarnated. The problem with this scenario is that we now know that the resistance fighters did not always act nobly and fairly towards civilians, Fascists and spies. My outspoken stance on this 'flaw' of the resistance does not represent even a remote attempt to discredit the enormous accomplishments and innate nobility of the cause of the anti-Fascist and anti-Nazi cause. The resistance achieved wonderful things, often protecting the civilian communities they were linked to, and providing for them at all costs, while also aiding the Allies to defeat the Nazis through courageous acts of guerrilla warfare, intelligence dispatch, sabotage and collaboration.

A propos empathy:

> One day this partisan helper brings the local Fascist Secretary in front of me, he's all excited, says, 'Hey Memi, look, you have to shoot this feller' . . . 'Hey hang on, slow down, shoot him? What's he done?' 'Oh I dunno what he done; I have orders to bring him to you, you shoot him'. Poor fascist Secretary! This little chap, maybe 5'2", his eyes popping out of his head, he had pissed himself judging from a dark stain on his crotch, well he . . . he says '*Signore*, I never hurt anyone, I have kids, please spare me . . .' He kneels; everyone starts asking questions, what is he doing, has he no dignity . . . I couldn't bring myself to do it. To shoot him. These summary executions, done at a moment's notice, no! So I found a way out. I said that when I had been imprisoned, this man had been kind to me and ordered our release. It wasn't true but I couldn't think of nothing else. As officer in charge I was able to convince my men to spare him. The others were reluctant, but I let him go.
>
> (Domenico Favero, interview 1 February 2002)

Here, a focus on the humiliation of the body and the act of killing and disposing of another's body elucidates some of the reactions these could evoke: fear and revulsion. In other words, the physical act of meting out guerrilla justice would be perceived as morally wrong by many; such moral and emotive turmoil seems to emerge from my grandfather Domenico's testimony and his decision to lie in order to not execute the prisoner. So as to be able to share his intense memories more spontaneously, this witness had asked permission to recount his experience in the local dialect: in the preface to the transcript the interviewers noted that 'unfortunately the liveliness of expression cannot survive on the printed page; in particular the liveliness and passion with which Signor Favero *relived* events and feelings' (Conte and Strazzer 2002: i, my emphasis).

The fact remains, however, that some members of the Communist brigades took advantage of their position in the imaginary of the Italians for personal gain or to enact their own personal vendettas against Fascists who had wronged them during the years of Mussolini's dictatorship. This accusation has been used time and again for the purpose of discrediting the morality of the resistance movement and to reconstitute the moral fibre of the Fascists (*pace* Pansa 2005; Mammone 2006). Yet memories of the conflict have crystallised into pat responses. When questioned on the fairness of the resistance experience, virtually all the veterans with whom I spoke dehumanised the Fascists and Germans as not quite worthy of mourning.

No victim status for the Nazi-Fascists, then ... But what about the myth of the good German? Where does that trope figure in an unforgiving attitude towards Germans? My work has thrown up more questions than answers, it seems. Of course, I would have been naïve to expect value-free stories and opinions from the close-knit veteran community. That messiness applies to us, too – us, on the other side of the recording device. Atmospheres and affects are shared and negotiated during the research encounter, but they have to have a foundation of sorts. They are not that precarious. I had not anticipated the almost complete lack of empathy towards wartime enemies, and yet there I was, nodding awkwardly. The fact that Fascists and anti-Fascists might have genuinely and spontaneously perceived their opponents – and the invading German soldiers – as not being quite as human as them might go some way towards explaining why they acted in certain ways, and how the perpetration of violent acts might have been perceived, received and elaborated in memory. The past 'collides with the present and with us, the witnesses to other people's pain' (Witcomb 2016: 218).

Contemporary anxieties about the war in Italy may not be entirely dictated by what one 'did' back then, but also by what one 'felt'. Old behaviour may be engendering tension in the present. One of my respondents, Lavinia, was a sixteen-year-old girl at the Armistice of 1943:

> Once I visited my Dad, held in a Nazi prison in Belluno, and someone said to me, 'People in those cells there, they wait for the firing squad'. I didn't fear for my safety though, and I have to say, the Nazis didn't touch a hair on my head. But I was so, so scared. Petrified. And then, when Liberation Day came I saw a German who didn't want to surrender and a partisan shot him and I cried, 'Serves you right!' What do you know – now it seems impossible that I had become so cynical, but at that moment I was just like that. I felt utter joy mixed with rage.
> (Interview 4 December 2010)

Lavinia's discourse centres on the themes of fear and the most extreme form of Schadenfreude: joy at seeing the enemy die. She now regrets her reaction, and seems ashamed of it, but *only in hindsight*. But would she have felt any differently *then* if she had thought about that man's family in Germany who were now without a father, spouse, son or brother?

To the lack of empathy of the anti-Fascists and veterans (especially those of Communist allegiance, it has to be said) corresponds the lugubrious rage of the 'other side'. Revisionist and hard-nosed right wing groups such as *Casa Pound* (named after American Fascist sympathiser and poet Ezra Pound) and *Silentes Loquimur* ('We speak silently') agitate for the rightful place of Fascist memories and understandings of the civil war to enter the national debate (see also Cassina Wolf 2012). The fact of the latter organisations' unsavoury neo-Nazi connections in Europe has doubtlessly done nothing to advance their agenda. Yet there are right wingers who do not want to pursue contemporary violence and aggressive racist policies: some simply want history to acknowledge that among those wearing a Fascist uniform, there were many who were coerced by circumstances (especially when they lived in the plains or in the cities of the centre-south) to join the RSI. And they are right: not everyone enlisted in the Fascist armed forces was there by choice. Not everyone relished the partisan witch hunt. Similarly, many contend that even those wearing the Black Shirt out of a personal commitment to the Duce and Fascism, and who then died for the cause of the Fatherland, also died a noble death. These men and women, too, deserve national mourning alongside the anti-Fascists (Pansa 2005). Their hidden graves, concealed monuments and controversial headstones should not, they argue, be marginalised and silenced.

Just as many Germans salved their own conscience about the killing of thousands of Italians by depicting them as 'traitors' and *Banditen* supporters (Schreiber 1996; Focardi 2005), most Fascists who perpetrated violence against the members of the resistance movement concealed their 'guilt' behind the shield of political and ideological belief. At least, that is what current interpretations agree on. But what if, as we have glimpsed above, the Fascists truly believed that the harm they were doing to the anti-Fascists *did not really matter*? Likewise, the partisans (and especially some militant Communist fighters) might not have found it so utterly repellent to engage in violent acts against the Fascists – the noxious Other collaborating with the Nazis. But what about the mass graves, the kangaroo courts and the suspected personal vendettas?

7.3.2 The poetics of exclusion

Infrahumanisation theories posit that in order to behave humanely towards an individual or social group, we must acknowledge their full humanity – that is to say, their capacity to feel, exist and act as we do (see Leyens et al. 2000; Haslam et al. 2005). The moment we perceive a group or person as inferior in emotional terms, we may feel entitled to judge them, criticise them, and to do things to them we would not do to our 'perceived' peers. The implications of infrahumanisation theories for the study and understanding of the civil war and German occupation are far-reaching. The fact that the activists and civilians during the years 1943–45 atomised in so many ingroups and excluded outgroups from their lifeworlds might mean that the Other's point of view, their hopes and fears, were discredited as less important than one's own. The infrahumanisation of the other side in a social and political conflict also afforded a relative ease to perpetrate violence against those who acted a certain way, or believed in a certain political and ideological cosmology 'other' than our own. The tropes of infrahumanisation abound in remembrance narratives. In partisan memoirs, we find frequent bestial epithets directed towards Fascists (see also Portelli 1997); the Germans' *bon mot* of choice to designate Italians was *Schwein* – pig (Wette 2006; Focardi 2013). Is it so far-fetched, then, to seek to frame and better understand war narratives within the cosmology and epistemology of infrahumanisation?

Fascist voices have been traditionally excluded from national narratives of the war – it is around these stories, it could be argued, that the densest of silences have gathered. In Zelmira's Fascist diary (Marazio 2004), I was struck by a stark reminder that the Fascists were people with friends and loved ones, too – which had been a tacit but inconspicuous theme in much of her remembrance. On page 63, Zelmira commented on the establishment of the activity of GAP[2] groups in Turin, born in order to create chaos in the city, to disrupt social life and to impede the re-organisation of Fascist forces, and, for her, to spread hatred and violence. Every day, Fascist victims fell to the stealthy hits of the Communist franc-tireurs. These victims, Zelmira wrote, had been people she used to work with, people with whom she had shared plans and hopes and dreams, and were now enclosed in wooden boxes draped in the Italian *Tricolore* flag. They fell to the invisible killers, were 'massacred in ambushes' or killed in confrontations in the streets.

Emotion, I would suggest, plays a key role in how we include or exclude persons and groups in our circles. Emotion is quintessentially social – socially produced, enacted and shared (Ahmed 2004a, b; Burkitt 2012: 459). Emotions, however, inform how we perceive the other and how we assess their humanity (Des Moulins 2004).

> The thought that it was enough to wear a uniform to turn your neighbour into your tormentor is still hard to accept. We [the Partisans] were dying of hunger, typhus, and fear. They [the Fascists] were laughing and enjoying themselves. I still remember the face of a little guy, half my size, who was hitting me while I was tied to a chair. If only I could move I would have beaten him to death. Their laughter was for us the worst torture, not to mention when they lined us up in front of the wall and told us it was our final hour, and then a shooter fired blanks, only to terrorize us. Our hearts jumped out of our chests.
> (Mario Nunziatini, XVIII Garibaldi Brigade, Forlì,
> quoted in Faure, Liparoto and Papi 2012: 256)

We are often quick to pass judgement on those who did not act the way we would have, or the way we expect others to act. Instead, by adopting an empathetic open-mindedness and reaching out to the stories of others, we can perhaps find it in ourselves to understand, and tolerate, difference. We can 'bring out prejudices to consciousness. Perhaps the better to change them' posits Lambek echoing Gadamer (Howes 1991: xi). Or maybe we should not be so quick to judge in the first place.

In the aftermath of a reprisal, Emanuele Artom wrote: 'A sad smell of burning all the way to Barge. Looking in that direction I thought about all the pain hidden in that smoke and ashes, made even blacker by the pure white of the snow' (Artom and Schwarz 2008: 114). Eerie, desolate, and hopeless: is this what a world at war *felt* like? Sherry Turkle has conceptualised quite beautifully the liminality of the everyday uncanny by commenting on how the Freudian *unheimlich* can trouble us into being unable to distinguish what is right and what is askew in our lifeworlds in quite mundane ways. In her discussion of liminality, she writes 'in traditional rites of passage, participants are separated from all that is familiar. We saw that this makes them vulnerable, open to the objects and experiences of their time of transition' (2005: 319–320). Germans found themselves at the mercy of locals and resistance fighters, turning from tolerated friend to mortal enemy overnight. A lack of language skills (for most) and ambiguous relationship with local (Communist) partisan formations disoriented Allied officers behind enemy lines. Yet some German soldiers deserted and joined the rank and file of the resistance, and Allied officers made friends for life with local Italians. The 'beauty' of the Italian war is that the full spectrum of human experience is represented – one just has to go and find it. I have grown quite attached to the characters in this book, to their worlds and emergent intentions, and I feel for them deeply. I wonder how disorienting the whole experience must have been for them all. I was lucky enough to hear from the voices of the protagonists about their intense, often scary memories of those twenty months, but digging deep in the archives, all sorts of affects and emotions come to the fore.

Elsewhere (De Nardi 2013), I wrote about an episode that happened during my fieldwork with veterans. At an interview with veterans Lavinia and Francesca, I learnt that aside from the famous, celebrated spaces and places of the local resistance, the surroundings of the town of Vittorio Veneto were home to a hidden underworld of 'disappeared'.

> In a certain cave, well, that's where *our boys* were hiding. Those who didn't feel up to joining the partisans in the mountains . . . They had to disappear off the face of the earth. Back then there was no path leading to the cave – as I discovered myself. Well, that's where those boys who couldn't face going all the way went. They were hiding there, and in other villages too.
>
> (Interview 4 December 2010)

My emphasis in the above passage indicates the affectionate tone of voice in which Francesca referred to those who stayed neutral out of fear and anxiety or due to political indifference – not 'deserters' or 'cowards', but rather 'our boys' – an idiom in the local dialect resonating with empathy, whereas the remainder of our exchange had been in Italian. Not only did she refer to 'our boys' as non-partisans, but she chose to include in her own brave story of resistance the story of those who chose not to resist actively – whereas the latter are consistently ignored in official commemorations of the conflict. Still, her warm, dialect-inflected narration expressed a deep understanding towards those who did not fight the cause.

For Cándida-Smith, 'vocal gestures shape . . . delivery of words. Patterns of speaking, . . . variation in force, pitch and tone contribute to an effort to convey meaning and not just information' (2003: 2). This applies to my whole veteran interview sample, but this particular example stood out for me, and, I feel, is essential to craft a discourse of tolerance and acceptance of others, even when they acted in ways that we would not share, approve of or even understand. In her sensitivity, activist Francesca is fully aware of the complexity of the choices and decisions facing individuals almost overnight in the confusing days after the Armistice; moreover, while 25 April is the commemoration day for former partisans, this day does not speak to others: namely, those who had fought against the resistance and believed in Fascism; those who, declaring themselves apolitical, had attempted to survive by sitting on the fence between partisans and Fascists (like my father's uncle under his chicken coop); and finally, 'those who remember not "the" Resistance but their own – at times partial – resistance; and those who do not want to remember . . .' (Ballone 2007: 418).

Individuals felt displaced due to several real and imagined factors: among these, belonging and exclusion from local communities and ideological groups. A sense of things not being quite right links the fates and experience of diverse individuals: the southern partisans, the Catholic and moderate partisans, the humane Fascist, the apolitical hideaway and the repenting German, to name but a few. But it also includes women who wanted to join armed formations, confused youths, last-minute partisan chancers, and the most feared category of all – spies.

7.4 A past we can know

In this book, I have sought to engage with the world-making role of materiality as a building block of social identities and cultural enactments. One of the questions I have posed is: what if the memory and postmemory of the Fascists and anti-Fascists is so fundamentally hardwired to reject or negate the proper humanity of their respective opponents in the civil war, that the very idea of taking responsibility for, or regretting wrongdoings and violent acts, appears genuinely superfluous? What if the veteran resistance fighters genuinely believe it was necessary to execute suspected spies, not out of a clear-cut conviction in their guilt, but in light of their marginality – their being 'not quite like us'? In other words, we, as social beings enacting identities in the everyday, share narratives about the war with members of our affective ingroup starting from a common set of knowledge and a shared materiality. After all, memory is grounded in materiality and the senses; through the senses, we make sense of the world around us and of persons and things interacting with us in the everyday. So if this context-specific dimension of remembrance is true, how do we re-enact stories of alien, alternate or Other materialities, bodies, identities and positionalities? How do we frame stories about the war that automatically 'other' the outsiders? What if our audience were to change – perhaps to include emotional outgroup members or 'neutral' individuals (say, foreigners)? How comfortable would we then feel with sharing feelings of *schadenfreude* about the enemy's demise or suffering?

Storytelling works as a social binder, asserting and keeping groups together – or apart. For Misztal, 'the reconstruction of the past always depends on present-day identities and contexts' (2003: 14). Moreover, '[t]he only past we can know is the one we shape by the questions we ask, and these questions are moulded by the social context we come from' (Kyvik 2004: 87). So far, so good. But there may well be cultural and psychological schemata influencing and shaping the past *and* the present experience of war and conflict. Social groups and mnemonic communities might harbour and nurture postmemory tenets that then become unquestioningly accepted and assimilated. This book has asked whether, and to what extent, if we perceive someone or something to be wrong, out of place, or aberrant, we are effectively crafting and ratifying present and future prejudice. What it those prejudices redefine old meanings and past understandings of how the world works?

In this book, I set out to investigate just how 'despite . . . differences in both the stories and how they are told, what all . . . share is a use of space and place to navigate the relationships between difficult events, others, and themselves' (Cole 2015: 5–6). It has been a rough ride! An attention to the dehumanising effect of competing or alien materialities, emplacements, affects and embodiments has drawn attention to the way that we, as humans, fundamentally discriminate against those who look, speak, smell, act or eat differently from us. While this is not exactly a noble human trait (not by today's standards, at any rate), we can work with our awareness of this tendency and listen to, and write, the stories of others with compassion and kindness – even when we cannot understand their stories, do not agree with them or simply cannot orientate ourselves in relation to the other's storytelling. Might we begin with embodiment? As Katz and Csordas (2003: 278) have argued, an emphasis on embodiment can 'serve as the common ground for recognition of the other's humanity'. Would this work in the case of wartime Europe, or is this proposition only valid for the non-Western other?

For Girard (1977), wartime victims act as the location for the emergence of law and community; by gathering around (the body of) the victim, drawn to the site of violence, the public, as witnesses, struggle to make sense of what happened. This can be seen as a more-than-representational process in which witnesses enact their own moral frameworks for making sense of right and wrong. On that note, let us return to Armando Baldini. Does our embodied imagination of Baldini as a human being made of flesh and bone, stripped of his regalia and uniform, a being about to die, bring us closer to him – do we forgive his uniform, tied to Fascism in its many evil connotations? To whom did Baldini's demise matter? If not closeness, the images inspire a certain degree of curiosity in us. The images channel affects: that is a start, at least. Is curiosity (another affect) not a reason why historians and anthropologists write books and their intended publics read them? Over and above the academic exercise and our own disciplinary epistemological anxieties, we humans care about the past. We want to know more about the past because it gives meaning to our present lives. We feel curious about an event such as Baldini's execution and become emotionally involved in the business of finding out what happened. We would like to know who took the pictures, and how it felt to be there. We want to know what the civil war and occupation were like – to understand the events with our heads and with our hearts, too.

The affective power of a photograph is able to reach out to new generations, and to continue telling the tale of the man who died, his killers, and their mutually implicated stories. The photographs become heralds of the two sides' intertwined destinies as well as those who did not commit to either one out of fear, lack of conviction, or apathy. These images convey powerful strands of a poetics of violence, exclusion and displacement. We feel a closeness to this troubled past, we 'brush' against people who were once alive and now breathe no longer. We want to be part of their lives. We want to know more; we want to see more. We want to see everything, uncover what was concealed, reveal what has been hidden – and find out why? The past is something that we encounter – something we find and get involved in. We engage with historical events because we care – but what is it that makes us care?

7.5 Engaging humanely with the materialities of others

Passerini (2005) has stressed how accustomed we have become to a conflation of the enemy with unproblematic stereotypes. In delineating the persistent trend to unify 'Nazis' with 'Germans', she agitates for a novel attention to distinct attitudes and behaviours within the German armed forces. To extend Passerini's invitation, it makes sense to attend to materiality's role in the construction of identities. If we do so, we might then consider the actors in a conflict as people from different parts of the world, each with their own backstory of material culture(s), epistemologies, religions, eating habits and dress sense. Identities and material cultures are, of course, profoundly intertwined. Anthropologists contend that it is vital 'to study the role materiality plays in the constitution of society both as a constraining mechanism but also as a constructive source and force for social relations, institutions and systems in the past as well as the present' (Fahlander and Oestigaard 2004: 11). In the case of the civil war and occupation in Italy, this book has explored some of the social, cultural and emotional consequences of foreign bodies moving through and across one's home turf. I have deployed materiality and identity-shaping processes as a framework to understand how mutually perceived alterity and foreignness affected perceptions of persons and places.

I have considered to what extent the other's difference and otherness were understood in a myriad of different ways, and postulated that individuals and social groups did not always cope well with the atomizing consequences of that difference. I feel it is now time to turn to the present – to the impact that the divided memory and complex misunderstandings arising during the war have on present-day society in Europe and beyond. What does everything we have encountered in this book tell us about remembrance practices in the present and the future of memory politics? In effecting a spatio-temporal incision into a problematic past, what ethnographies of present affects have been unearthed? Some of us might refuse to accept or acknowledge a trait of our personality as social beings. Then the othering and infrahumanization of those we perceive to be our enemies defines the gap in our understanding of war events, even the bloodiest ones. If we acknowledge this human weakness, then we could begin to react to this imbalance and attempt to fill the gap between hearts and nations. We can attempt a dialogue with the other side based on our common tendencies and traits as human beings as well as political animals. Using Levinas' paradigm of the 'interhuman' serves as a good starting point: 'the interhuman, properly speaking, lies in a non-indifference of one to another, in a responsibility of one for another' (1998: 100). If we cannot yet muster sympathy for the Other, perhaps we can begin by establishing non-indifference.

The makings of postmemory can lay the foundations for that non-indifference to the fate and grief of others. Postmemory, however painful, should not be seen as a burden or barrier: rather, we should treat postmemory as a *possibility*. The realm of postmemory is where we can make a real difference. We cannot change the past, but we can work with postmemory towards reconciliation through our non-indifference. In doing (post)memory work with veterans of the civil war in Italy, we can begin to disrupt, problematize and unravel the multiple, divided, messy tapestry of wartime memories and legacies (De Nardi 2014, 2015b).

If, for instance, Italians could bring themselves to face their interhuman responsibilities towards others and metabolise the deep-seated causes of the impossibility or reluctance to acknowledge the faults of one's own political side, they could 'move on'. As an Italian studying the consequences of wartime prejudice on social division within my own cultural group, I propose that we learn to put ourselves in the Other's shoes and rethink what we assume the Other to be. A newly found compassion could go some way towards a mutual understanding of what makes one 'Italian' and to a feeling of closure, of making peace with the violent wartime past. By attending to the side of our human nature that denies full, proper personhood and humanity to those who differ from us, we might perhaps overcome our tendencies to judge them as such. We should embrace and even cultivate the awareness that the callousness deriving from infrahumanisation practices may blind us to the fact that others ('the Other side') also hoped, suffered and regretted things. As Levinas postulated, 'is our relation with the other a *letting be*?' (1998: 6, emphasis in original).

Figure 7.1 The River Sile, Veneto. On its shores a bitter civil war was fought by partisans vs. Fascists, whose memory still divides communities today (see section 6.4).

Photo: Sarah De Nardi

In Italy, the stark polarisation of memory of the civil war could then, as it has in Germany, lead the way to a long, painful but ultimately cathartic process of reconciliation. In the preceding chapters, I have shown how the role and attitudes of the opposed fighting sides during the war in Italy were complex; we have explored the dense forests of place or placelessness, competing material cultures, incompatible embodiments, differing ways of remembering and engaging with other persons, other groups, and with the material legacies of the war. Far from being schematic and clear-cut, one finds wildly diverging accounts of accountability and personal and moral conduct attributed to the Fascist and Nazi enemy. It is important to dispel the myth that historical sources must either conform or disprove theories, arguments or opinions held about the war. I have not attempted to confirm or dispel stereotypes and clichés about the war, as that would be a pointless endeavour: they constitute the mythologies of the recent past we live by. I have, rather, attempted to glimpse the complex lived, fleshly and emotional realities informing the clichés, colouring the stereotypes and grounding accepted versions of events in the imagination. I have sought to complicate rather than unpick the emotional and affective threads in the complex human tapestry of the war. I have pointed to the fact that there is no easy, quick way to reconcile painful memories and legacies with our present and future. That is because the poetics of conflict experience constitutes a never-ending, open-ended world of inferences, imagination and hopes which can never be defined, proved or disproved – only approached with an open mind and open heart.

Notes

1 'Questo divieto era doloroso, perché fra noi, in ognuna delle nostre menti, pesava un segreto brutto: lo stesso segreto che ci aveva esposti alla cattura, spegnendo in noi, pochi giorni prima, ogni volontà di resistere, anzi di vivere. Eravamo stati costretti dalla nostra coscienza ad eseguire una condanna, e l'avevamo eseguita, ma ne eravamo usciti distrutti, destituiti, desiderosi che tutto finisse e di finire noi stessi; ma desiderosi anche di vederci fra noi, di parlarci, di aiutarci a vicenda ad esorcizzare quella memoria ancora così recente. Adesso eravamo finiti, e lo sapevamo: eravamo in trappola, ognuno nella sua trappola, non c'era uscita se non all'in giù'.
2 Communist partisan urban guerrilla groups, or Gruppi di Azione Partigiana.

Appendix

Il Messaggero, 25 July 1966

*Five hundred people 'infoibate' down a vertical
cave in the Cansiglio plain*

Four young speleologists [. . .] claim to have found hundreds and hundreds of dead civilians, Germans and Republicans in an hourglass-shaped cave reaching a depth of 285 meters. They (claim) the bodies had been thrown in during the stormy final phase of the war.

The four cavers, the first ever to descend into the opening, have allegedly investigated the extent of knowledge about the cave among the population of the area. Bus de la Lun or Lum, translatable into Italian as Hole of the Light or of the Moon, has long been known to the locals due to the occurrence of will o' the wisp in its interior.

The cavers interviewed people who 'know the story'; among other things they heard from a person who, under the influence of alcohol, allegedly confessed to having personally thrown soldiers into the cave; finally, they have collected the testimonies of numerous farmers who say they see the elderly relatives of the 'disappeared' praying near the Bus de la Lun even now, after all these years.

At 180 m below the entrance, there are reports of the recovery [by whom?] of plenty of putrefied corpses. [. . .]

Ultimately we have collected a series of stories that, if taken seriously, leads to the following conclusion: in 1945, over a hundred people, both soldiers and civilians, were thrown down the cave to their death (!!)

Il Messaggero, 3 August 1966

A fanciful tale debunked: No corpses in Bus de la Lum

At our explicit request fifteen speleologists from Friuli and Trieste have carried out an exploration of Bus de la Lum, the vertical cave on Pian del Cansiglio and the place of recovery, according to rumours, of the bodies of some five hundred people thrown into the abyss during the last war.

[. . .] At a depth of 225 meters the speleologists found an obstruction, a pebble and crushed stone platform which blocks the way to further descent. On this platform, reaching a surface of some 30 square meters, the explorers found no sign either of skeletons, nor of objects. [. . .] Readers will remember that in our report days ago we advanced several doubts about an alleged en masse disposal of bodies down Bus de la Lum. However, some cavers from the local rescue centre have alleged the recovery of corpses set in ice blocks with their military uniforms still intact [whose? Black Shirts? Germans?]

[. . .] Moreover, the population of neighbouring villages in Pian del Cansiglio has nurtured for years the idea of Yugoslavian-style infoibamento at the Bus de la Lum, as the grim fate reserved to numerous people who disappeared during the murky last phase of the war.

La Tribuna, 11 March 1989

Here comes the harsh rebuke of the ex-partisans:
'No atrocities on Pian Cansiglio'

Those murder victims represent one of Italy's darkest histories. [. . .]

The partisans, who lived the twenty months of the resistance, deny any atrocities while admitting that a dozen Fascists, plus three captured spies, were tried, found guilty, executed and made to disappear into the cave. [. . .]

According to the former partisans: 'There are no forgotten massacres here, but rather specific facts which we can explain'. Thus: No Fascist was thrown alive down the 200-something metres of the 'Bus'.

La Tribuna, 21 August 1989

The cave of controversy

And 'the Bus de la Lum (sp) in Cansiglio, where during the War of Liberation were thrown an unknown quantity of civilians' bodies (or 'collaborators' as some prefer to call them). The crux of the ongoing controversy between the families of the victims and the ex-partisans lies in the number of 'infoibati' and their conditions at the point in which they ended up down into the cave (were they dead or alive?)

Spokespersons of the committee for the funeral and reburial of the remains have claimed: 'Without animosity, we demand this historical memory not be erased, or much less denied'.

The truth. Which side, then, is right? Antonio Costalonga and Lino Pin, two partisans who fought in Cansiglio, claimed: 'To our knowledge nothing remotely near hundreds of people ended up into the Bus de la Lum. We were at war, and it may have happened that, for reasons of public order, we buried some dead individuals that way. It is almost certain that even some partisans ended up in there' pointed out Costalonga. 'Therefore, we do not see why, after 45 years, anyone would want to speculate on a tragedy that has cost us all so much suffering'.

'We have nothing to hide' – say the ANPI representatives of Vittorio Veneto. 'We were the first to flat out refuse a German proposal to cover the Bus de la Lum with cement to bury the bodies and the memory of the dead forever'.

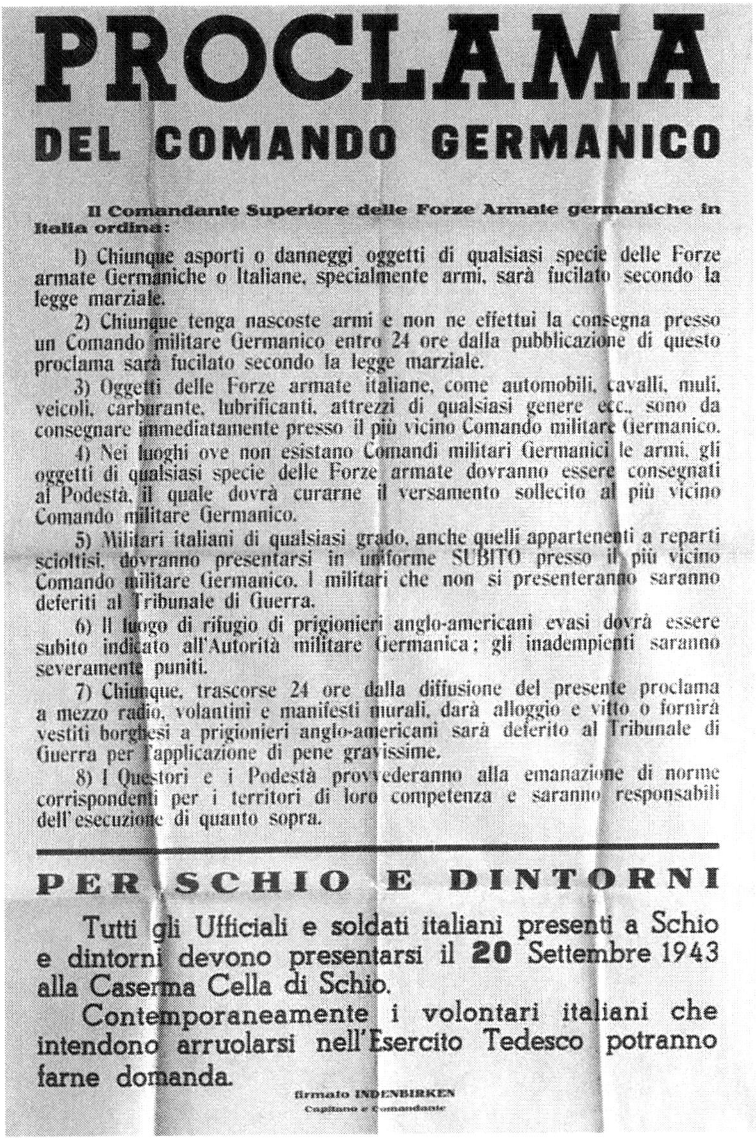

PROCLAMA

DEL COMANDO GERMANICO

Il Comandante Superiore delle Forze Armate germaniche in Italia ordina:

1) Chiunque asporti o danneggi oggetti di qualsiasi specie delle Forze armate Germaniche o Italiane, specialmente armi, sarà fucilato secondo la legge marziale.

2) Chiunque tenga nascoste armi e non ne effettui la consegna presso un Comando militare Germanico entro 24 ore dalla pubblicazione di questo proclama sarà fucilato secondo la legge marziale.

3) Oggetti delle Forze armate italiane, come automobili, cavalli, muli, veicoli, carburante, lubrificanti, attrezzi di qualsiasi genere ecc., sono da consegnare immediatamente presso il più vicino Comando militare Germanico.

4) Nei luoghi ove non esistano Comandi militari Germanici le armi, gli oggetti di qualsiasi specie delle Forze armate dovranno essere consegnati al Podestà, il quale dovrà curarne il versamento sollecito al più vicino Comando militare Germanico.

5) Militari italiani di qualsiasi grado, anche quelli appartenenti a reparti sciolti, dovranno presentarsi in uniforme SUBITO presso il più vicino Comando militare Germanico. I militari che non si presenteranno saranno deferiti al Tribunale di Guerra.

6) Il luogo di rifugio di prigionieri anglo-americani evasi dovrà essere subito indicato all'Autorità militare Germanica; gli inadempienti saranno severamente puniti.

7) Chiunque, trascorse 24 ore dalla diffusione del presente proclama a mezzo radio, volantini e manifesti murali, darà alloggio e vitto o fornirà vestiti borghesi a prigionieri anglo-americani sarà deferito al Tribunale di Guerra per l'applicazione di pene gravissime.

8) I Questori e i Podestà provvederanno alla emanazione di norme corrispondenti per i territori di loro competenza e saranno responsabili dell'esecuzione di quanto sopra.

PER SCHIO E DINTORNI

Tutti gli Ufficiali e soldati italiani presenti a Schio e dintorni devono presentarsi il **20** Settembre 1943 alla Caserma Cella di Schio.

Contemporaneamente i volontari italiani che intendono arruolarsi nell'Esercito Tedesco potranno farne domanda.

firmato INDENBIRKEN
Capitano e Comandante

Figure A.1 Schio (Vicenza), 1943. German poster declaring the establishment of martial law in the town and announcing a draft of Italian men into the forces of the Salo' Republican Army.

Source: Wikicommons

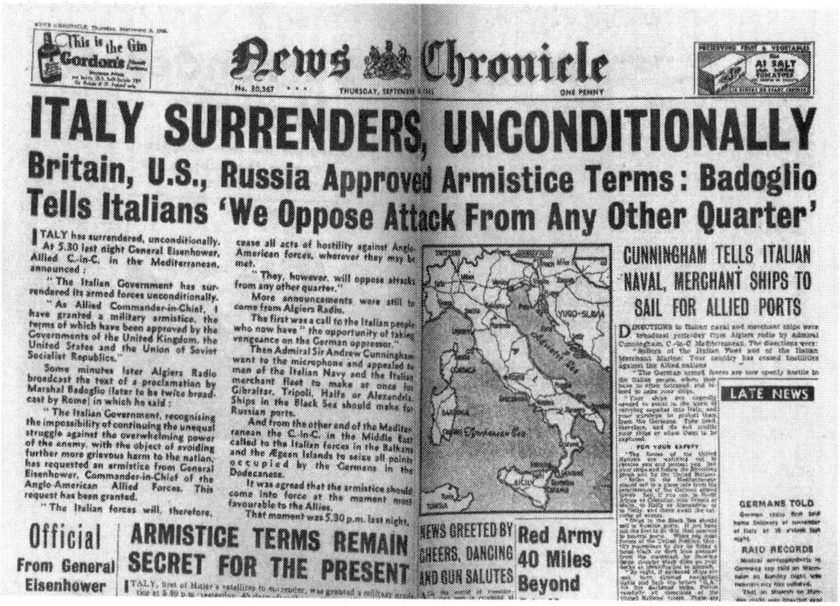

News Chronicle

ONE PENNY

ITALY SURRENDERS, UNCONDITIONALLY

Britain, U.S., Russia Approved Armistice Terms: Badoglio Tells Italians 'We Oppose Attack From Any Other Quarter'

ITALY has surrendered, unconditionally. At 5.30 last night General Eisenhower, Allied C.-in-C. in the Mediterranean, announced:

"The Italian Government has surrendered its armed forces unconditionally.

"As Allied Commander-in-Chief, I have granted a military armistice, the terms of which have been approved by the Governments of the United Kingdom, the United States and the Union of Soviet Socialist Republics."

Some minutes later Algiers Radio broadcast the text of a proclamation by Marshal Badoglio (later to be twice broadcast by Rome) in which he said:

"The Italian Government, recognising the impossibility of continuing the unequal struggle against the overwhelming power of the enemy, with the object of avoiding further more grievous harm to the nation, has requested an armistice from General Eisenhower, Commander-in-Chief of the Anglo-American Allied Forces. This request has been granted.

"The Italian forces will, therefore, cease all acts of hostility against Anglo-American forces, wherever they may be met.

"They, however, will oppose attacks from any other quarter."

More announcements were still to come from Algiers Radio.

The first was a call to the Italian people who now have "the opportunity of taking vengeance on the German oppressor."

Then Admiral Sir Andrew Cunningham went to the microphone and appealed to men of the Italian Navy and the Italian merchant fleet to make at once for Gibraltar, Tripoli, Haifa or Alexandria. Ships in the Black Sea should make for Russian ports.

And from the other end of the Mediterranean the C.-in-C. in the Middle East called to the Italian forces in the Balkans and the Ægean Islands to seize all points occupied by the Germans in the Dodecanese.

It was agreed that the armistice should come into force at the moment most favourable to the Allies.

That moment was 5.30 p.m. last night,

Official From General Eisenhower

ARMISTICE TERMS REMAIN SECRET FOR THE PRESENT

NEWS GREETED BY CHEERS, DANCING AND GUN SALUTES

Red Army 40 Miles Beyond

CUNNINGHAM TELLS ITALIAN NAVAL, MERCHANT SHIPS TO SAIL FOR ALLIED PORTS

LATE NEWS

GERMANS TOLD

RAID RECORDS

Figure A.2 *News Chronicle*: Italy's unconditional surrender is big news.

Source: Wikicommons

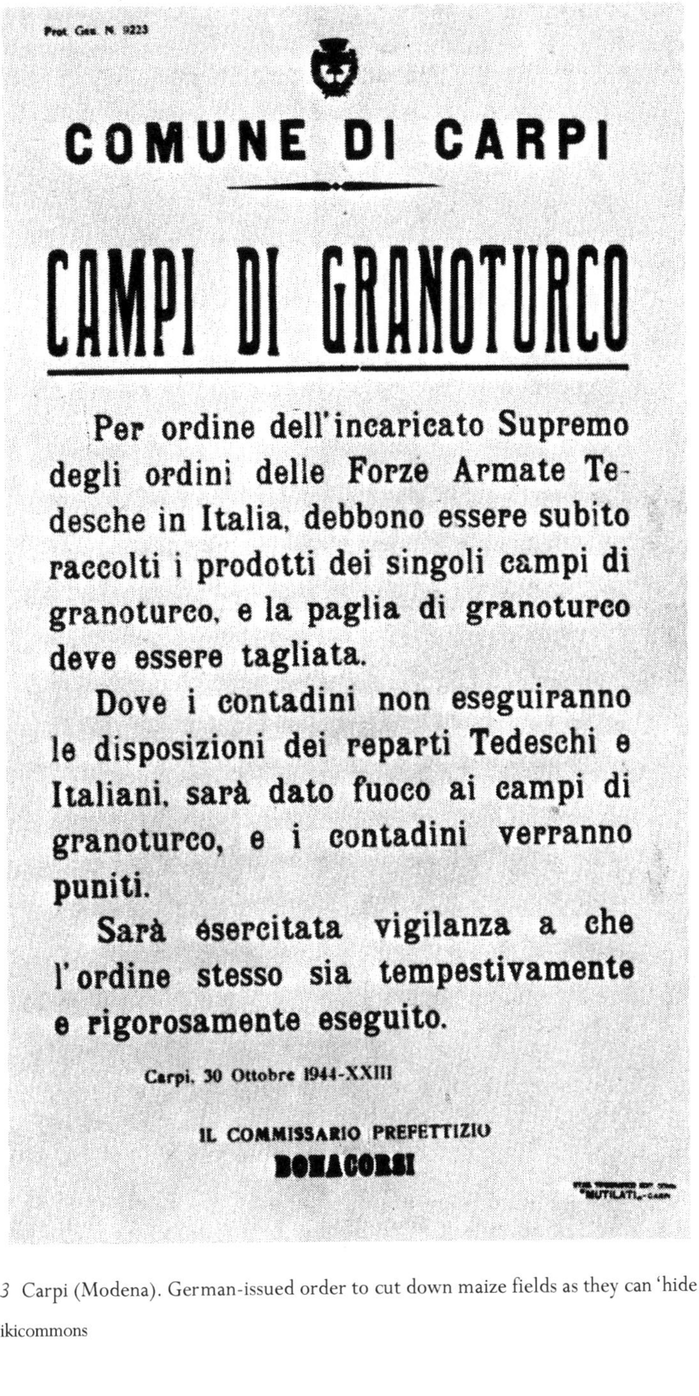

Prot. Gen. N. 9223

COMUNE DI CARPI

CAMPI DI GRANOTURCO

Per ordine dell'incaricato Supremo degli ordini delle Forze Armate Tedesche in Italia, debbono essere subito raccolti i prodotti dei singoli campi di granoturco, e la paglia di granoturco deve essere tagliata.

Dove i contadini non eseguiranno le disposizioni dei reparti Tedeschi e Italiani, sarà dato fuoco ai campi di granoturco, e i contadini verranno puniti.

Sarà esercitata vigilanza a che l'ordine stesso sia tempestivamente e rigorosamente eseguito.

Carpi, 30 Ottobre 1944-XXIII

IL COMMISSARIO PREFETTIZIO
BONACORSI

Figure A.3 Carpi (Modena). German-issued order to cut down maize fields as they can 'hide men'.

Source: Wikicommons

Figure A.4 Poster inviting Italians to work in Germany.

Source: Wikicommons

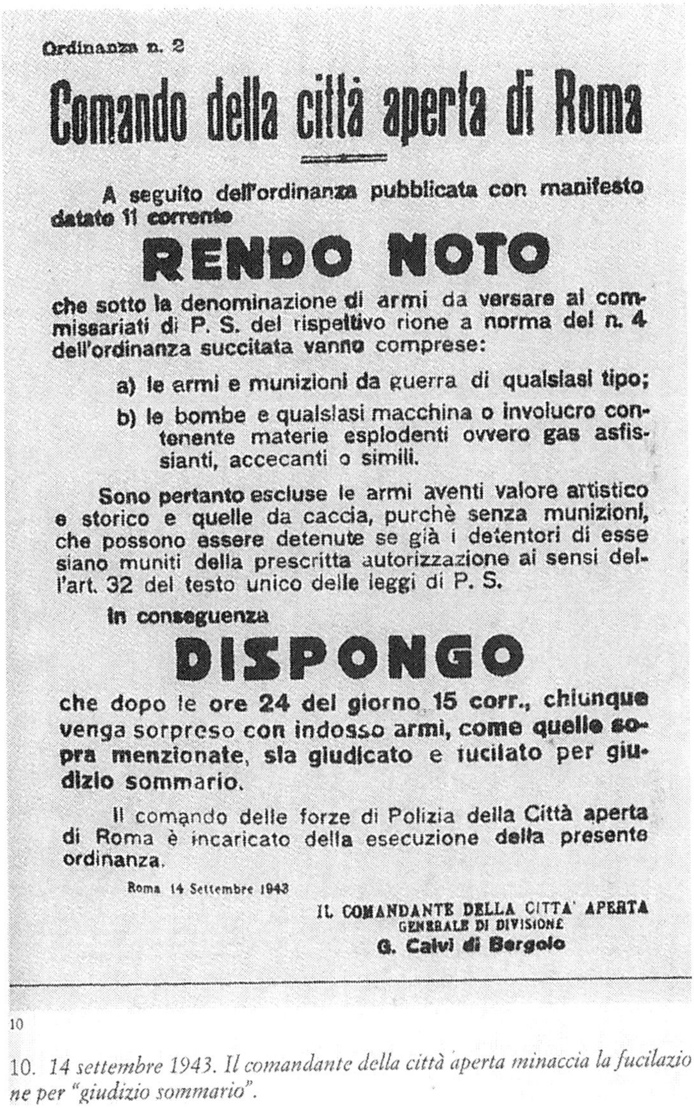

Ordinanza n. 2

Comando della città aperta di Roma

A seguito dell'ordinanza pubblicata con manifesto datato 11 corrente

RENDO NOTO

che sotto la denominazione di armi da versare ai commissariati di P. S. del rispettivo rione a norma del n. 4 dell'ordinanza succitata vanno comprese:

a) le armi e munizioni da guerra di qualsiasi tipo;

b) le bombe e qualsiasi macchina o involucro contenente materie esplodenti ovvero gas asfissianti, accecanti o simili.

Sono pertanto escluse le armi aventi valore artistico e storico e quelle da caccia, purchè senza munizioni, che possono essere detenute se già i detentori di esse siano muniti della prescritta autorizzazione ai sensi dell'art. 32 del testo unico delle leggi di P. S.

In conseguenza

DISPONGO

che dopo le ore 24 del giorno 15 corr., chiunque venga sorpreso con indosso armi, come quelle sopra menzionate, sia giudicato e fucilato per giudizio sommario.

Il comando delle forze di Polizia della Città aperta di Roma è incaricato della esecuzione della presente ordinanza.

Roma 14 Settembre 1943

IL COMANDANTE DELLA CITTA' APERTA
GENERALE DI DIVISIONE
G. Calvi di Bergolo

10

10. *14 settembre 1943. Il comandante della città aperta minaccia la fucilazione per "giudizio sommario".*

Figure A.5 Rome Open City proclaim.

Source: Wikicommons

Bibliography

Adorno, T., Frenkel-Brunswik, E., Levinson, D. and Sanford, N. 1950. *The Authoritarian Personality*. New York: Harper & Brothers.

Agamben, G. 2002. *L'Aperto: L'Uomo e l'Animale*. Turin: Bollati Boringhieri.

Ahmed, S. 2004a. Collective feelings: Or, the impressions left by others. *Theory Culture Society* 21 (2): 25–42.

Ahmed, S. 2004b. Affective economies. *Social Text* 22: 114–139.

Ahmed, S. 2010. Happy objects. In M. Greg and Seigworth, G. J. (eds.) *The Affect Theory Reader*. Durham, NC: Duke University Press, 29–51.

Altoè, Lorenzo. Interview with author on 18 December 2011.

Amantia, A. and Svaluto Moreolo, M. 2004. *Renato De Zordo e la Resistenza a Perarolo: Memorie Documenti Testimonianze*. Belluno: ISBREC.

Anderson, B. and Harrison, P. 2010. The promise of non – representational theories. In B. Anderson and Harrison, P. 2000 (eds.) *Taking – Place: Non Representational Theories and Geography*. Farnham: Ashgate, 1–36.

Anderson, B. and McFarlane, C. 2011. Assemblage and geography. *Area* 43 (2): 124–127.

Anderson, J. 2010. *Understanding Cultural Geography: Places and Traces*. London: Routledge.

Andrews, G. J., Kearns, R. A., Kontos, P. and Wilson, V. 2006. 'Their finest hour': Older people, oral histories and the historical geography of social life. *Social and Cultural Geography* 7 (2): 153–179.

Anico, M. and Peralta, E. (eds.) 2009. *Heritage and Identity: Engagement and Demission in the Contemporary World*. London: Routledge.

Ankersmit, F. 1996. Can we experience the past. In R. Torstendahl and Veit-Brause, I. (eds.) *History – Making: The Intellectual and Social Formation of a Discipline*. Stockholm: Almqvist and Wiksell International, 47–76.

Ankersmit, F. 2005. *Sublime Historical Experience*. Stanford: Stanford University Press.

Anna, G. Interview with author on 3 August 2011.

Antze, P. and Lambek, M. 1996. Introduction: Forecasting memory. In P. Antze and Lambek, M. (eds.) *Tense Past: Cultural Essays in Trauma and Memory*. London: Routledge, x–xxxviii.

Appadurai, A. 1986. Introduction: Commodities and the politics of value. In A. Appadurai (ed.) *The Social Life of Things: Commodities in Cultural Perspective*. Cambridge: Cambridge University Press, 3–63.

Artom, E. and Schwarz, G. 2008. *Diario di un Partigiano Ebreo. Gennaio 1940–Febbraio 1944*. A cura di Guri Schwarz. Turin: Bollati Boringhieri.

Askins, K. 2009. That's just what I do: Placing emotion in academic activism. *Emotion Space and Society* 2 (2009): 4–13.

Bibliography 191

Assmann, J. and Czaplicka, J. 1995. Memory and cultural identity: New German critique. *Cultural History/Cultural Studies* 65: 125–133.

Atkinson, R. 2007. *The Day of Battle: The War in Sicily and Italy 1943–1944*. London: Barnes & Noble.

Azzalini, Aldo Bruno. Interviews with author on 23 December 2010 and on 15 January 2011.

Bachelard, G. 1992 [1958]. *The Poetics of Space*. Boston: Beacon Press.

Bachelard, G. 1958. *La Poétique de l'Espace*. Paris: Presses Universitaires de France [Beacon, 1969 English Paperback edition].

Bakhtin, M. M. 1981. *The Dialogic Imagination: Four Essays*. Holquist, M. (ed.), translated by Caryl Emerson and Michael Holquist. Austin: University of Texas Press.

Baldissara, L. and Pezzino, P. 2009. *Il Massacro. Guerra ai Civili a Monte Sole*. Bologna: Il Mulino.

Baldoli, C. 2009. *A History of Italy*. London: Palgrave.

Ballone, A. 2007. La Resistenza. In M. Isnenghi (ed.) *I Luoghi della Memoria. Strutture ed Eventi dell'Italia Unita*. Rome: Laterza. Online at https://docs.google.com/viewer?a=v&pid=sites&srcid=ZGVmYXVsdGRvbWFpbnxtYXN0ZXJlc3R1ZGlvc2l0YWxpYW5vc3xneDo3YzdiNjRjMDU1MWQ5MzBk&pli=1. Last accessed on 10 April 2015.

Banchieri, R. 2008. Memorie. In M. Sega (ed.) *Eravamo Fatte di Stoffa Buona: Donne e Resistenza in Veneto*. Venice: nuovadimensione, 175–184.

Barad, K. 2007. *Meeting the Universe Half Way*. Durham, NC: Duke University Press.

Barad, K. 2013. Posthumanist performativity: Toward an understanding of how matter comes to matter. *Signs: Journal of Women in Culture and Society* 28 (3): 801–831. Online at http://uspace.shef.ac.uk/servlet/JiveServlet/downloadBody/66890-102-1-128601/signsbarad.pdf. Last accessed on 1 May 2014.

Bartrop, P. 2014. *Encountering Genocide: Personal Accounts from Victims, Perpetrators, and Witnesses*. Santa Barbara: ABC – CLIO.

Bates, M. 1996. *The Wars We Took to Vietnam: Cultural Conflict and Storytelling*. Berkeley: University of California Press.

Battaglia, R. 1953. *Storia della Resistenza Italiana*. Turin: Einaudi.

Battaglia, R. 1957. *The Story of the Italian Resistance*. London: Oldhams.

BBC News. 13 January 2007. Italy convicts Nazis of massacre. Online at http://news.bbc.co.uk/1/hi/world/europe/6259987.stm.

BBC News. 29 September 2015. Drawings of WW2 exploding chocolate bar bombs discovered. Online at http://www.bbc.co.uk/news/uu-34399018.

BBC News. 30 September 2015. Drawings reveal Germans' World War Two boobytrap bombs, by Nick Higham. Online at http://www.bbc.co.uk/news/uk-34396939.

Beatty, A. 2014. Anthropology and emotion. *Journal of the Royal Anthropological Institute* 20 (3): 545–563.

Beaumont, J. 1995. *The Politics of a Divided Society: Australia's War, 1914–1918*. St. Leonards: Allen & Unwin.

Behan, T. 2009. *The Italian Resistance: Fascists, Guerrillas and the Allies*. London: Pluto Press.

Belco, V. 2008. *War, Massacre, and Recovery in Central Italy 1943–1948*. Toronto: University of Toronto Press.

Bell, Ian. Imperial War Museum, Accession no. 19875.

Bell, Lorenzo. Interviewed by Myers Brown. Library of Congress, Accession no. AFC/2001/001/51535.

Bell, M. M. 1997. The ghosts of place. *Theory and Society* 26: 813–836.

Bendix, R. 2000. The pleasures of the ear: Towards an ethnography of listening. *Cultural Analysis* 1. Online at http://socrates.berkeley.edu/~caforum/volume1/vol1_article3.html.

Bernacchi, A. Interviewed by S. Khan on 26 February 2007. Library of Congress, Accession no. AFC/2001/001/01792.

Bernhard, P. n.d. Tagebuchsarchiv Accession no. 3310.

Bibliography

Bille, M., Hastrup, F. and Sørensen, T. 2010 (eds.) *An Anthropology of Absence: Materializations of Transcendence and Loss*. Berlin: Springer.

Black, M. 2003. Expellees tell tales. *History and Memory* 25 (1): 77–110.

Bocca, G. 1977. *Partigiani della Montagna*. Milan: Feltrinelli.

Bolt, B. 2008. A performative paradigm for the creative arts? *Working Papers in Art and Design* 5. Available online https://www.herts.ac.uk/__data/assets/pdf_file/0015/12417/WPIAAD_vol5_bolt.pdf. Last accessed on 16 August 2016.

Bondi, L. 2005a. Making connections and thinking through emotions: Between geography and psychotherapy. *Transactions of the Institute of British Geographers* 30 (4): 433–448.

Bondi, L. 2005b. Troubling space, making space, doing space. *Group Analysis* 38: 137–149.

Bondi, L. 2014. Understanding feelings: Engaging with unconscious communication and embodied knowledge. *Emotion Space and Society* 10: 44–54.

Bondi, L., Cameron, L., Davidson, J. and Smith, M. 2009 (eds.) *Emotion, Place and Culture*. Aldershot: Ashgate.

Bondi, L., Davidson, J. and Smith, M. 2005. Introduction: Geography's 'emotional turn'. In J. Davidson, Smith, M. and Bondi, L. (eds.) *Emotional Geographies*. Aldershot: Ashgate, 1–16.

Borer, T. A. 2003. A taxonomy of victims and perpetrators: Human rights and reconciliation in South Africa. *Human Rights Quarterly* 25 (4): 1088–1116.

Bornat, J. 2001. Reminiscence and oral history: Parallel universes or shared endeavour? *Ageing and Society* 21 (2): 219–241.

Bourdieu, P. 1986. The forms of capital. In J. Richardson (ed.) *Handbook of Theory and Research for the Sociology of Education*. New York: Greenwood, 241–258.

Boston Museum of World War II. Online at http://www.museumofworldwarii.com/resistance. Last accessed on 4 October 2013.

Bosworth, R. 2006. *Mussolini's Italy*. London and New York: Penguin.

Braidotti, R. 2006. Posthuman, all too human: Towards a new process ontology. *Theory, Culture & Society* 23 (7–8): 197–208.

Bravo, A. and Bruzzone, A. M. 2000. *In Guerra Senza Armi. Storie di Donne 1940–1945*. Rome: Laterza.

Brennan, T. 2004. *The Transmission of Affect*. Ithaca: Cornell University Press.

Brescacin, P. P. 2010. *La Colonna d'Oro del Menare' e il Tesoro di Conegliano*. Vittorio Veneto: Tipse.

Brescacin, P. P. 2013. *Quel Sangue Che Abbiamo Dimenticato*. Volume 1. Vittorio Veneto: Tipse.

Brescacin, P. P. 2014. *Quel Sangue Che Abbiamo Dimenticato*. Volume 2. Vittorio Veneto: Tipse.

Brescacin, P. P. (ed.) and Tillman, H. 2001. *Missione Beriwind in Cansiglio*. Vittorio Veneto: Istituto per la Storia della Resistenza e della Società Contemporanea del Vittoriese (ISREV).

Brescacin, P. P. 2013. *Quel Sangue che Abbiamo Dimenticato. Volume I*. Vittorio Veneto: Tipse.

Brighton, S. 2011. Applied archaeology and community collaboration: Uncovering the past and empowering the present. *Human Organization* 70(4): 344–354.

Buchli, V. 2015. *An Archaeology of the Immaterial*. London: Routledge.

Burkitt, I. 2012. Emotional reflexivity: Feeling, emotion and imagination in reflexive dialogues. *Sociology* 46(2): 458–472.

Busato, E. Interviewed by the author on 8 August 2011.

Butler, J. 2009. *Frames of War: When Is Life Grievable?* London: Verso.

Calvino, I. 1964. *Il Sentiero dei Nidi di Ragno*. Turin: Einaudi.

Cameron, E. 2012. New geographies of story and storytelling. *Progress in Human Geography* 36(5): 573–592.

Cándida-Smith, R. 2002. Introduction: Performing the Aarchive. In R. Cándida-Smith (ed.) *Art and the Performance of Memory: Sounds and Gestures of Recollection*. New York: Routledge, 1–12.

Canella, Bruno. Interview with author on 23 December 2010.

Canetti, E. 1960. *Crowds and Power*. London: Macmillan.
Canetti, E. 1984 [1960]. *Crowds and Power*. NewYork: Farrar, Straus and Giroux.
Cappelletto, F. 2003. Long term memory of extreme events: From autobiography to history. *Journal of the Royal Anthropological Institute* (N.S.) 9: 241–260.
Cappelletto, F. 2005. Introduction. In F. Cappelletto (ed.) *Memory and World War II: An Ethnographic Approach*. Oxford: Berg, 1–38.
Cassina Wolf, E. 2012. *L'Inchiostro dei Vinti. Stampa e Ideologia Neofascista, 1945–1953*. Turin: Mursia.
Ceccarelli, M. 2011. *Giornale del Tempo di Guerra. 12 Giugno 1940–7 Maggio 1945*. Bologna: Il Mulino.
Chumley, L. and Harkness, N. 2013. Introduction: Qualia. *Anthropological Theory* 13 (1–2): 3–11.
Ciapetti, S. 2007. *Il Salviatino. Ricordi di Guerra di un'Adolescente 1940-1945*. Archivio dei Diari di Pieve Santo Stefano, Accession no. MG/07.
Cimberle, E. 2004. *Il Passaggio*. Bassano del Grappa: Attiliofraccaroeditore.
Citton, R. Rev. n.d. *Note Riassuntive del Periodo Bellico 1943–1944–1945*. Unpublished diary.
Classen, C. 1993. *Worlds of Sense: Exploring the Senses in History and Across Cultures*. London: Routledge.
Classen, C. and Howes, D. 2006. The sensescape of the museum: Western sensibilities and indigenous artifacts. In E. Edwards, Gosden, C. and Phillips, R. (eds.) *Sensible Objects: Colonialism, Museums and Material Culture*. Oxford: Berg, 199–220.
Cobb, S. 2013. *Speaking of Violence: The Politics and Poetics of Narrative in Conflict Resolution*. Oxford: Oxford University Press.
Cole, T. 2015. (Re)Placing the past: Spatial strategies of retelling difficult stories. *Oral History* 42 (1): 30–49.
Coleman, P., Nowak, A., Vallacher, R., and Bui-Wrzosinska, L. 2007. Intractable conflict as an attractor: Presenting a dynamical model of conflict, escalation, and intractability. *American Behavioral Scientist* 50: 1454–1475.
Connerton, P. 1989. *How Societies Remember*. Cambridge: CUP.
Connolly, W. 2013. The 'new materialism' and the fragility of things. *Millennium: Journal of International Studies* 41 (3): 399–412.
Conte, S. and Strazzer, C. 2002. *Intervista a Domenico Favero, ex – Partigiano, e al Signor Bruno Arsiè, ex – Fascista*. Unpublished interview.
Conte, S. and Strazzer, C. 2003. *Intervista a Domenico Favero, ex-Partigiano, e al Signor Bruno Arsiè, ex-Fascista*. Unpublished interview.
Conway, M. 1996. Autobiographical memory. In E. Ligon Bjork and Ligon Bjork, R. (eds.) *Memory*. San Diego: Academic Press, 165–196.
Cooke, P. (ed.) 1997. *The Italian Resistance: An Anthology*. Manchester: Manchester University Press.
Cooke, P. 2000. Recent work on Nazi massacres in Italy during the Second World War. *Modern Italy* 5 (2): 211–218.
Cooke, P. 2009. *The Legacy of the Italian Resistance*. London: Palgrave Macmillan.
Cooke, P. 2011. *The Legacy of the Italian Resistance*. London: Palgrave Macmillan.
Coole, D. and Frost, S. (eds.) 2010. *New Materialisms: Ontology, Agency, and Politics*. Durham: Duke University Press.
Coombes, A. 2013. Witnessing history/embodying testimony: Gender and memory in post-apartheid South Africa. *Journal of the Royal Anthropological Institute* (N.S.) 17: 92–112.
Cornish, P. and Saunders, N. (eds.) 2014. *Bodies in Conflict: Corporeality, Materiality and Transformation*. London: Routledge.
Cronin, A. 2014. Between friends: Making emotions intersubjectively. *Emotion, Space and Society* 10 (2014): 71–78.
Crouch, D. 2015. Affect, heritage, feeling. In E. Waterton and Watson, S. (eds.) *The Palgrave Handbook of Contemporary Heritage Research*. Basingstoke: Palgrave Macmillan, 177–190.

Bibliography

Csikszentmihalyi, M. 1993. Why we need things. In S. Lubar and Wingery, W. (eds.) *History from Things: Essays on Material Culture*. Washington, DC: Smithsonian Institution Press, 20–29.

Csordas, T. 1990. Embodiment as a paradigm for anthropology. *Ethos* 18 (1): 5–47.

Csordas, T. (ed.) 1994. *Embodiment and Experience: The Existential Ground of Culture and Self*. Cambridge: Cambridge University Press.

Cubitt, G. 2007. *History and Memory*. Manchester: Manchester University Press.

Curti, G. H. 2008. From a wall of bodies to a body of walls: Politics of affect – politics of memory – politics of war. *Emotion, Space and Society* 1 (2008): 106–118.

Dallan, M. Interview with author on 20 December 2010.

Dant, T. 1999. *Material Culture in the Social World: Values, Activities, Lifestyles*. Buckingham, Philadelphia: Open University Press.

Darnton, R. 1991. *The Great Cat Massacre and Other Episodes in French Cultural History*. Harmondsworth: Penguin.

Davidson, J. and Bondi, L. 2004. Spatialising affect, affecting space: Introducing emotional geographies. *Gender, Place and Culture* 11 (3): 373–374.

de Certeau, M. 1984. *The Practice of Everyday Life*. Berkley: University of California Press.

de Certeau, M. 1986. *Discourse on the Other*. Minneapolis: University of Minnesota Press.

de Certeau, M. 1988. *The Writing of History*. New York: Columbia University Press.

Deleuze, G. 1991. *Bergsonism*. Boston: MIT Press.

Deleuze, G. and Guattari, F. 1987. *A Thousand Plateaus*. Minneapolis, MN: The University of Minnesota Press.

De Marchi, N. 2000. *Partigiani in Montagna*. Treviso: ISTRESCO.

Demoulin, S. 2002. Differential association of uniquely and non-uniquely human emotions to the ingroup and the outgroup. *Group Processes and Intergroup Relations* 5(1): 105–117.

De Nardi, S. 2013. 'No-one had asked me about that before': a focus on the body and 'other' Resistance experiences in Italian World War Two storytelling. *Oral History* 41(2): 73–83.

De Nardi, S. 2014. An embodied approach to Second World War storytelling mementoes: Probing beyond the archival into the corporeality of memories of the Resistance. *Journal of Material Culture* 19(4): 443–464.

De Nardi, S. 2015a. The enemy as confounding other: Interpersonal perception and displacement in memories of the Resistance and German occupation of Italy, 1943–1945. *History and Anthropology* 26(2): 234–254.

De Nardi, S. 2015b. When research and family clash: the role of autobiographical emotion in the production of stories about the Italian civil war. *Emotion Space and Society* 17: 22–29.

De Paris, W. 2005. *Memorie e Scritture Private*. Belluno: ISBREC.

DeSilvey, C. 2006. Observed decay: Telling stories with mutable things. *Journal of Material Culture* 11 (3): 318–338.

Diken, B. and Carsten Bagge, L. 2005. Becoming abject: Rape as a weapon of war. *Body and Society* 11 (1): 111–128.

Di Pompeo, C. 2009. *Diario Dedicato alla Mia dolce Antonietta*. Unpublished diary. Archivio dei Diari di Pieve Santo Stefano, Accession no. DG/08.

Di Scala, S. M. 1999. 'Resistance mythology'. In 'Behind enemy lines in World War II, the resistance and the OSS in Italy'. *Journal of Modern Italian Studies* 4 (1): 67–72.

Dixon, J. and Durrheim, K. 2000. Displacing place-identity: A discursive approach to locating self and other. *British Journal of Social Psychology* 39: 27–44.

Dolphijn, R. and van der Tuin, I. 2012. *New Materialism: Interviews and Cartographies*. Ann Arbor, MI: MPublishing, University of Michigan Library.

Domanska, E. 2006. The material presence of the past. *History and Theory* 45 (3): 337–348.

Domenico, R. 1999. The many meanings of anti – Fascism. In 'Behind enemy lines in World War II, the resistance and the OSS in Italy'. *Journal of Modern Italian Studies* 4 (1): 54–59.

Dougherty Delano, P. 2000. Making up for war: Sexuality and citizenship in wartime culture. *Feminist Studies* 26: 33–68.

Drozdzewski, D. 2012. Knowing (or not) about Katyń: The silencing and surfacing of public memory. *Space and Polity* 16: 303–319.

Drozdzewski, D. 2015. Retrospective reflexivity: The residual and subliminal repercussions of researching war. *Emotions, Space and Society* 17: 30–36.

Dudley, S. 2009. Museum materialities: Objects, sense and feeling. In S. Dudley (ed.) *Museum Materialities. Objects, Engagements, Interpretations*. London: Routledge, 1–18.

Durando, D. 2007. *[…] Ohimè, Gente, Udite!* Unpublished diary. Archivio dei Diari di Pieve S. Stefano, Accession no. DG/07.

Edwards, E. 2009. Photographs and history: emotion and materiality. In S. Dudley (ed.) *Museum Materialities. Objects, Engagements, Interpretations*. London: Routledge, 21–38.

Edwards, E., Gosden, C. and Phillips, R. 2006. Introduction. In E. Edwards, Gosden, C. and Phillips, R. (eds.) *Sensible Objects: Colonialism, Museums and Material Culture*. Oxford: Berg, 1–34.

Edwards, E. and Hart, J. (eds.) 2004. *Photographs Objects Histories: On the Materiality of Images*. London: Routledge.

Eufemia, F. 1972. Unpublished diary. Archivio dei Diari di Pieve Santo Stefano, accession no. DP/T2.

Evans, M. 2012. Feeling my way: Emotions and empathy in geographic research with fathers in Valparaíso, Chile. *Area* 44: 503–509.

Fahlander, F. and Oestigaard, T. 2004. Introduction: Material culture and post – disciplinary sciences. In F. Fahlander and Oestigaard, T. (eds.) *Material Culture and Other Things: Post – Disciplinary Studies in the 21st Century*. Lindome: Bricoleur Press, 1–8.

Fahlander, F. and Oestigaard, T. (eds.) 2014. *The Materiality of Death. Bodies, Burials, Beliefs*. Oxford: BAR International Series 1768.

Faure, S., Liparoto, A. and Papi, G. (eds.) 2012. *Io Sono l'Ultimo. Lettere di Partigiani Italiani*. Turin: Einaudi.

Favero, G. 1993. *Inesorabile Piombo Nemico*. Roncade: Piazza.

Favero, G. 2003. *Inesorabile Piombo Nemico*. Roncade: Edizioni Piazza. Available online: http://www.roncade.it/download/2008/Inesorabile%20Piombo%20Nemico.pdf. Last accessed 26 July 2016.

Fentress, J. and Wickham, C. 1992. *Social Memory*. Oxford: Blackwell.

Focardi, F. 2005. *La Guerra della Memoria*. Rome: Laterza.

Focardi, F. 2013. *Il Cattivo Tedesco e il Bravo italiano*. Rome: Laterza.

Foot, J. 2009. *Fratture d'Italia*. Milan: Rizzoli.

Fowler, C. 2013: *The Emergent Past: A Relational Realist Archaeology of Early Bronze Age Mortuary Practices*. Oxford: OUP.

Frazer, M. 2008. Memoria della Resistenza nei racconti di donne. In M. T. Sega (ed.) *Eravamo Fatte di Stoffa Buona: Donne e Resistenza in Veneto*. Venice: nuovadimensione, 159–174.

Frettlorh, Robert. Imperial War Museum, Accession no. 19590.

Frisch, M. 1990. *A Shared Authority: Essays on the Craft and Meaning of Oral and Public History*. Albany: State University of New York Press.

Gamble, C. 2015. *Archaeology: The Basics*. London: Routledge.

Gehler, M. 1996. *Verspielte Selbstbestimmung? Die Südtirolfrage 1945/46 in US Geheimdienstberichten und Osterreichischen Alden*. Innsbruck: Wagner.

Gentile, C. 2012. *Wehrmacht und Waffen-SS im Partisanenkrieg: Italien 1943–1945*. Padeborn: Schoeningh Ferdinand Verlag.

Gibson, M. 2004. Melancholy objects. *Mortality* 9 (4): 285–299.

Ginsborg, P. 1990. *A History of Contemporary Italy: Society and Politics 1943–1988*. London: Penguin.

Girard, R. 1977. *Violence and the Sacred*. Baltimore, MD: John Hopkins University Press.
Giust, Giuseppe. Interview with author on 8 March 2010.
Groeger, J. 1997. *Memory and Remembering: Everyday Memory in Context*. London: Longman.
Halbwachs, M. 1992 [1926]. *On Collective Memory*. Chicago: University of Chicago Press.
Hallam, E. and Hockey, J. 2001. *Death, Memory and Material Culture*. Oxford: Berg.
Hancock, S. 2009. Virginia Woolf's glasses: Material encounters in the literary/artistic house museum. In S. Dudley (ed.) *Museum Materialities. Objects, Engagements, Interpretations*. London: Routledge, 114–127.
Hammermann, G. 2004. *Gli Internati Militari Italiani in Germania 1943–45*. Bologna: Il Mulino.
Haslam, N., Bain, P., Douge, L., Lee, M. and Bastian, B. 2005. More human than you: Attributing humanness to self and others. *Journal of Personality and Social Psychology* 89 (6): 937–950.
Heeresarchiv Potsdam. Record no. RH 19–IX Oberkommando Heeresgruppe B (Italien).
Heidegger, M. 1953. *Sein und Zeit*. Tübingen: Niemeyer Verlag.
Heidegger, M. 1996 [1926]. *Being and Time*. Albany: State University of New York Press.
Heidegger, M. 1998 [1946]. Letter on humanism. In W. McNeill (ed.) *Pathmarks*. Cambridge: Cambridge University Press, 239–276.
Henare, A. J., Holbraad, M. and Wastell, S. 2007. Introduction. In A. Henare, Holbraad, M. and Wastell, S. (eds.) *Thinking Through Things: Theorising Artefacts Ethnographically*. London: Routledge, 1–31.
Henig, D. 2012. Iron in the soil: Living with military waste in Bosnia – Herzegovina. *Anthropology Today* 28 (1): 21–23.
Hill, L. 2013. Archaeologies and geographies of the post – industrial past: Landscape, memory and the spectral. *Cultural Geographies* 20: 379–396.
Hirsch, M. 1996. Past lives: Postmemories in exile. *Poetics Today* 17(4): 659–686.
Hirsch, M. 2008. The generation of postmemory. *Poetics Today* 29: 103–128.
Hodder, I. 2012. *Entangled: An Archaeology of the Relationships between Humans and Things*. Oxford: Wiley.
Hoskins, J. 1993. *The Play of Time: Kodi Perspectives on Calendars, Exchange and History*. Berkeley: California University Press.
Hoskins, J. 1998. *Biographical Objects: How Things Tell the Stories of People's Lives*. London: Routledge.
Howes, D. (ed.) 1991. *The Variety of Sensory Experience: A Sourcebook in the Anthropology of the Senses*. Toronto: University of Toronto Press.
Ianelli, M. n.d. *Coi Partigiani in Casa: 1936–1944*. Archivio dei Diari, Accession no. 2356.
Ingold, T. 1993. The temporality of landscape. *World Archaeology* 25 (2): 152–174.
Ingold, T. 2000. *The Perception of the Environment*. London: Routledge.
Ingold, T. 2007. Materials against materiality. *Archaeological Dialogues* 14 (1): 1–16.
Ingold, T. 2011. *Being Alive: Essays on Movement, Knowledge and Description*. London: Routledge.
Jackson, A. and Mazzei, L. 2011. *Thinking with Theory in Qualitative Research: Viewing Data Across Multiple Perspectives*. London: Routledge.
Jackson, M. 1996. *Things as They Are: New Directions in Phenomenological Anthropology*. Bloomington: Indiana University Press.
Jackson, M. 2002. *The Politics of Storytelling: Violence, Transgression, and Intersubjectivity*. Copenhagen: Museum Tusculanum Press.
Jay, M. 2011. In the realm of the senses: An introduction. *The American Historical Review* 116 (2): 307–315.
Jentsch, E. 1906 (25 August). On the psychology of the uncanny (der Unheimlich). *Psychiatrisch-Neurologische Wochenschrift* 8(22): 195–198.
Jones, O. 2011. Geography, memory and non-representational geographies. *Geography Compass* 5: 875–885.
Kalb, D., Marks, H. and Tak, H. 1996. Historical anthropology and anthropological history: Two distinct programs. *Focaal* 26–27: 5–13.

Katz, J. and Csordas, T. 2003. Phenomenology ethnography in sociology and anthropology. *Ethnography* 4(3): 275–288.

Kavanagh, G. 2000. *Dream Spaces: Memory and the Museum*. London: Leicester University Press.

Kearney, R. 1998. *Poetics of Imagining*. New York: Fordham University Press.

Kerby, A. 1991. *Narrative and Self*. Bloomington: Indiana University Press.

Kesselring, A. 1970 [1954]. *A Soldier's Record*. Westport, CT: Greenwood Press.

Kidron, C. 2012. Breaching the wall of traumatic silence: Holocaust survivor and descendant person – object relations and the material transmission of the genocidal past. *Journal of Material Culture* 17 (1): 3–21.

Kivimäki, V. and Tepora, T. 2009. War of hearts: Love and collective attachment as integrating factors in Finland during World War Two. *Journal of Social History* 43(2): 285–305.

Klinkhammer, L. 1996. *Stragi Naziste in Italia 1944–1945*. Rome: Donzelli Editore.

Koonz, C. 1994. Between memory and oblivion: Concentration camps in German memory. In J. R. Gillis (ed.) *Commemorations: The Politics of National Identity*. Princeton: Princeton University Press, 258–280.

Kyvik, G. 2004. Prehistoric material culture, presenting, commemorating, politicising. In F. Fahlander and Oestigaard, T. (eds.) *Material Culture and Other Things: Post – Disciplinary Studies in the 21st Century*. Lindome: Bricoleur Press, 87–102.

LaCapra, D. 2001. *Writing History, Writing Trauma*. Baltimore: John Hopkins University Press.

Langer, M. 1989. *Merleau – Ponty's Phenomenology of Perception: A Guide and Commentary*. Basingstoke: Macmillan.

Langhardt-Söntgen, R. 2011. *Partisanen, Spione und Banditen: Abwehrkämpfe in Oberitalien 1943–1945*. Dresden: Winkelried.

Latour, B. 1993. *We Have Never Been Modern*. Translated by Catherine Porter. Cambridge, MA: Harvard University Press.

Lavinia, F. Interviews with author on 4 August 2010 and on 23 December 2010.

Law, J. 2004. *After Method: Mess in Social Sciences Research*. London: Routledge.

Layolo, L. 1998. La Guerra Civile. In V. Pianca (ed.) *Geografia della Resistenza*. Vittorio Veneto: Tipse, 80–84.

Leach, J. 2007. Differentiation and encompassment: A critique of Alfred Gell's theory of the abduction of creativity. In A. G. Henare, Holbraad, M. and Wastell, S. (eds.) *Thinking Through Things: Theorising Artefacts Ethnographically*. London: Routledge, 167–188.

Lefebvre, H. 2004 [1992]. *Rhythmanalysis: Space, Time and Everyday Life*. Translated by S. Elden and G. Moore. London and New York: Continuum.

Legg, S. 2005. Contesting and surviving memory: Space, nation, and nostalgia in Les Lieux de Mémoire. *Environment and Planning D: Society and Space* 23: 481–504.

Lemon, A. 2013. Touching the gap: Social qualia and Cold War contact. *Anthropological Theory* 13 (1–2): 67–88.

Lepre, A. 1995. *Mussolini L'Italiano*. Rome: Laterza.

Levi, P. 1975. *Il Sistema Periodico*. Turin: Einaudi.

Levinas, E. 1998 [1991]. *Entre Nous: Thinking – of – the – Other*. Translated by M. B. Smith and Barbara Harshaw. New York: Columbia University Press.

Lewis, L. 1985. *Echoes of Resistance: British Involvement with the Italian Partisans*. Tunbridge Wells: Costello.

Leyens, J. 2009. Retrospective and prospective thoughts about infrahumanization. *Group Processes & Intergroup Relations* 12 (6): 807–817.

Leyens, J., Paladino, P., Rodriguez-Torres, R., Vaes, J., Demoulin, S., Rodriguez-Perez, A. and Gaunt, R. 2000. The emotional side of prejudice: The attribution of secondary emotions to ingroups and outgroups. *Personality and Social Psychology Review* 4 (2): 186–197.

Leys, R. 2000. *Trauma: A Genealogy*. Chicago: University of Chicago Press.

Lipsitz, G. 1990. Listening to learn and learning to Listen: Popular culture, cultural theory and American Studies. *American Quarterly* 42(4): 615–637.

Lorenzon, Rina. Interview with author on 4 August 2010.

Lorimer, H. 2005. Cultural geography: The busyness of being 'more – than representational'. *Progress in Human Geography* 29 (1): 83–94.

Lotto, A. 2008. Tra Tedeschi e Italiani. Storie di donne bellunesi. In M. T. Sega (ed.) *Eravamo Fatte di Stoffa Buona: Donne e Resistenza in Veneto*. Venice: nuovadimensione, 121–136.

Low, S. M. and Lawrence-Zúñiga, D. 2003 (eds.) *The Anthropology of Place and Space: Locating Culture*. London: Blackwell.

Lowenthal, D. 1985. *The Past is a Foreign Country*. Cambridge: Cambridge University Press.

Lowenthal, E. 2015. *Mani in Alto, Bitte. Memorie di Ico, Partigiano, Ebreo*. Rome: Zona.

Lutz, C. 1996. Engendered emotion: Gender, power, and the rhetoric of emotional control in American discourse. In R. Harre and W. G. Parrott (eds.) *The Emotions: Social, Cultural and Biological dimensions*. Thousand Oaks: Sage, 151–171.

Luzzatto, S. 2014. *Partigia. Una Storia della Resistenza*. Bologna: Il Mulino.

MacLure, M. 2008. Broken voices, dirty words: On the productive insufficiency of voice. In A. Jackson and Mazzei, L. (eds.) *Voice in Qualitative Inquiry: Challenging Conventional, Interpretive, and Critical Conceptions in Qualitative Research*. London: Routledge, 97–113.

Macpherson, H. 2010. Non – representational approaches to body – landscape relations. *Geography Compass* 4: 1–13.

Maddrell, A. 2013. Living with the deceased: Absence, presence and absence – presence. *Cultural Geographies* 20: 501–522.

Maistrello, F. 2001. *Partigiani e nazifascisti nell'Opitergino 1944–1945*. Verona – Istituto per la Storia della Resistenza: Cierre Edizioni, 65–67.

Mammone, A. 2006. A daily revision of the past: Fascism, anti-Fascism and memory in contemporary Italy. *Modern Italy* 11 (2): 211–226.

Marazio, Z. 2004. *Il Mio Fascismo. Storia di una Donna*. Rome: Verdemare.

Marcella, D. Interview with author on 20 October 2012.

Margalit, G. 2010. *Guilt, Suffering, and Memory: Germany Remembers Its Dead of World War Two*. Translated by H. Watzmann. Bloomington: Indiana University Press.

Marzona, Cesare. Interview with author on 1 May 2011.

McCormack, D. 2003. An event of geographical ethics in spaces of affect. *Transactions of the Institute of British Geographers* 28: 488–507.

McCormack, D. 2010. Remotely sensing affective afterlives: The spectral geographies of material remains. *Annals of the Association of American Geographers* 100: 640–654.

McSorley, K. (ed.) 2012a. *War and the Body: Militarisation, Practice and Experience*. London: Routledge.

McSorley, K. 2012b. Introduction. In K. McSorley (ed.) *War and the Body: Militarisation, Practice and Experience*. London: Routledge, 1–39.

McSorley, K. 2014. Towards an embodied sociology of war. *The Sociological Review* 62(S2), 107–128.

Melanco, G. 2002. *Annarosa Non Muore*. Belluno: ISBREC.

Meneghin, Francesca. Interview with author on 4 August 2010.

Merleau-Ponty, M. 1996 [1962]. *Phenomenology of Perception*. London: Routledge.

Meskell, L. 2002. Negative heritage and past mastering in archaeology. *Anthropological Quarterly* 75 (3): 557–574.

Meskell, L. 2010. An anthropology of absence: Commentary. In M. Bille, Hastrup, F. and Soerensen, T. F. (eds.) *An Anthropology of Absence. Materializations of Transcendence and Loss*. New York: Springer, 207–212.

Meyer, M. 2012. Placing and tracing absence: A material culture of the immaterial. *Journal of Material Culture* 17(1): 103–110.
Miller, D. 2008. *The Comfort of Things*. London: Routledge.
Miller, D. 2009. *Stuff*. London: Polity Press.
Miller, D. and Parrot, F. 2009. Loss and material culture in South London. *Journal of the Royal Anthropological Institute* 15 (3): 502–519.
Misztal, B. 2003. *Theories of Social Remembering*. Maidenhead: Open University Press.
Mochmann, I. and Larsen, S. 2005. Kriegskinder in Europa. *Aus Politik und Zeitgeschichte* (APUZ): 18–19: 2005. Online at http://www.bpb.de/apuz/29076/kriegskinder-in-europa?p=all. Last accessed on 2 June 2014.
Moles, K. 2009. A landscape of memories: Layers of meaning in a Dublin park. In M. Anico and Peralta, E. (eds.) *Heritage and Identity: Engagement and Demission in the Contemporary World*. London: Routledge, 129–140.
Morgan, P. 2009. 'I was there too': Memories of victimhood in wartime Italy. *Modern Italy* 14 (2): 217–231.
Morgan, S. 1999. War, civil war and the problem of violence in Calvino and Pavese. In H. Peitsch, Burdett, C. and Gorrara, C. (eds.) *European Memories of the Second World War*. Oxford: Berghahn Books, 67–77.
Morris, P. (ed.) 2007. *Women in Italy 1945–60*. Basingstoke: Palgrave.
Moshenska, G. 2008. Ethics and ethical critique in the archaeology of modern conflict. *Norwegian Archaeological Review* 41 (2): 159–175.
Moshenska, G. 2010. Gas masks: Material culture, memory, and the senses. *Journal of the Royal Anthropological Institute* 16: 609–628.
Moshenska, G. 2012. MR James and the archaeological uncanny. *Antiquity* 86 (334): 1192–1201.
Mullings, B. 1999. Insider or outsider, both or neither: Some dilemmas of interviewing in a cross-cultural setting. *Geoforum* 30 (4): 337–350.
Munn, N. 1996. Excluded spaces: The figure in the Australian Aboriginal landscape. *Critical Inquiry* 22(3): 446–465.
Munn, N. 2013. The becoming past of places. Spacetime and memory in nineteenth century, pre-Civil War New York. *HAU: Journal of Ethnographic Theory* 3(2): 359–380.
Muzaini, H. and Yeoh, B. S. A. 2005. War landscapes as 'battlefields' of collective memories: Reading the reflections at Bukit Chandu, Singapore. *Cultural Geographies* 12 (3): 345–365.
Nasini, C. 2012. *Una Guerra di Spie. Intelligence Anglo-americana, Resistenza e Badogliani nella Sesta Zona Operativa Ligure Partigiana 1943–1945*. Trento: Tangram.
Navaro-Yashin, Y. 2009. Affective spaces, melancholic objects: Ruination and the production of anthropological knowledge. *Journal of the Royal Anthropological Institute* (N.S.) 15: 1–18.
Navaro-Yashin, Y. 2012. *The Make-Believe Space: Affective Geography in a Postwar Polity*. Durham, NC: Duke University Press.
Neisser, U. 1993. Five kinds of self-knowledge. In U. Neisser (ed.) *The Perceived Self: Ecological and Interpersonal Sources of Self-Knowledge*. Cambridge: Cambridge University Press, 306–403.
Neitzel, S. and Welzer, H. 2013. *Soldaten: On Fighting, Killing and Dying: The Secret Second World War Tapes of German POWs*. New York: Simon & Schuster.
Neri Sernieri, S. 1995. A past to be thrown away? Politics and history in the Italian resistance. *Contemporary European History* 4 (3): 367–381.
Nora, P. 1981. *Les Lieux de Memoire*. Paris: Gallimard.
Nordstrom, C. 1997. *A Different Kind of War Story (The Ethnography of Political Violence)*. Philadelphia: University of Pennsylvania Press.
Norman, N. 2015. Online at http://www.vcita.com/society/2015/feb/18/defensive-architecture-keeps-poverty-unseen-and-makes-us-more-hostile.

Bibliography

Olick, J. 2008. Collective memory: A memoir and prospect. *Memory Studies* 1(1):23–29.

Oliva, G. 2002. *Foibe: le Stragi Negate degli Italiani della Venezia Giulia e dell'Istria*. Milan: Mondadori.

Olsen, B. 2003. Material culture after text: Re-membering things. *Norwegian Archaeological Review* 36 (2): 87–104.

Origo, I. 2000. *The War in Val D'Orcia: An Italian War Diary 1943–1944*. London: Allison & Busby.

Osborne, B. S. 2001. Warscapes, landscapes, inscapes: France, war and Canadian national identity. In I. Black and Butlin, R. (eds.) *Place, Culture and Identity*. Quebec: LUP, 311–333.

Ott, S. 2005. Remembering the resistance in popular theatre: A Basque controversy. In F. Cappelletto (ed.) *Memory and World War Two: An Ethnographic Approach*. London: Berg, 65–86.

Paladino, P. M., Leyens, J., Rodriguez, R., Rodriguez, A., Gaunt, R. and Demoulin, S. 2002. Differential association of uniquely and non-uniquely human emotions to the ingroup and the outgroup. *Group Processes and Intergroup Relations* 5 (1): 105–117.

Pansa, G. 2003. *Il Sangue dei Vinti. Quello che Accadde in Italia Dopo il 25 Aprile*. Milan: Sperling & Kupfer.

Pansa, G. 2005. *Il Sangue dei Vinti*. Milan: Longanesi.

Passerini, L. 2005. Memories of resistance, resistances of memory. In H. Peitsch, Burdett, C. and Gorrara, C. (eds.) *European Memories of the Second World War*. Oxford: Berghahn Books, 288–296.

Pavone, C. 1994 Edition[1991]. *Una Guerra Civile. Saggio Storico sulla Moralità nella Resistenza*. Turin: Universale Bollati Boringheri.

Peitsch, H. 1999. Studying European literary memories. In H. Peitsch, Burdett, C. and Gorrara, C. (eds.) *European Memories of the Second World War*. Oxford: Berghahn Books, x–xiii.

Perin, Clorinda. Interview with author on 25 August 2010.

Perin, Gildo. Interviews with author on 14 August 2010 and on 25 August 2010.

Petersen, R. 2005. Memory and cultural schema: Linking memory to political action. In F. Cappelletto (ed.) *Memory and World War Two: An Ethnographic Approach*. London: Berg, 131–154.

Pezzino, P. 2005. The Italian resistance between history and memory. *Journal of Modern Italian Studies* 10 (4): 396–412.

Pickering, M. and Keightley, E. 2012. Communities of memory and the problem of transmission. *European Journal of Cultural Studies* 16 (1): 115–131.

Pilotto, R. Interview with author on 8 August 2011.

Pink, S. 2009. *Doing Sensory Ethnography*. London and Los Angeles: Sage.

Pirjevec, J. 2009. *Foibe: Una Storia d'Italia*. Turin: Einaudi.

Pizzol, Renato. Interview with author on 24 September 2011.

Portelli, A. 1997. *The Battle of Villa Giulia: Oral History and the Art of Dialogue*. Madison: University of Wisconsin Press.

Portelli, A. 2003. The massacre at the Fosse Ardeatine: History, myth, ritual and symbol. In K. Hodgkin and Radstone, S. (eds.) *Contested Pasts: The Politics of Memory*. London: Routledge, 30–40.

Proctor, R. W. and Dutta, A. 1995. *Skill Acquisition and Human Performance*. Thousand Oaks, CA: Sage.

Proia, Liviano. Interview with author on 6 August 2011.

Pucci, E. 1992. Review of Paul Ricoeur's oneself as another: Personal identity, narrative identity and 'selfhood' in the thought of Paul Ricoeur. *Philosophy Social Criticism* 18: 185–209.

Pupo, R. 2005. *Il Lungo Esodo. Istria: Le Persecuzioni, le Foibe, l'Esilio*. Milan: Rizzoli.

Quazza, G. 1976. *Resistenza e Storia d'Italia. Problemi e Ipotesi di Ricerca*. Milan: Feltrinelli.

Radstone, S. 2005. Reconceiving binaries: The limits of memory. *History Workshop Journal* 59: 134–150.

Radstone, S. 2007. Trauma theory: Contexts, politics, ethics. *Paragraph* 30 (1): 9–29.

Reddy, W. 1999. Emotional liberty: Politics and history in the anthropology of emotions. *Cultural Anthropology* 14 (2): 256–288.

Reddy, W. 2001. *The Navigation of Feeling: A Framework for the History of Emotions*. Cambridge: Cambridge University Press.

Renshaw, L. 2010. The scientific and affective identification of republican civilian victims from the Spanish Civil War. *Journal of Material Culture* 15 (4): 449–463.

Renshaw, L. 2011. *Exhuming Loss: Memory, Materiality and Mass Graves of the Spanish Civil War*. Walnut Creek: Left Coast Press.

Residori, S. 2008. 'Gli ideali superano la paura': Le donne Vicentine nella Resistenza. In M. T. Sega (ed.) *Eravamo Fatte di Stoffa Buona*. Venice: nuovadimensione, 69–98.

Residori, S. and Crestani, A. 2003. *I Busi: Intervista ad Attilio Crestani*. Vicenza: ISTREVI, Istituto Storico della Resistenza nel Vicentino Ettore Gallo (Video).

Richard, A. and Rudnyckyj, D. 2009. Economies of affect. *Journal of the Royal Anthropological Institute* (N.S.) 15: 57–77.

Ricoeur, P. 1976. *Interpretation Theory: Discourse and the Surplus of Meaning*. Fort Worth: Texas Christian University Press.

Ricoeur, P. 1991. *A Ricoeur Reader: Reflection and Imagination*. Edited by M. J. Valdés. New York: Harvester Wheatsheaf.

Ricoeur, P. 1996. *The Hermeneutics of Action*. Edited by R. Kearney. London: Sage.

Riley, M. and Harvey, D. 2005. Landscape archaeology, heritage and the community in Devon: An oral history approach. *International Journal of Heritage Studies* 11 (4): 269–288.

Ritchie, D. 2003. *Doing Oral History*. Oxford: Oxford University Press.

Rival, L. 2001. Encountering nature through fieldwork: Expert knowledge, modes of reasoning, and local creativity. *Journal of the Royal Anthropological Institute* (N.S.) 20: 218–236.

Röhrs, M. 2009. *I Tedeschi. Das Bild der Deutschen in Italienischen Kriegserinnerungen*. Tübingen: Tübinger Vereinigung für Volkskunde.

Rose, M. 2002. Landscapes and labyrinths. *Geoforum* 33: 455–467.

Rose, M. 2002. The seductions of resistance: Power, politics, and a performative style of systems. *Environment and Planning D* 20(4): 383–400.

Rosenwein, B. 2006. *Emotional Communities in the Early Middle Ages*. Ithaca: Cornell University Press.

Rosenwein, B. 2010. Problems and methods in the history of emotions. *Passions in Context* 1 (2010/I). Available online http://www.passionsincontext.de/uploads/media/01_Rosenwein.pdf. Last accessed 14 August 2016.

Ross, John. Interviews with author on 10 March 2010 and on 12 March 2010.

Rusconi, G. E. 1997 [1995]. Le radici dei difficili rapporti tra Resistenza e Alleati. In P. Cooke (ed.) *The Italian Resistance: An Anthology*. Manchester: Manchester University Press, 153–156.

Salerno, M. and Zarankin, A. 2014. Discussing the spaces of memory in Buenos Aires: Official narratives and the challenges of site management. In A. Gonzalez-Ruibal and Moshenska, G. (eds.) *Ethics and the Archaeology of Violence*. New York: Springer, 89–112.

Sartorelli, T. 1987. *Una Famiglia Un Paese*. Unpublished diary. Archivio dei Diari di Pieve S. Stefano, Accession no. MP/87.

Saunders, N. 2000. Bodies of metal, shells of memory: 'Trench art' and the Great War re-cycled. *Journal of Material Culture* 5(1): 43–67.

Saunders, N. (ed.) 2004. *Matters of Conflict: Material Culture, Memory and the First World War*. London: Routledge.

Saunders, N. 2009. People in objects: Individuality and the quotidian in the material culture of war. In C. White (ed.) *The Materiality of Individuality*. London: Springer, 37–55.

Scalfari, E. 2008. Nella memoria di quello che fu il Gennaio 1943. Camelot Destra Ideale. Online at http://www.camelotdestraideale.it/2008/05/29/eugenio-scalfari-io-o-smesso-di-essere-fascista-solo-quando-ne-sono-stato-espulso/Blog entry posted on 29 May 2008 at 4:39 pm. Last accessed on 15 January 2016.

Scarry, E. 1985. *The Body in Pain: The Making and Unmaking of the World*. Oxford: Oxford University Press.

Scates, B., Tiernan, C. and Wheatley, R. 2014. The railway men: Prisoner journeys through the traumascapes of World War II. *Journal of War & Culture Studies* 7 (3): 206–222.

Scheer, M. 2012. Are emotions a kind of practice (and is that what makes them have a history)? A Bourdieuian approach to understanding emotion. *History and Theory* 51: 193–220.

Schiffer, M. 1999. *The Material Life of Human Beings: Artifacts, Behavior, and Communication*. London: Routledge.

Schreiber, G. 1996. *Deutsche Kriegsverbrechen in Italien. Täter, Opfer, Strafverfolgung*. Munich: Beck.

Schreiber, G. 2000. *La vendetta tedesca 1943–1945: le rappresaglie naziste in Italia*. Milan: Mondadori.

Secchia, P. and Nizza, E. 1968. *Enciclopedia dell'Antifascismo e Resistenza*. Rome: La Pietra.

Sedgwick Kosofsky, E. 2003. *Touching Feeling: Affect, Pedagogy, Performativity*. Durham, NC: Duke University Press.

Sega, M. T. 2008. *Eravamo Fatte di Stoffa Buona: Donne e Resistenza in Veneto*. Venice: nuovadimensione.

Semelin, J. 1993. *Unarmed against Hitler: Civilian Resistance in Europe 1939–1943*. Westport, CT: Praeger.

Seremetakis, N. 1994 (ed.) *The Senses Still: Perception and Memory as Material Culture in Modernity*. London and Chicago: The University of Chicago Press.

Simonsen, K. 2010. Encountering O/other bodies: Practice, emotion and ethics. In B. Anderson and Harrison, P. 2000 (eds.) *Taking – Place: Non Representational Theories and Geography*. Farnham: Ashgate, 221–240.

Smith, M. 2007. *Sensing the Past: Seeing, Hearing, Smelling, Tasting, and Touching in History*. Berkeley: University of California Press.

Spagnol, T. 2005. *Memoriette del Tempo Nero. A Cura di Pier Paolo Brescacin*. Vittorio Veneto: Tipse.

Stargardt, N. 2011. Beyond 'consent' or 'terror': Wartime crises in Nazi Germany. *History Workshop Journal* 72 (1): 190–204.

Stark, T. 1997. Richard Kearney's hermeneutic imagination. *Philosophy Social Criticism* 23 (2): 115–130.

Stephens, George. Imperial War Museum, Accession no. 24630.

Stewart, K. 2007. *Ordinary Affects*. Durham, NC: Duke University Press.

Stewart, S. 1994. *On Longing: Narratives of the Miniature, the Gigantic, the Souvenir, the Collection*. London: Duke University Press.

Stoller, P. 1989. *The Taste of Ethnographic Things: The Senses in Anthropology*. Philadelphia: University of Pennsylvania Press.

Stoller, P. 1997. *Sensual Scholarship*. Philadelphia: University of Pennsylvania Press.

Stone, Norman. 1996. Leicester Oral History Archive, Community History Collection. Interview 654, CH/122/211. Recording Date: 1/3/1996.

Straw, W. 1999. The thingishness of things: Keynote address for the interrogating subcultures conference, University of Rochester, March 27, 1998. In *– Visible Culture: An Electronic Journal for Visual Studies* 2. Online at http://www.rochester.edu/in_visible_culture/issue2/straw.htm.

Suleiman, S. R. 2006. *Crises of Memory and the Second World War*. Harvard: Harvard University Press.

Sylvester, C. (ed.) 2011. *Experiencing War*. Oxford: Routledge.

Sylvester, C. 2012. War experiences/War practices/War theory. *Millennium: Journal of International Studies* 40 (3): 483–503.

Taffarel, Giuseppe. Interviews with author on 4 August 2010 and on 11 August 2010.

Taussig, M. 1991. Tactility and distraction. *Cultural Anthropology* 6 (2): 147–153.

Thelen, D. 1990. Introduction: Memory and American history. In D. Thelen (ed.) *Memory and American History*. Bloomington: Indiana University Press, vii–xix.

Thompson, P. 2000. *The Voice of the Past: Oral History*. Oxford: Oxford University Press.

Thrift, N. 2000. Still life in nearly present time: The object of nature. *Body and Society* 6: 34–57.

Thrift, N. 2004. Intensities of feeling: Towards a spatial politics of affect. *Geografiska Annaler Series B* 86: 57–78.

Tilley, C. 2004. *The Materiality of Stone*. London: Berg.

Tiso Olivero, Aida. Interview with author on 2 July 2011.

Togni, F. 1988. *Avevamo Vent'anni (Anche Meno)*. Unpublished diary. Archivio dei Diari di Pieve Santo Stefano, Accession no. MG/88.

Tolia-Kelly, D. 2004. Locating processes of identification: Studying the precipitates of re-memory through artefacts in the British Asian home. *Transactions of the Institute of British Geographers* 29: 314–329.

Tolia-Kelly, D. 2006. Affect – an ethnocentric encounter? Exploring the 'universalist' imperative of emotional/affectual geographies. *Area* 38 (2): 213–217.

Tolia-Kelly, D.P. In press. Feeling and being at the (postcolonial) museum: presencing the affective politics of 'race' and culture. *Sociology*.

Tolson, R. 2007. *A Soldier Poet*. Oxford: Tolson Publications.

Tomsich, G. 1995. *Cantavo Giovinezza*. Unpublished diary. Archivio dei Diari di Pieve Santo Stefano, Accession no. MP/93.

Trentmann, F. 2009. Materiality in the future of history: Things, practices, and politics. *Journal of British Studies* 48 (2): 283–307. Online at http://eprints.bbk.ac.uk/2805/1/2805.pdf.

Tudor, M. 2004. *Special Force: SOE and the Italian Resistance 1943–1945*. Newtown: Emilia Publishing.

Turcato, G. and Zanon Dal Bo, A. (eds.) 1976. *1943–1945, Venezia nella Resistenza*. Venice: Comune di Venezia.

Turkle, S. 2007. *Evocative Objects: Things We Think With*. Cambridge, MA: MIT Press.

Valdevit, G. 1997. *Foibe. Il Peso del Passato*. Venice: Marsilio.

Valentine, G. and Sadgrove, J. 2012. Lived difference: An account of spatio – temporal processes of social differentiation. *Environment and Planning A* 44 (9): 2049–2063.

van Alphen, E. 1997. *Caught by History: Holocaust Effects in Contemporary Art, Literature, and Theory*. Stamford: Stamford University Press.

van Boeschoten, R. 2005. 'Little Moscow' and the Greek civil war: Memories of violence, local identities and cultural practices in a Greek mountain community. In F. Cappelletto (ed.) *Memory and World War II: An Ethnographic Perspective*. London: Berg, 39–64.

van Heekeren, D. 2015. Senses of magic: Anthropology, art and Christianity in the Vula'a lifeworld. In K. Ram and Houston, C. (eds.) *Phenomenology in Anthropology: A Sense of Perspective*. Bloomington: Indiana University Press, 248–267.

Veder, R. 2013. Walking through Dumbarton Oaks: Early twentieth-century bourgeois bodily techniques and kinesthetic experience of landscape. *Journal of the Society of Architectural Historians* 72 (1): 5–27.

Vendramini, F. 1993. Taped interview of 9 October 1993 with Al Materazzi and Giuliana Foscolo, Tapes 1 and 2. ISBREC Archive, Belluno, Cat. no. 17/93a – 93b.

Venohr, W. 2002. *Die Abwehrschlacht: Jugenderinnerungen 1940–1955*. Berlin: Junge Freiheit Verlag.

Vicchi, G. 1984. L'esperienza di un emiliano nella Resistenza Bellunese. In ISBREC (ed.) *Tedeschi, Partigiani e Popolazioni nell'Alpenvorland 1943–1945*. Belluno: ISBREC, 493–502.

Vicchi, Giorgio. Interview with author on 20 December 2010.

Viganò, R. 1949. *L'Agnese Va A Morire*. Milan: Bompiani.

von Uexküll, J. 1926. *Theoretical Biology*. New York: Harcourt, Brace & Co.

von Widmann, M. and Wiltenburg, M. 2006. Kinder des Feindes. *Spiegel Online*, 22/12/2006. Online at http://www.spiegel.de/spiegel/print/d-49976912.html. Last accessed on 5 June 2014.

Walkerdine, V. 2009. Steel, identity, community: Regenerating identities in a South Wales town. In M. Wetherell (ed.) *Identity in the 21st Century: New Trends in Changing Times*. Basingstoke: Palgrave, 59–75.

Walkerdine, V. 2010. Communal belongingness and affect: An exploration of trauma in an ex-industrial society. *Body and Society* 16 (1): 91–116.

Ward, D. 1999. Fifty years on: Resistance then, resistance now. In 'Behind enemy lines in World War II, the resistance and the OSS in Italy'. *Journal of Modern Italian Studies* 4 (1): 59–64.

Waterton, E. 2013. Landscape and non-representational theories. In P. Howard, Thompson, I. and Waterton, E. (eds.) *The Routledge Companion to Landscape Studies*. London: Routledge, 66–75.

Watson, S. 2007. History museums, community identities and a sense of place: Rewriting histories. In S. Knell, MacLeod, S. and Watson, S. (eds.) *Museum Revolutions*. London: Routledge, 160–172.

Wetherell, M. 2013. *Affect and Emotion: A New Social Science Understanding*. London: Sage.

Wette, W. 2006 [2002]. *Wehrmacht: History, Myth, Reality*. Translated by D. L. Schneider. Cambridge, MA: Harvard University Press.

Whatmore, S. 2006. Materialist returns: Practising cultural geography in and for a more – than – human world. *Cultural Geographies* 13: 600–609.

White, H. 1966. The burden of history. *History and Theory* 5 (2): 111–134.

White, H. 1992. Historical emplotment and the problem of truth. In S. Friedlander 2002 (ed.) *Probing the Limits of Representation: Nazism and the 'Final Solution'*. Cambridge, MA: Harvard University Press, 37–53.

White, L. 2000. Telling more: Lies, secrets and history. *History and Theory* 39 (4): 11–22.

Winter, D. 1979. *Death's Men: Soldiers of the Great War*. Harmondsworth: Penguin.

Witcomb, A. 2010. Remembering the dead by affecting the living: The case of a miniature model of Treblinka. In S. Dudley (ed.) *Museum Materialities: Objects, Engagements, Representations*. London: Routledge, 39–52.

Witcomb, A. 2016. Beyond sentimentality and glorification: Using a history of emotions to deal with the horror of war. In D. Drozdzewski, De Nardi, S. and Waterton, E. (eds.) *Memory, Place and Identity: Commemoration and Remembrance of War and Conflict*. London: Routledge, 205–220.

Withy, K. 2009. *Heidegger on Being Uncanny*. Dissertation by Katherine Withy, University of Chicago, Illinois. Available at https://muse.jhu.edu/article/615339

Wodak, R. 2006. Discourse-analytic and socio-linguistic approaches to the study of nation(alism). In G. Delanty and Krishan, K (eds.) *The Sage Handbook of Nations and Nationalism*. London: Sage, 104–117.

Wool, Z. 2013. On movement: The matter of U.S. soldiers' being after combat. *Ethnos* 78 (3): 403–433.

Woolf, S. 2005. Historians: Private, collective and public memories of violence and war atrocities. In F. Cappelletto (ed.) *Memory and World War Two: An Ethnographic Perspective*. London: Berg, 177–194.

Wright, C. 2004. Material and memory: Photography in the western Solomon Islands. *Journal of Material Culture* 9 (1): 73–85.

Wylie, J. 2002. An essay on ascending Glastonbury Tor. *Geoforum* 33: 441–454.

Wylie, J. 2005. A single day's walking: Narrating self and landscape on the South West Coast Path. *Transactions of the Institute of British Geographers* 30: 234–247.

Zanfranceschi, Nedda. Interview with author on 13 October 2010.

Zangrandi, G. 2001. *I Giorni Veri*. Recco, Genova: Le Mani.

Zanolin, R. and Brescacin, P. 2013. *I Ragazzi di Polcenigo*. Vittorio Veneto: Tipse.

Index

Names in **bold** indicate narrators quoted from oral history interviews and/or written sources

absence ii, 33, 76, 78, 90, 13, 133; absence-presence 8, 109, 116, 122, 123–4, 130, 133, 137; Law's presence, manifest absence and otherness 10; materiality (absence) 12, 14, 138, 146, 162, 163, 164, 165, 167
activists, activism (in the resistance movement), 20, 30, 45, 76, 103, 104, 150
Adorno, Theodor (historian, theory of crowds) 103, 104
affect (definition) 4, 6, 7, 10, 25; affect (role) 21, 25, 40, 69, 80, 98, 101–6, 123, 130–1, 164; affect and memory 5, 8, 10, 65, 78, 99, 106, 112, 128, 167, 173; affect and storytelling 11, 13, 15, 16, 38, 63, 86, 92, 93–4, 95, 98, 100, 106, 108, 111–12, 125, 132–3, 168, 176; affect as political catalyst 4, 5, 13, 20, 28–9, 42, 105; affectual events 20; melancholia (affect) 72, 76, 86, 124, 139, 158, 164
Ahmed, Sara (affect theory) 5, 69, 95, 102, 105, 118
Aliboni, Fulvio (deserting RSI soldier) 149
Allies, Allied 2, 6, 7, 8, 13, 16, 17, 18, 19, 94, 104, 136, 148, 150, 155, 158, 172, 176; Allied bombings 28, 42, 46, 47, 59–60, 109; Allied-held southern Italy 25, 41; Allied landings 24, 28, 142; Allied missions in Italy 90, 107, 109, 130, 135; Allied prisoners of war in Italy 25, 27; Allied reaction to Armistice announcement 27; Allies on Germans 56, 57; Allies' role in Italian imagination 59–60, 63
Alpenvorland (Reich-annexed area) 26, 27, 59, 126, 135, 136, 139
alterity 15, 48, 75, 99, 113, 119, 121, 171, 179; *see also* Otherness

Altoè, Lorenzo (veteran partisan) 69, 134, 145, 158
Anglo-Americans 17, 25, 28, 42, 43, 59, 142, 162; amphetamine use among Anglo-Americans 135
Ankersmit, Frank (historian) 125
anti-Fascism, anti-Fascists 21, 22, 45, 48, 70, 111, 147, 153; anti-Fascism during the Regime 24; Giustizia e Libertà (party) 29; organisation after armistice 25, 26, 29, 42, 43
Archivio dei Diari di Pieve Santo Stefano, Diary Archive at Pieve Santo Stefano 35
Armistice Day (capitulation day) 2, 6, 16, 18, 19, 21, 25, 29, 30, 43, 46, 142, 147, 150, 153, 158, 162, 163, 173, 177; Armistice radio announcement 25; Artom on the Armistice 105; Bell on the armistice 27; Cimberle on the Armistice 34; De Zordo on the Armistice 26; Donnelly on the Armistice 60; **Otto A.** on the Armistice 28
Artom, Emanuele (partisan, Jewish resistance fighter) 26, 29, 45, 49–50, 65, 72, 80, 81, 105, 125, 135, 150, 151; Artom on place 165, 175
assemblage (concept) 5, 11, 35, 109, 110, 114, 120, 122, 128, 137
autobiography 33, 112
autoethnography 21
Azzalini, Aldo (partisan) 64, 71

Bachelard, Gaston (philosopher) 1, 8, 95
Baldini, Armando (RSI officer) 1–4, 6, 7, 8, 10, 14, 20, 66, 92, 121, 168, 178, 179
Banchieri, Rosetta (partisan) 23, 83
Barad, Karen (philosopher, theory of intra-action) 99, 102, 122, 141

Barletta (town) 58
Bassano del Grappa (town) 100
being-in-the-world-at-war 102, 104
Bell, Ian (British soldier) 27
Bell, Lorenzo (US soldier) 94
Belluno (town) 21, 26, 27, 47, 55, 62, 70, 107, 108, 135, 139–40, 154, 173
Berlin-Rome Axis 24
Bernacchi, Alfredo (Fred) (US soldier) 59
body, bodies 6, 11, 14, 16, 68, 73, 101, 140–2, 162, 177, 178; body and identity 36, 70, 83, 84, 179; body-at-war 15; body-in-conflict 7, 68, 85, 127, 134, 143, 177; body in pain 12, 50, 85, 87, 151, 172; body memory 69, 71, 96, 137; at Buss de la Lum 89, 90–2, 115; disposal of dead bodies 85, 86, 87, 88, 111; female body 75–80, 136, 154; Jewish body 80–3; *see also* embodiment
Bondi, Liz (social scientist) 103, 113
Brescacin, Pier Paolo (historian) 2, 3, 78, 87, 90, 109, 110, 140; Brescacin on Colonna D'Oro 109–10
Brigate Nere, Black Brigades (Fascist infantry) 21, 49
Buffalo Division (US Army) 94
Buss De la Lum (site) 87–92, 93, 115, 140

Calvino, Italo (author) 96, 99, 169; *Sentiero dei Nidi di Ragno* [path of the spider nests] 96
Cándida-Smith, Richard (historian) 177
Canella, Giordano Bruno (Bruno) (partisan) 12, 131; on his wife's letter-poem 131–2
Canetti, Elias (historian, theory of crowds) 103, 104
Cansiglio (Forest) 70, 78, 88, 90–1, 153, 183–4
Cappelletto, Francesca (social antrhopologist) 55, 100, 167
Cassino, Monte Cassino 35, 71, 147; remembered by Frettlorh (Wehrmacht veteran) 160–1
Castelfranco Veneto (town) 39
Ceccarelli, Magda (witness) 12, 51, 59, 129, 171
Celentano, Francesco (Italian national, German prison camp internee) 56
Chappell, Howard (US OSS Head of Mission Taccoma) 107–8
Ciapetti, Sonia (witness) 27–8, 124, 129, 154
Cimberle, Emilio (RSI soldier) 30, 34
civil war (Italian) 31, 46, 113, 121, 124, 165, 179, 181; Cimberle's anti-civil war sentiment 34; civil war genesis 24–5, 121; Spanish Civil War 68

Cobb, Sara (conflict resolution scholar) 4, 6, 98, 99, 170
Comitato di Liberazione Nazionale (CLN) 29
Cortina D'Ampezzo (town) 77
Crestani, Attilio (partisan) 135
Csordas, Thomas (anthropologist, embodiment theory) 14
Curti, Giorgio Hadi (cultural geographer) 101

Dallan, Marcella (partisan) 38
De Bin, Aldo (partisan) 134–5, 156
de Certeau, Michel (philosopher) 3–4, 12, 15, 16, 20, 95–6, 98, 101, 112, 158, 163, 164, 167, 169
dehumanisation 44, 45, 79, 85, 178; Fascists dehumanisation (by others) 46; partisan dehumanisation 85
De Marchi, Nino (partisan) 61, 63, 64, 65, 74, 90
De Paris, Wilma (partisan) 76, 77, 78, 135–6
Deserters 13, 29, 51, 52, 54, 176
De Zordo, Renato (partisan) 26, 60
Di Pompeo, Corrado (witness) 35, 130–1
Domanska, Ewa (historian, theory of absent present) 14, 124, 130
Donnelly, John (British soldier) 60
Douglas-Taylor, Peter (British soldier) 53–4
Durando, Danilo (RSI soldier) 55
dwelling (Ingold's theory) 11, 36, 43, 45, 47, 61, 68, 78, 120, 153, 160

Edwards, Elizabeth (visual anthropologist) 121, 137
embodiment 4, 5, 7, 14–15, 35, 40, 43–5, 47, 50, 65, 68, 70, 75, 76, 101–2, 121, 127, 141, 171, 178; *see also* body
emotion (in wartime experience) 10, 14, 22, 25, 28, 43, 45, 50, 55, 143, 164; emotional absence-presence 123; emotional ingroups and outgroups (infrahumanization theory) 15, 84, 174, 175, 178; emotional practises 15, 103, 105; emotional regimes (Reddy) 15, 28, 101; emotion as political catalyst 4, 103, 104; empathy 53, 65, 86, 165, 168, 172, 173, 175–6; memory-emotion 38, 69, 98, 119–20; primary and secondary emotions 45, 174, 175; storytelling and emotion 87, 97, 100, 102–3, 108, 111, 133, 136–7, 161, 168
ethnography 4, 5, 7, 8, 10, 12, 14, 17, 21, 33, 34, 38, 90, 104, 109, 116, 118, 120, 123, 127, 164, 167, 168, 180; ethnographic encounter 111, 113, 120, 123, 137;

ethnographic-place-as-event (pink) 10; photographic ethnography 4, 179
experience (wartime) 95–9, 121, 125, 142, 143, 154, 168, 169; abject, abjection (dystopian wartime experience) 49, 75, 79, 88, 92, 115, 159, 160, 171; alienation (in wartime experience) 4, 26, 41, 65, 78, 101, 135, 147, 153, 156, 178; disorientation (in wartime experience) 55, 70, 113, 120, 141–2, 146–7, 162, 178; displacement (in wartime experience) 4, 10, 27, 30, 55, 75, 144, 147, 153, 162, 164, 167, 170, 179; experiential approach 15, 19–21, 101–6, 113, 116, 123, 137; Jewish experience 81, 82, 83, 115, 127, 158, 166; loss (experience) 38, 41, 80, 85, 100, 117, 122–3, 128, 131, 133, 134, 137, 141, 150, 163; trauma 78

family 20, 21–2, 76, 82, 98, 112, 113, 131, 155, 173
Fascism (Italian regime) 10, 25, 29, 31, 81, 90, 127, 171, 177, 178; dehumanisation (Fascists) 46, 85, 173; Fascist materiality 26, 56, 78, 124, 156, 157; Fascists (Italian) 2, 7, 8, 18, 24, 35, 48–50, 56, 59, 89, 126–7, 174, 175, 177; Fascist women 49, 77, 79; interaction with Fascists 31, 34, 40, 53, 54–5, 62, 77, 79, 134, 146, 165, 168, 172; killed Fascists 111, 112, 140; Mussolini and Petacci's execution 170, 171; Neofascists (on Buss de la Lum) 90, 92; partisans infiltrating Fascist rank and file 158; Roncade Fascist killings 159, 160
Favero, Domenico (Memi) (partisan) 16, 65, 71–2, 85–6, 87, 90, 172
Favero, Gianni (historian, author) 49, 52, 159, 160
Frescura, Lavinia (partisan) 65, 74, 151, 168, 173, 176
Frettlorh, Robert (Wehrmacht soldier) 71, 147, 160, 161
Frisch, Michael (historian) 12; 'More History' theory 12
Fucini, Renato (RSI soldier) 34

Germans in Italy during war 58, 64, 72, 73, 80, 116, 136, 139, 145, 147, 157–8, 174; dehumanisation of Italians 36, 72, 73; fair fight by Germans 49, 53, 55; German booby traps 129; German deserters 51, 52, 54, 55, 56, 84; German loot 109–10; German reflexivity 57–8, 71, 148; German resistance prisoners 85, 86, 87; Germans after the Armistice 25, 26, 27–8; Germans vs. Austrians 51; Gufo Nero (deserters' brigade in resistance with German elements) 13; hostility towards Germans 46, 55, 57, 58, 70; militaristic masculinity in German army 70; myth of the good German 168, 173; Nazi Germans 81, 106, 152, 179; SS (Sicherheitsdienst des Reichsführers-SS) 51, 52, 57, 58
Giust, Giuseppe (partisan) 65, 73, 90, 91, 141, 144, 155
GNR, Guardia Nazionale Repubblicana 2
Golden Column of Menarè 109, 110, 114
Gufo Nero (deserters' brigade in the resistance) 13

Hancock, Nuala (cultural heritage scholar) 31, 123
hearsay (phenomenon) 13, 23, 26, 97, 99, 107, 108, 109, 168
Heidegger, Martin (phenomenologist) 19, 114, 118, 142, 143; being-in-the-world 10, 142
Hirsch, Marianne (historian and philosopher) 20; postmemory theory 18, 160, 164, 167, 178, 180
historiography 4, 20, 94, 106, 114, 125, 162, 168
history 15, 22, 43; embodied histories 76, 124; everyday history 2, 22, 95, 96, 167; historicity (Heidegger) 118; history and storytelling 13, 14, 94; mainstream history 91, 97, 101, 125, 136, 163, 164, 168, 170; more history (Frisch) 12
Holewa, Herbert Franz (Wehrmacht soldier) 70–1

Ianelli, Margherita (Marzabotto) 131, 152
identity (role) 40, 43, 92, 101, 110, 118, 120; identity and language (in German-speaking Italy) 27, 48; identity and materiality 4, 6, 12, 15, 43, 46, 68, 102, 115, 108, 119, 170; identity and politics 30, 34, 45, 48, 52, 65, 81–2, 110, 160, 162; identity and war 16, 18, 19, 21, 40, 41, 44, 52, 78, 114, 129, 169; identity in storytelling 97–8, 168, 177, 179
imagination, imaginary (role) 5, 6, 7, 8, 12, 15, 16, 24, 38, 48, 88, 90, 92, 94, 95, 99, 102, 107, 108, 110, 114, 136, 137, 159, 167, 168, 169, 172, 182
Imperial War Museum archive (London) 35
infrahumanisation theory 44, 45, 70, 85, 171, 174, 180
Ingold, Tim (anthropologist) 11, 95, 98, 101, 106, 118, 150

interhuman theory (Levinas) 180
interviews, interviewing 36, 47, 86, 102, 120, 137, 168; interview materiality 15, 16–17, 34, 123, 128, 137, 164; interview practise 16–17, 33, 100, 114, 122, 164
intra-action (Barad) 99, 102, 122, 141

Jew, Jewish experience 29, 45, 51, 80, 81, 83, 115, 127, 158, 166; Fascist Racial Laws (1943) 82; Jewish resistance 45, 49, 80, 82, 158

killing (act) 10, 14, 20, 34, 49, 50, 51, 53, 61, 70, 87, 88, 108, 138, 146, 159, 171, 172; Suicide 81

landscape 43, 55, 69, 120, 134, 139, 141, 148, 153, 158, 162, 165, 169; hostile landscape perception 139, 144, 147, 153, 165; woods, woodland in resistance stories 11, 63, 71, 74, 78, 83, 89, 135, 136, 143, 146, 151, 156
Langhardt-Soentgen, Rainer (Wehrmacht soldier) 53, 58
Lesegno (town) 42
Levi, Primo (activist, author, partisan) 63, 80, 81, 82, 165, 166; Levi the partisan 82, 165–6
Levinas, Emmanuel (philosopher) 8, 31, 118, 163, 167, 168, 170, 171, 180
Lowenthal, Enrico (Ico) (partisan) 45, 51, 62, 73, 80, 82, 83, 84, 130, 144156, 158
Luzzatto, Sergio (author) 165, 166; *Partigia* 166

Maniago (town) 54
mapping practises 36, 38, 95–6, 98, 130, 141
Marazio, Zelmira (witness) 31, 79, 93, 126, 127, 175
Marinello, Caterina (witness) 126–7
Marzabotto (SS civilian massacre) 42, 131, 152
Marzona, Cesare (partisan) 134
Materazzi, Al (US OSS Agent) 107–8
materiality (definition) 4, 7, 12, 14, 16, 70; absent-present materiality 124, 129, 130, 131; American materiality 130; autobiographical materiality 21, 32–6, 37, 39, 69, 80, 83, 86, 170; Fascist materiality 126–8; interview materiality 120, 121, 122–3; materiality significance 6, 10, 24–5, 43, 118, 169, 177, 179; memory and materiality 33–6, 38, 49, 95, 115, 124; ruination (materiality) 149, 154; storytelling materiality 94, 96–100
Melanco, Giovanni (author, *Annarosa Non Muore*) 147

mementoes (things about the war) 11, 38, 96, 98, 115, 123, 128, 131, 133; interview mementoes 120, 122, 137, 169; mementoes as evocative objects 16, 117, 120–1
memory 111, 119, 123, 130, 136, 158, 162, 165, 167–8, 169, 173; divided war memory 6, 10, 20, 21, 22, 30, 46, 69, 87–91, 180, 181; Fascist counter-memory 2, 20, 174; history and memory 14; Italian counter-memory 2, 15, 87–91, 125, 177; materiality and memory 33, 36, 45, 49, 68, 69, 91, 96, 101, 115, 117, 120–1, 124–5, 128, 135, 137, 164; memory and storytelling 8, 11, 15, 20, 97–8, 120, 137, 150; memory and trauma 20–1, 87–8, 166; memory as mapping practise 38; places in memory 87, 88, 165; social memory 14, 30, 68, 98, 99, 107, 110, 133, 141
Menarè (locality) 109, 137
Meneghin, Francesca (partisan) 176–7
Merleau-Ponty, Maurice (phenomenologist) 31, 150, 163; *phenomenology of perception* 31, 150, 163
Moshenska, Gabriel (conflict archaeologist) 117, 149

Neitzel, Sonke and Welzer, Harald (historians, authors of *Soldaten*) 51–3, 58, 70, 73, 85, 87, 95, 97, 100, 170
new materialism (theory) 119
Nordstrom, Carolyn (military historian) 102, 104; being-in-the-world-at-war 102, 104
Nunziatini, Mario (partisan) 175

Olivero, Aida (partisan) 26–7
Operation Eiche (Germany, Mussolini freed from prison) 29
Operation Husky (Allies) Sicily landings 24
Origo, Iris (author, witness) 28, 97, 107
otherness 10, 45, 75, 95, 97, 99, 113, 119, 121, 143, 180; Fascists' otherness 48, 49, 51; German's otherness 51, 65, 84; otherness (violence) 55; *see also* alterity
OVRA (Secret Fascist Police) 24

Paris, Rosina (partisan) 54
partisan (definition) xiv; **Cimberle** (Fascist) on the partisans 34; Communist partisans 2, 22, 31, 111, 114, 155, 172, 174, 175, 176, 182; female partisans 75–8; Garibaldi brigades 1, 2, 22, 31, 82, 83, 155; killed partisans 2, 9, 26, 40, 67, 85, 126, 139; mountain partisans (trope) 36–7, 133, 145, 155, 169; partisan actions 12, 19, 21–2, 27, 29–31, 32, 42,

47–54, 62, 66, 70, 73, 74, 79, 82, 84–8; *Partisanengefahr* (danger posed by partisans) 58; partisan memoirs 44, 129, 147, 156; partisan places 124, 130, 134; partisans 90, 94, 100, 104, 111, 140, 144, 146, 150, 151, 160
Passerini, Luisa (social historian) 44, 179
Pavone, Claudio (partisan, historian) 29, 40, 46, 50, 100, 168; *Una Guerra Civile* [A Civil War] 40, 46
Perarolo (town) 26
perception (role) 5, 41, 45, 46, 50, 55, 61, 68–9, 84, 87, 101, 129, 141, 143, 169, 179; materiality (perception) 6, 7, 11, 21, 30, 38, 44, 107, 136
Perin, Gildo (partisan) 62
Peter G. (Wehrmach soldier) 36
Peterle, Rosina (partisan) 54
phenomenology 2, 5, 19, 43, 69, 101, 114, 118, 123, 164
Pink, Sarah (ethnographer) 10, 33, 169
Pizzol, Renato (partisan) 70, 104, 153
Porzus bloodshed (inter-partisan violence) 31
Pozzi, Cesare (activist) 32
Proia, Liviano (partisan) 67, 70, 74, 123

Qualia (theory) 96, 99, 102

Reddy, William (history of emotions) 15, 28, 101, 102
reflexivity 30, 33, 34, 65, 90, 98, 170
resistance movement 2, 11, 12, 13, 14, 15, 16, 19, 22, 31, 43, 44, 45, 47, 75, 111–12, 139, 144, 148; catholic resistance 45; geographical distribution of resistance activity 36–7; Jewish resistance 45, 49, 80–2, 158; materiality (resistance) 123, 124, 129, 130, 134, 146, 156; patriotic war, class war and civil war (Pavone) 46; resistance (development) 24–5, 30, 42, 48, 102, 104; resistance mythology 24, 30, 36, 44, 47, 100, 156, 172; unarmed resistance 20, 28, 37, 105
responsibility (historical) 44, 85, 108, 123, 177, 180
Revine (town) 33
revisionism 172, 173
Rhodes, Dusty (British soldier) 60
Ricoeur, Paul (philosopher) 8, 45, 94, 95, 98, 113, 114, 168, 170
Röhrs, Matthias (historian) 54
Roncade (town) 48, 52, 55, 159, 160
Rosenwein, Barbara (scholar, history of emotions) 28, 111–12

Ross, John Dr. (British SOE operative, partisan) 12, 62, 74, 108, 155
Rossi, Gio Batta (RSI officer) 48
RSI, Repubblica Sociale Italiana (Fascist state) 29, 34, 56, 88, 111, 114
ruination 143, 149, 151, 159
rumour/s (role) 12–13, 24, 26–7, 93, 95, 105, 107, 109, 113, 130, 165, 168–9, 183; see also hearsay

Santa Giustina Bellunese (town) 27
Sartorelli, Teresa (witness) 53, 79
Saunders, Nicholas (conflict archaeologist) 117, 120, 128
Scalfari, Eugenio (former President of the Italian Republic and one-time Fascist) 127
Semelin, Jacques (historian) 20, 97
Sense of place 15–16, 25, 30, 35, 36, 38–9, 68, 71, 78, 80, 120, 124, 143; placelessness i, 124, 147, 150, 181
Seremetakis, Nadia (anthropologist) 101, 114; resistance as an affective event 29
sex 4, 71–3, 77, 80
sleep 54, 63, 74, 122, 134, 143, 155, 156, 157; sleep deprivation 122, 134–5, 143
SOE, Special Operations Executives (British) 10, 29, 74, 155
Spagnol, Tito Antonio (partisan) 90
spies 11, 18, 22, 42, 62–4, 65, 80, 88, 89, 90, 171, 177
staffetta/e (resistance messengers) 107, 136
Stargardt, Nicholas (German historian) 13
Stephens, George (British soldier) 35, 57, 61, 64, 71
Stoller, Paul (anthropologist) 14
Stone, Norman (British soldier) 142
storytelling 13, 38, 92, 93, 94–6, 97, 98, 99, 101, 137, 141, 146, 178; storytelling and memory 8, 11, 15, 20, 97–8, 120, 137; storytelling as mapping practise 98
Sylvester, Carolyn (conflict sociologist) 7

Taffarel, Giuseppe (partisan) 33, 145
Tagebuchsarchiv Emmendingen (German Diary Archive) xv, 28, 35, 46, 58, 72, 80, 147, 149
Tilman, Harold (British SOE Head of Mission Simia, partisan) 61, 74
Togni, Fernando (RSI soldier, Fascist) 127
Tolia-Kelly, Divya (cultural geographer) 38, 120; Re-memory theory 120
Tolson, Richard (British SOE operative, partisan) 155

Tomsich, Gustavo (Fascist, RSI officer) 48
Treviso (town) xv, 21, 46, 60, 77, 151;
　Bombing by the Allies 46–7, 60, 151
Trichiana (town) 136
Tudor, Malcolm (SOE historian) 10, 27
Turkle, Sherry (anthropologist) 8, 16, 95, 122

Umwelt (theory) 5–6, 141
uncanny, the 6, 20, 62–3, 142

Valsalega (locality) 70
Vendramini, Ferruccio (historian) 107, 108
Veneto (region) 15, 27, 52, 55, 74, 88
Vicchi, Giorgio (partisan) 55, 83, 144, 153, 156
Vittorio Veneto (town) 1, 2, 21, 33, 54, 64, 109, 176, 185

war stereotypes 59, 82, 85, 179, 182
Wehrmacht 8, 28, 29, 35, 49, 51, 52, 53, 55, 58, 68, 70, 72, 84, 86, 87, 146
Wetherell, Margaret (social scientist) 5, 101
Whatmore, Private Denys (British soldier) 56, 74
White, Hayden (Holocaust historian) 115
White, Luise (historian) 7, 95, 100
Witcomb, Andrea (cultural geographer) 173
Wolff, Kark (Wehrmacht officer) 58
Wool, Zoe (conflict anthropologist) 6, 150

Zanfranceschi, Nedda (partisan) 60, 72, 151, 153
Zangrandi, Giovanna (author, partisan) 77
Zanolin, Raimondo (partisan) 52, 53, 54, 55, 74, 146